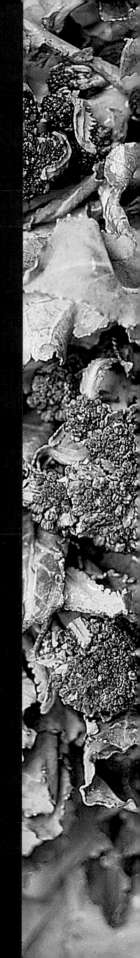

Allegra McEvedy's **COLOUR** cookbook

Kyle Cathie Limited

Allegra McEvedy's
COLOUR cookbook

with **Fred Dickieson**

photography by Georgia Glynn Smith

to the very loving memory of The Best Da in the world

First published in Great Britain in 2006 by

Kyle Cathie Limited
122 Arlington Road
London NW1 7HP

general.enquiries@kyle-cathie.com
www.kylecathie.com

ISBN 1 85626 668 0

ISBN (13-digit) 978 1 85626 668 0

A Cataloguing in Publication record for this title is available
from the British Library.

Printed in China by C & C Offset

Project Editor Kyle Cathie

Copy Editor Catherine Ward

Designed by Mary Evans

Photography by Georgia Glynn Smith

Cooking by Allegra McEvedy and Fred Dickieson

Styling by Wei Tang

Production by Sha Huxtable and Alice Holoway

acknowledgements

From the first synapse shock that started the idea for this book to publication has been a four year journey that I would never have completed had it not been for the kindness and help of many people.

Quiet spaces are a near impossibility in our house, so I really appreciate the Garnett family (including Shona and Chris) at Cannwood, and Ron and Tim in upstate New York for lending me theirs.

On the food front every good cook knows that you're only as good as your ingredients, and after years of searching I now have Kings amongst suppliers. The father and son team of Vince and Chris at Muscatt and John at Stenton's made for the best combination of butchers a girl could ever wish for. The Fish Shop at Kensington Place really care and know about their wares and bent over backwards to get me what I wanted (which on one occasion was an hour lesson on trout-boning from the Portuguese masters Carlos and Ramiro). Souhale and Joe are just two of the best local suppliers I know, and a very grateful mention indeed to David Williams for his beautiful foliage from the South coast.

It's not only their goods, but their good nature that makes my suppliers special – the fact that they are always on the end of the phone to answer my random and often quite bonkers questions when I know what busy lives they lead. Of these great men and women there is one to whom I owe much inspiration: my veg man Rushton not only took the time to understand where I was coming from and what I needed, but then unfailingly sent box after box of the most breath-taking and awe-inspiring fruit and veg I have ever had the pleasure to work with. The proof, as they say, is in the photos.

To be fair though, someone else had something to do with what I think are some of the most knock-out, super-sharp and imaginative pictures of food I have ever seen. Georgia has brought my idea to life to an extent I never even dreamed of and when the pics came through both Fred and I got all teared up. It makes me unbelievably proud that these photos are in my book, but even prouder that the Glynn Smith family and the McSmither family are now friends for life.

Everyone needs a beautiful assistant and Georgia certainly has one of the calibre she deserves in the shape of Helen McArdle, who is not only beautiful but talented too. Mark my words – this girl will go far.

There's one final component to the pics that finish them off and bring them together, and for that we have to thank Wei for her bowls, bits and backgrounds – I just never knew there were that many shades of yellow.

Martine at Deborah Mckenna did a fine job of selling this book, and Kyle did an ever better one of buying it. Kyle is the kind of publisher that a creative person dreams of – understanding how important the small things are and matching you pound for pound for eccentric behaviour. Not only could this book literally not have happened without her, but if it had come to fruition elsewhere, it wouldn't have been anything like as good. As with any strong and successful person she has a great team around her: Catherine, the proofreader down in Jersey did a spectacular and sensitive job; Sophie Allen has been unflinching, thorough and kind when it came to editing Fred's and my pencil marks (and a quick thank-you to my godmother Camilla for the pencils). Mary Evans, the designer, has immersed herself so totally in this book that she knows it as well as I do, and her simple layouts have really made sense of my somewhat jumbled thoughts.

Professional support is one thing, but good emotional support is harder to come by. I've been blessed with great friends, and my sister Floss has been the backbone of my life, particularly in this last very painful year, but when Susi and I got married, somewhere between the shooting and proofing of this book, I knew that the final piece had dropped in to place and we were both set for life. The sun she brings into the room with her lifts me when it's all got a bit much, and her patience at my work schedule has been a lesson in understanding. Roll on the rest of our lives.

And now for the rest of my support team: my dad always said that I'd be in jail by now if it wasn't for Lorraine. So much better than a PA, more honest than a friend and just always there for me. As the deadline for delivering the book got closer and Fred and I started looking stresseder and stranger, Lorraine walked in with a warehouse full of stationary and filing, sat down and typed and edited for 52 hours straight until the book had safely gone. What a woman.

Matt Cranston is an old friend of Fred's and mine, and a really talented chef who, when we were wobbling about something in the kitchen, was always there to be a third brain.

It's been touching how all the ever-extending Leon family have been so enthusiastic and supportive about the writing of this book, especially Super Chef Benny for understanding when I just couldn't be there.

Not wishing to sound like a cliché, I'd like to thank everyone I know, on the grounds that pretty much everyone I know tested recipes for the book. You are simply the best group of friends and family one could ever have, and I've told you before how sexy you all are. True heartfelt thanks to all of you, especially my mother-in-law Sarah Smither who by sheer bad luck ended up getting 11 soups to test, and that's enough soup for 66 people (sorry about that, Sarah).

And the last shout must go out to our Fred, who has been my best friend and workmate for so many years, and more recently was a stupendous Best Man. I feel we've had enough fun together making this book for a life-time, and for reasons both practical and emotional I just couldn't have done it without you.

Pa would be proud of us.

beginner's notes

● Red chillies are the bigger ones with a medium heat. The little ones, also know as bird's eye, have a seriously potent kick and are generally less available. This book uses the big ones unless otherwise stated. The same applies to green chillies.

● Butter unsalted versus salted. I don't care either way, as I do like a pinch of salt in my sweets. But if you opt for unsalted as many are on salt-reduced diets, do check the taste for seasoning.

● In most recipes I have used organic caster and granulated sugars as well as organic flours.

● All eggs are free-range, as are the chickens.

● S & P. Seasoning is an integral part of cooking (except puddings) so it is worth using the good stuff – sea salt (like Maldon) and black pepper from a grinder please.

The thinking behind Allegra McEvedy's Colour Cookbook:

each season has a palette of colours associated with it, and if you eat by colour by season you will naturally be giving your body what it needs at that time of year.

Why are tomatoes red, and what does that redness do for you?
Why is a pink grapefruit better for you than a yellow one? Are
black grapes really more nutritious than red ones (yes) and what
is it that makes pumpkins quite so vibrantly orange?

For most of us, when we sit down to a plate of food, our first impressions come from appearance and then from smell, long before flavour comes into play. The decision about whether we like what we see is made up of several components, such as texture, height and complexity of appearance, but far and away the most important is colour. What in the world can be more unappetising than mangetout that have been overcooked to the colour of primordial swamp food, or a slice of roast beef that's as grey and dry as an elephant's ear?

The factors we use to judge raw food are a little different – texture still plays a part, and so can smell, but again colour is paramount. There are a lot of people in the food supply business who realised this a long time ago, and unfortunately have been trying to subtly dupe us ever since, with an assortment of devices such as chemical preservative sprays and even genetic modification.

Yet it isn't just the food suppliers who are at fault. Joe Public has been lazy, choosing to go for the easy, obvious option: 'Wouldn't a summer berry pavlova be delicious after the Christmas turkey!'. We rarely stop to work out that those strawbs have come a minimum of 4,000 miles and have been squirted with all sorts of funniness to keep them in pristine condition for a scary amount of time. And that's before you go into a secondary layer of challenging thought about the ecological impact of the transportation and packaging involved just so that we Brits can have strawbs out of our natural season....

The real tragedy is that strawberries in mid-winter don't do any kind of justice to their seasonal counterpart flavour-wise, nor for that matter do they do your body much good. A strawberry

that has been flown in from Morocco, if you're lucky, or South Africa, if you're not, will contain less than ten per cent of the iron, vitamin C and immune-building antioxidants than one bought locally in summer. A study of oranges showed that one freshly picked and bought from the grower contained around 180mg of vitamin C, whereas an identical-looking orange bought from a supermarket had less than 1mg. And that same supermarket will try to flog you twelve kinds of vitamin supplements that you just don't need if you take what nature is giving you.

Staying with oranges, they realised that eating oranges did you good as long ago as the seventeenth century. In 1895, scientists discovered that, specifically, it was the vitamin C that was beneficial. By 1937 there was a general acknowledgement that you need ascorbic acid to maximise the absorption of vit C, and the latest thoughts are that actually it's bioflavonoids that get the most out of it. To me, it's no mean coincidence that an orange contains all three of these nutrients, so let's just hold our hands up, stop trying to play God to our bodies and do what nature tells us – she got it right in the beginning. I'm not anti-science – far from it. The more we understand, the better informed we can be, but all this knowledge should bring us back to a beautiful, simple orange rather than a cupboard full of pharmaceuticals. You are what you eat...energy is brainpower, and the phrase 'food for thought' cannot be taken too lightly.

The riddle is that nearly everything that tastes good looks good, but not everything that looks good, tastes good. Once you're aware of those Dutch hothouses and unnecessary food miles, all you have to do is use a bit of nous. This is an age of mass imports and exports in which we rely on directions and instructions for just about everything. To successfully get through the tricks and pitfalls of your weekly veg shop you have to rely on your instincts a bit more as to what tastes good. What it all boils down to is colour + common sense = flavour = good for you.

Until comparatively recently, seasonality wasn't an issue: you couldn't transport fresh food successfully, so cooks had no choice but to buy locally, and in the many centuries before vitamin and mineral supplements were available on the shelves, those basic, local ingredients played a large part in people staying healthy and that, in a beautiful brown nutshell, is the essence of this book. For a long time now I have been interested in promoting local, British, seasonal food. Not in a bash-you-round-the-head-with-a-limp-turnip kind of a way, but because it simply makes sense. When I lived and worked in New York, I spent hours every week perusing the greenmarkets that are farm-direct, so when I came back home I was keen to use and work with London's farmers' markets. I would wander round the stalls on a Saturday morning looking for fruit and veg that were just coming into season, and watching the old stuff go out. Nature is like an annual miracle – just when we're tiring of off-white root veg, we begin to get the first greens of spring, which hand over to the summer reds, then fantastic autumnal oranges, to be passed back to winter's finest. How can any cook get bored with such a relentless barrage of change?

The structure of this book is simple, and was simply derived. I made a list of every major indigenous fruit and veg, and then marked out each one's season on a chart.

Fairly quickly a pattern of colour emerged: we get a fat hit of dark green midwinter, with the market being flooded with

curly kale, watercress, Brussels sprouts (and their fantastic tops), cavolo nero, leafy broccoli, Swiss chard and so on. Some of it was going, some of it was just arriving, but it was all there at the same time. In a similar fashion, after a long hot summer, it's all about sun-rich, heat-swollen, orac-laden deep purple: cherries, grapes, blackberries, Victoria plums and damsons. I'm a cook, not a data analyst, but clearly this was not rocket science.

Antioxidants are so last millennium; 21st century free-radical cleaning up is done by oracs — these are foods with high Oxygen Radical Absorbance Capacity. Free radicals are the natural by-product of the body's metabolic process, but we also absorb them through our skin, through breathing in the air and via processed foods. There will always be free radicals, attaching themselves to our healthy cells and rusting them, but there are thousands of micronutrients that Mother Nature provides which are good for you, and orac is the collective term for them and their good work. Eat a diet packed with oracs and keep the rusting at bay. As your guide, look to the colour coding created by the heat and love of the spring, summer and autumn sun — yellows, deep reds, purples and rich oranges.

But this is nature that we're talking about, and seasons are not highly disciplined. The X-factor is the weather, both in the short and the long term. In the immediate future the arrival date of any given ingredient can vary up to about a month. Looking forwards, global warming is a serious worry, and at this stage no one quite knows how it will affect our climate's natural seasons. A couple of summers ago, the highest British temperature ever was recorded in Great Yarmouth — over 100°F. A great day for some, but a scary one for anyone who's environmentally aware.

In whatever month you go into your local supermarket, you will be affronted by the same spectrum of hyper-real colours. If you head for the organic section and really squint you may be able to pick up a more realistic hue. Head for your local street market and the likelihood of seeing the seasonal shades is much higher. Go to your local farmers' market and it's unavoidable. That's not to say that a potter round the stalls in summer will yield a purely red shopping basket, but if you could have a crow's view of the year, red would be the characteristic tint of the season.

For reasons that I'll go into later, we have five seasons: the usual suspects, and then a bonus Christmas season at the end just for laughs, which is what Christmas should be about. Each chapter has around thirty recipes which reflect what's seasonal, beautiful and delicious at that time of year, and most importantly why you should be eating it at its seasonal zenith to get the most out of it.

The recipes are not worthy – I am a cook not a nutritionist; I don't care how good for you olive oil is – I couldn't live without butter. So the recipes are all about flavour, and it just so happens that you're doing yourself a favour too. And to be fair, a few of them aren't especially good for you at all, they're just good to eat.

Each chapter starts with a list of Seasonal Superstars, which I hope will be a bit of an eye-opener, or at least will make you think a bit more about your shopping and cooking. If the language gets a bit flowery and gay, it's probably because Fred wrote it. These lists give you a bit of a run-down on what it is, exactly, that each season's produce can do for you, and why adding it to your diet will make you, and those you love, feel bouncier and bonnier than ever before.

winter

Nowadays, there are a reassuring amount of cookbooks that are divided into seasons, rather than starters, mains etc., which as we're all learning is the right way to approach cooking. Having done a quick flip through a bunch of them I noticed they invariably start with spring: a season more associated with happiness and joy than sluggish winter, thus starting on an altogether more upbeat note. But for me it was always going to be winter first, and I've distilled my thinking down to three reasons.

Firstly, I'm holding my hands up to having a juvenile rebellious reflex still to go against the grain. At the age of 35 I instinctively squirm when anyone starts a sentence, 'You should...' even if it's as innocent as, 'You should go and see this exhibition/try this restaurant'. It may be a hangover from my 'should do better' days at school but, for whatever reason, I have a problem with being told what to do and with swimming with the shoal.

The second reason is altogether more foodie and veg-related: according to the Gregorian Calendar the year starts with the lion's share of winter still to come. Even though spring may be a more joyful and uplifting season to kick off with, if we are being true to our year, the beginning of our journey should be wintery. And what's wrong with that? Winter, as we will discover, has as much to extol as it's more obviously charming seasonal counterparts and, being a bit of an underdog supporter (Go on the Hoops – QPR have been my team for all my life), I'm proud to be backing winter.

And the final reason is that I have split my year into five seasons, and as the last is Christmas, then we must start in January, which in anybody's book (in this case mine) is definitely not spring.

So off we trot in the deep midwinter, for this season is all about depth: there are two greens in my book, but as there are an infinite number in the world (not to mention that green's the single colour most associated with nature), I think that's ok. The deep, dark, forest greens of winter could not be more different than that of the young shoots of spring, and I definitely find the winter green more attractive than the paler, youthful shade. Watercress, chard, kale, spinach and broccoli utterly radiate goodness and whenever we get a box of cavolo nero in at work, I just want to put my face in it and have a good nuzzle around. Obviously I don't, though, for a number of reasons, including Health and Safety laws or being thought of as a vegetable pervert. It's the kind of green that just screams of goodness: vitamins, minerals and trace elements.

There are plenty of really exciting leaves and heads to get us through the sleepy months of the year – have a go at chard, cima di rape or purple-sprouting broccoli for a bit of a change from spinach, but if I had to eat only one green veg for the entire winter, I'd stand by my cabbage.

Now don't just groan and turn over like a housewife with a headache; this mighty head is to be truly revered, as indeed it used to be by the Romans. I'm not saying they deified it, applauded it at the Circus Maximus and marched through Gaul with it on a banner, but at least they appreciated it for what it does, which is plenty. Just for a minute let's leave aside the white cabbage, which is the slightly dull cousin in the family, and concentrate instead on the darker heads: Savoy, being the most famous, or Hispi, which verges on being more like winter greens.

Then there's the resplendent January King, a real native stunner with leaves that go from green to purple as the colour travels up the veins; the aforementioned cavolo nero, a loose, floppy head from Italy but now grown here too; and of course winter's favourite slow-cook, red cabbage. All of these have flavour, character and goodness in abundance, so don't let too many years of tasteless coleslaw put you off. I'm not going to force the info or the cabbage down your throat – instead I'll just let you come across some very convincing evidence in the winter superstars....

There's a second colour that creeps into our winter palette, that which stealthily moves up the leaves of our January King cabbage, and which has a much more ethereal feel than the earthy green. It's a special kind of purple that you see at the beginning of the year, in purple-sprouting broccoli, some kinds of sage and on the leaves of many hardy plants. It's a dusky mauve that reminds me of dew-laden daybreaks, fairies and forests. Then as winter moves on, a deeper shade starts taking over, led by the best winter leaf of all, the radicchio. The tougher, bitter salad heads we see at this time of year are so much more flavourful and potent than their summer counterparts, and with the bitterness comes a host of healing characteristics that leaves the summer foliage standing.

The way to get through winter is not to fight it, but to go with it, make the most of what nature is offering and look for the beauty that's out there, rather than lamenting what's not.

And spend a lot of time in front of the fire in the pub.

Artichokes – contain substances that are proven to be good for the kidneys (by encouraging diuresis) and the liver (by promoting detoxification), as well as helping to lower levels of blood cholesterol.

Broccoli – is the king of the crucifer family and our winter superfood. Great for combating all that our bodies encounter in life. They also strengthen the blood and circulatory system.

Brussels sprouts/tops – not only can you enjoy the little bundles of greatness that are brussels, but their tops are crammed with goodness too: antioxidants, vitamins A, C and E and folic acid, which are the building blocks of all genes and red blood cells.

Cabbage – has been renowned since Roman times as a cure-all. One of their many micronutrients incites all cells in the body to grow anew and thus helps to keep our blood healthy.

Cavolo nero – if green is the colour of the winter oracs, then cavalo blue green is its mightiest hue. As all the brassicas, the abundance of sulphur in cavolo nero maintains happy joints.

Celeriac – may be a bit ugly, but it has vitamins, iron, iodine (which is needed by the thyroid to manage all our hormones) and lowers cholesterol.

Celery – is both a stimulant and a diuretic, acting on the kidneys and bladder. It also works as an antiseptic in these eliminatory organs. The magnesium in celery is necessary for metabolising calcium.

Chard – is filled with iron and vitamins A and B, all of which are essential in the production of haemoglobin (red blood cells). Without haemoglobin, the oxygen we breathe in would not go to the cells for rebuilding and replenishing. The more new red blood cells we have, the more old ones with high blood fat can be replaced.

Cima di rape – contains lots of calcium and considerable amounts of folic acid, which is crucial for making healthy genetic material, along with zinc, which keeps our reproductive system strong – this is the veg for mothers-to-be.

January King cabbage – strengthens the blood and is loaded with vitamin B3, making it great for keeping our energy levels stable and constant renewal of skin cells, plus it is an inspiration to behold.

Flatleaf parsley – greenest of the greens and packed with vitamins A, B, C, calcium and iron. It stimulates liver function and helps to regulate the appetite for smooth digestion. Like all the greens, it is wanted by the blood and circulatory system. Love it!

Hispi cabbage – like all cabbages, it is high in the kind of multinutrients that are particularly good for our cardiovascular system. They have a calming effect on stomach problems and help to lower blood sugar to keep your energy levels stable.

Kale – is packed with protective phytochemicals that help you stave off illness and keep your body tickety-boo. Importantly, it also includes glucosinolates, which increase the activity of the enzymes that help the body eliminate nasty, free radicals.

Leeks – are rich in phosphorus, which is what the body needs to construct tiny nerves for the cellular communication system as well as making the strong bits: bones and teeth.

Purple-sprouting broccoli – is one of the top 10 Superfoods. Powerful oracs with a veil of purple, all the antioxidants a body could ever want and damn fine colour and flavour too. This is just what you need in winter.

Radicchio/trevisse – is the tonic for the damage we do to our livers on a daily basis: excessive fat, alcohol and salt. Radicchio and trevisse empower the liver so we can maximise the energy from the food we eat. The happier the liver, the happier and less weighed down with extras the body is.

Red cabbage – is a powerful antioxidant that strengthens the immune system, perfect for fighting all those viruses we encounter over the cold damp winter months.

Rocket – is filled with peppery chlorophyll and vitamin C, which help your body fight the perils of winter by healing your wounds, as well as keeping the skin in great shape with all that vitamin A.

Rosemary – stimulates the circulation to keep our winter blood flowing, whilst strengthening the capillaries. Bioflavinoids help with the absorption of vitamin C. Both stress and winter hat-head can cause dandruff, which rosemary is thought to soothe.

Sage – is antiseptic, antibacterial and it also strengthens the mucous membranes – healthy lungs, big breaths.

Spinach – what more can we say? Loaded with calcium for bones and teeth, and with potassium, which keeps the heartbeat regular; its iron is good for the muscles, blood and nervous system. A great source of energy.

Thyme – is the herb of choice for the winter, as it contains omega 3s and fatty acids. Thymol, the volatile constituent of thyme, is a powerful antiseptic. Added to this is a much-needed dose of vitamin A.

Watercress – is a good friend to our blood and circulation. It empowers the upper respiratory system and acts as an expectorant upon it. It also keeps a harmonious lymphatic/immune system balance – out, damn cold, out I say.

brodo di nonna - grandma's CHICKEN soup

This is all about making you feel better – the panacea broth is the backdrop for tortellini – bellybutton pasta. If you have an Italian deli near you, you may ask for *tortellini per brodo*, which are a third of the size of our supermarket versions and rather cute in soups.

We are all familiar with that moment when we know that we're coming down with something, whether it is flu or the dreaded cold. This simple exercise in chicken and stock will have you set up for days, particularly if you add some chicken thighs to your stock for added sustenance. You end up with a nourishing broth with a side of gently puréed veg, which is soft and warming when reheated with some buttered toast.

This cure-all needs no further introduction, but a good last thought is to add a splash of red wine to the broth in your bowl before you drink it.

serves 6

FOR THE BROTH
1kg chicken bones, raw
1 carrot, topped and tailed
1 white onion, peeled and cut in half
1 celery stick, cut in half
1 courgette, topped and tailed
6 garlic cloves, peeled
1 sprig of rosemary
1 sprig of thyme
2 bay leaves
1 teaspoon salt
2 tablespoons extra virgin olive oil (or 40g butter)

FOR THE BRODO DI NONNA
300g tortellini, fresh (not dried)
10g flatleaf parsley, chopped
30g Parmesan cheese, grated
S & P

● Put all the broth ingredients except the oil or butter into your favourite large-ish stockpot and cover with water. Put onto a low flame and cook gently for 1½ hours – no boiling please, only steaming. Skim occasionally.

● Turn off the heat and take the vegetables out of the stock with a slotted spoon. Put them into a food processor along with the extra virgin or butter and some seasoning. Pulse until you have a smooth purée.

● Let the vegetable purée cool and store in the fridge or freezer until needed for future ailments.

● Strain the stock and throw away the bones.

● When you want to serve, heat the broth to just below boiling. Add the tortellini and cook as per the instructions on the packet – usually 2–3 minutes.

● Mix the parsley and Parmesan in now, adjust the seasoning and then ladle the hot brodo into warmed bowls. All that is left is to start feeling a bit better about the world.

Shelf Life: Both broth and purée, 3–4 days. **Best Kept:** The broth should be kept in the fridge, along with the puréed veg.

HAM hock, cavolo nero and pearl barley BROTH

Cavolo nero is a tall, thin cabbage with leaves like long, droopy bunny's ears, a puckered texture and a chlorophyll-laden colour. It works particularly well in a slow-cook situation, like this mighty broth. If broths conjure up images of what my dad used to call 'loo water soups', then think again. This is wall-to-wall goodness, providing everything you need to keep yourself healthy and energised, due to the slow-release qualities of the pearl barley.

serves 6

FOR THE HAM HOCK STOCK
1 ham hock
3 celery sticks, snapped
   in half
3 carrots, trimmed, peeled
   and cut in half
2 onions, halved
2 bay leaves
2 branches of thyme
1 whole head of garlic,
   cloves peeled

TO FINISH
30g sage, roughly chopped
100g pearl barley
250g cavolo nero or savoy
   cabbage, trimmed and
   thinly sliced
a drizzle of extra virgin
   olive oil, to serve
S & P

● Put the ham hock and 4–5 litres of water into a pot with all of the veg, herbs and garlic. Bring to the boil, skim, then turn down the heat and leave to simmer for 4 hours, skimming off any scum that comes to the surface during the cooking process.

● When the ham is falling off the bone it is cooked. Using your favourite grappling device for large boiled meats (mine being a spider), take the ham out and leave it to cool on a plate.

● Take out the vegetables and put to one side; throw away the thyme and bay leaves.

● Put the veg into a food processor and pulse until they are in nice small chunks. Or you could chop them small with a knife – very easy because they are so soft.

● Put the ham stock back on the stove and bring to a simmer. Give a final skim to remove the fat. Add the sage and pearl barley, cooking the barley according to the time on the packet.

● Remove the bigger bits of fat off the ham hock and then, with your fingers or with a sharp knife, shred the meat into soup-sized hunks. Cholesterol lovers can add a bit of the fat, but all the goodness is in the stock with the barley.

● Add the shredded ham hock and the veg to the stock and check the seasoning.

● About 25 minutes before the barley is cooked, stir in the cavolo nero. Cover the broth with a lid and continue simmering until the barley and cavolo are cooked – it will be longer than the pre-defined 25 minutes, as the cabbage will have lowered the temperature, probably nearer 40 minutes. A liberal seasoning with S & P will be the making of this dish.

● Serve in big bowls with a drizzle of your best extra virgin and some crusty bread.

Shelf Life: 4–5 days. **Best Kept:** In a cold larder or fridge.

hispi SLAW

Despite the Asian sounding name, hispi is one of the oldest varieties of cabbage native to England, where it is also known by the much more lovely name of sweetheart cabbage.

The Cabbage Collective is one of the mightiest in our fields, and its nutritional character traits are beguiling. The Romans believed cabbages to be a panacea for pretty much everything. They have been used across Europe for thousands of years by the Celts, Slavs, Germans and Basques. They always feature right near the top of those '100 Greatest Vegetables of All Time' surveys... and with good reason. They are high in the kind of antioxidants that are particularly good for our cardiovascular system, great for stomach problems and also help to lower our blood sugar levels. They contain vitamins A, B, C and E, plus the elusive vitamin K that is essential for getting our blood to clot. And because it's eaten raw in this dish, 100 per cent of the nutrients are available for us to use. Cabbages take care of the community that is our body. This frisky little number works as a much fresher, healthier and desirable 'slaw than the ones we have come to accept. Zingy, nutty, crunchy, hispi.

serves 6

4 tablespoons mixed seeds (the standards are sesame, pumpkin and sunflower, but you can branch out with radish, dill or hemp)

1 hispi or sweetheart cabbage, quartered, cored then finely shredded

1 packet sprouting pulses (mung, chickpea, aduki, lentil – they tend to come in mixed punnets and are seriously good for you and seriously yum)

2 punnets mustard cress

4 tablespoons crème fraîche

4 tablespoons All Purpose Peanut Sauce (page 226)

juice of 2 limes

S & P

● Preheat the oven to 200°C/400°F/gas 6.

● Mix your seeds with a pinch of salt, spread them out on a small baking tray and put in the oven for around 5 minutes until toasted and golden. Take out of the oven and leave to cool.

● Mix together the shredded cabbage, sprouts and mustard cress.

● In a different bowl, whisk together the crème fraîche, peanut sauce, lime juice and S & P.

● Dress the cabbage, sprouts and mustard cress with the peanuty cream and sprinkle over the toasted seeds.

● Taste and correct the seasoning. If the dressing is a little sticky, add a splash of water to restore the creaminess.

Shelf Life: Have to eat it the same day once it's dressed. **Best Kept:** In the fridge, tightly covered.

SOUSED mackerel salad

This just smacks of all things Baltic, and as the folks round there really know how to live through a freezing winter, taking a leaf out of their Book of Natural Survival is no bad thing.

It's the oils in the fish – those helpful omegas – combined with the supercharged cabbage that make for a powerful antioxidant combination.

The standard Russian salad found in buffets and sorry institutions is a mix of overcooked root veg and peas bound with gruesome amounts of mayo; but my accompaniment to the finest of fish, has nothing in common with that one, it just displays some Russian, Baltic or even Scandinavian sympathies.

serves 6

12 cocktail sticks

FOR THE MACKEREL

12 mackerel fillets (175–225g each) – ask the fishmonger to cut the bones out

6 bay leaves

12 sprigs of thyme

1 small white onion, finely sliced

2 teaspoons black peppercorns

120ml cold tea (no milk)

120ml cider vinegar

1^1/$_2$ tablespoons brown sugar

1 tablespoon chopped dill

^{1}/$_2$ teaspoon chopped red chilli

salt

FOR THE PICKLED RED CABBAGE

^{1}/$_4$ teaspoon caraway seeds

3 tablespoons sour cream

35g cornichons, sliced

1 hard-boiled egg, grated

230g red cabbage, cut into 1cm dice

S & P

● Wash the mackerel fillets under cold running water and dry on kitchen paper.

● Lightly salt the flesh of the fish. Split the bay leaves down the centre and place half a leaf and a sprig of thyme across the tail end of each fillet.

● Roll each fillet up individually, beginning at the tail end, and pierce with a cocktail stick to retain the shape. When you stand it up it should look like a roll-mop; the bay and thyme should be sticking out of the top. It will probably take you a couple of fillets to perfect the technique and teach those slippery fish who's boss.

● Scatter the onions in a lightly greased, high-sided frying pan and sit the rolls on top. It should be a tight fit, with the rolls sitting snugly. Sprinkle with peppercorns.

● Mix together the tea and vinegar, then stir in the sugar, dill and chilli and pour over the fish.

● Cover loosely with a foil dome and cook on the hob on a medium flame for 15 minutes, or until the fish is tender and opaque.

● In a medium-sized bowl, mix the caraway seeds with the sour cream, cornichons, grated egg and red cabbage. Add a tablespoon of water if necessary to loosen everything up. Taste and correct the seasoning.

● Take the fish off the heat, pull the foil off and leave to cool down in the liquid for 10 minutes. Serve warm, not forgetting to pull out the cocktail sticks. The fish may be gently reheated if being eaten later, and are actually pretty nice cold too. A bit of warm, crusty bread works for me, but if we are staying within the region, go dense and dark.

Shelf Life: Fish, 3 days; salad, 2 days. **Best Kept:** Fridge it.

smoked mack attack

The omega 3 fatty acids and huge shot of vitamin D present in oily fish are now recognised to be life-enhancing. Not only famously good for joints, the effect they have on the heart is affirmed by this small sentence: 'Eskimos, whose diet includes more oily fish than anyone else's worldwide, have the lowest global rate of cardiovascular disease.' (*The Complete Guide to Nutritional Health*.) Eating oily fish as a regular part of your diet can decrease your chance of having a heart attack by around a third. And there is growing support for the belief that it can increase brain development if included in a child's diet. This recipe really is a double hitter: watercress is great for the joints and for arthritis, as well as being a friend to our blood and circulation.

serves 6

120g smoked salmon, sliced

140g smoked mackerel fillet

1 bunch of watercress
   (about 160g)

3 eggs

2 tablespoons of your
   favourite toasted seeds
   (pumpkin or sesame are
   very good)

6 slices of rich seed loaf or
   rye bread (Ryvita crisp
   bread works at a push,
   but it's a touch crackly)

S & P

FOR THE DRESSING

1 teaspoon wasabi powder
   or 1 tablespoon wasabi
   paste

2 tablespoons crème fraîche

juice of 1 lime

black pepper

● Tear the salmon into thick strips.

● Peel the skin from the mackerel and throw it away. Break the mackerel into small hunks and take out any bones along the way.

● Wash and drain the watercress. If it is large and long, give it a few chops.

● Soft-boil the eggs (5 minutes in boiling water). Tip into the sink just forcefully enough to crack the shells (making them easier to peel), then put them back in the pan and run the cold tap over them until all the heat has been taken out of them. Peel.

● Knock up the dressing; mix the wasabi powder with 1 tablespoon of water to make a paste. Stir in the crème fraîche, lime juice and a bit of black pepper for extra zoom.

● Mix the watercress, fish, seeds and dressing together in a bowl. Put a nice pile of this salad on each of your toasted breads or crispbreads. Cut the eggs in half and put one half, yolk-side up, on top of the salad. Season with a little bit of S & P atop the yolk. A perfect lunchtime energy boost.

Shelf Life: No, no, no. **Best Kept:** Don't keep it, just eat it.

SKATE and spinach salad
with anchovy and CAPER dressing

This is a special salad with healing properties, not to mention bucketloads of flavour.

My lovely Pa suffered from heart fibrillations, which could go on for weeks or months before they stopped. Not once, not twice, but three times when I served him a simple supper of poached fish (John Dory, if you're interested) the fibrillations stopped that very night.

Despite what people who read this book may think, there's nothing hippy woo-woo about my outlook on life, and even my dad (a no-nonsense consultant psychiatrist) found the correlation between his irregular heartbeat stopping and eating such plain, fresh fish somewhat overwhelming evidence.

serves 6

FOR THE FISH

1.2kg skate, preferably in
   1 or 2 wings only (little
   ones are a bit of a pain)
1/2 red onion, roughly
   chopped
25g flatleaf parsley
4 slices of lemon
S & P

FOR THE SALAD

1.5kg whole leaf spinach

FOR THE DRESSING

8–10 good anchovies,
   drained
2 tablespoons capers,
   washed and drained
1 teaspoon dill seeds
   (if you see them in the
   shop buy 5 packets as
   they're a bit hard to find,
   but don't stress if you
   can't find them)
juice of 1 lemon
60g flatleaf parsley, chopped
1 garlic clove, finely chopped
10 tablespoons extra virgin
   olive oil
S & P

● Preheat the oven to 180°C/350°F/gas 4.

● Season the fish well on both sides. Put the skate, with the fleshier side up, into a sufficiently large roasting tray with sides at least 8cm high.

● Scatter the onion, parsley and lemon slices into the tray, more around the wings than on them. Pour in enough water to come two thirds of the way up. Give the skate a little wiggle, so that it is lifted up from the base of the pan and some water gets underneath it to prevent it from sticking.

● Cover the tray with foil, sealing around the edges, and cook in the oven for 30 minutes.

● Put a large, covered pan of salted water onto a high heat for the spinach.

● Now for the dressing. Finely chop up the anchovies and capers and mix them in a bowl with the dill seeds, lemon juice, parsley and garlic. Slowly pour in the extra virgin, stirring constantly with a fork.

● Just before the water reaches boiling, get ready with a colander or spider for draining the spinach, and have a sinkful of cold water on hand. When the water is boiling, take the lid off and put the spinach in. Push down with a spider/slotted spoon. Stir the spinach for 2–3 minutes and then lift out the leaves (or drain in a colander in a separate sink) and drop them straight into your sinkful of cold water. Leave for a few minutes to take the heat out of the leaves.

● Lift the spinach out of the water and put it in a colander. Now, taking a handful at a time, squeeze out as much of the excess water as possible from the spinach. Roughly chop the squeezed balls and put them into a bowl.

● Take the skate out of the oven, unfoil and leave to cool for 10 minutes.

● Once the fish has had time to rest, drain off the cooking liquor and either throw it away or keep as a soup base.

● Have your plates ready and laid out (this one is definitely an individually plated salad). Mix the spinach with a few generous tablespoons of the ancho-caper dressing and divide between the plates, putting a small pile in the middle of each one.

● Using a palette knife, carefully remove the fish fillets from the thin layer of bamboo-like cartilage, starting on the thick side. Gently ease the knife underneath the flesh and draw it towards the edge of the fin following the grain of the fish. As you get a tranche off, lay it on one of your piles of spinach.

● Carefully remove the layer of cartilage and throw it away. Now divide the rest of the skate flesh among the salads.

● Drizzle each salad with ancho-caper dressing and serve with a wedge of lemon. Eat while the fish is still warm – it's not supposed to be hot. What the French call a *salade tiède*.

Shelf Life: Not really a keeper. **Best Kept:** Fish in the fridge.

horenso goma-ae

The Japanese standard Horenso Goma-ae (Spinach and Sesame dressing) is a favourite of mine. You can find it in various forms in Japanese restaurants, but if you want to see it for real go to Japan. There they stack the carefully blanched tender spinach leaves perfectly in a pile, roll them up like a roulade and then slice it. What you get is a slice of goodness in a light pool of silky sesame sauce, the consistency of a daydream, inducing a zen-like calm.

The sauce involves thousands of sesame seeds, but I don't feel that's an issue as they are neither very expensive nor an endangered species.

serves 6

200g sesame seeds
600g whole leaf spinach
4 teaspoons sugar
2 teaspoons fish sauce
4 tablespoons dark soy
    sauce
5 teaspoons light soy sauce
3 tablespoons rice wine
    vinegar
juice of 1 lime
salt

● Preheat the oven to 200°C/400°F/gas 6.

● Bring 3 litres salted water to the boil. Wash the spinach really well and drain.

● Sprinkle the sesame seeds on a baking tray and put in the oven for 15 minutes, or until golden. Keep a close eye and move them about for even colouration.

● Before you blanch the spinach, have a spider or colander to hand and a sinkful of cold water. Blanch the spinach in the boiling water for 2–3 minutes – you may need to do this in 2 batches. When it is cooked, either drain it into a separate sink, or scoop it out with the spider. Then immerse it straight away in the sink of cold water. Leave for 5 minutes.

● Drain the spinach in the colander, then take out a handful at a time, squeezing tightly into balls to wring out the excess water.

● Take the sesame seeds out of the oven and leave to cool.

● Put the cooled seeds into the blender with the sugar, fish sauce and dark soy. Blend until very smooth, adding enough water to get to the consistency of double cream.

● Now for the ultimate touch: pass the sesame paste through a fine sieve, again maybe in 2 loads. You will end up with a concrete lump in the sieve, and a super-silky sesame dressing below. The concrete lump is loaded with flavour, but sadly plays no more part in this dish. We couldn't bear to throw it away, so we stuffed it under the skin of a chicken breast and baked in the oven. Great little cook's snack.

● Dress the spinach with the light soy, rice wine vinegar and lime. Toss it well, making sure every leaf has a fine patina. Spoon a pool of sesame dressing on the bottom of the plate and then, with the precision of a sushi master, create a beautiful shape with your spinach in the middle. You can serve it with grated radish on top – *arigato*.

Shelf Life: Sesame dressing, 2 days; dressed spinach, 24 hours. **Best Kept:** Fridge, but the fresher the better.

haggis for the modern woman

Haggis lovers are like Radio 4 listeners: there are a lot more out there than you think, and they turn up in the funniest places. After I'd done an early slot on the *Today* programme I was blown away by the number of calls I got from friends, family and acquaintances from all walks of life – esteemed colleagues and pub low-lives, hippy tripped-out friends in the furthest corners of Scotland, and of course our vicar, Father Huw.

Anyway, I only recently found out that both my sisters regularly feed haggis to their families, and all the kids (whether two-and-a-half or sixteen years old) love it. I'm not sure the kids would dig the subtle nuance of my pickly, celery salsa, though – they would probably opt for a more traditional neeps 'n' tatties cardiac stuffer.

This recipe is designed as a starter, and a light, elegant, delicious starter at that. For it is up to the modern woman to yank haggis into a less heart-stopping arena, and one of the best jobs celery does is to help the immune system – especially when eaten at this time of year, when it is at its most pungent and powerful.

This is for the alternative Burns Night crew, going down nicely with a glass of New Zealand pinot.

serves 6

20g fresh thyme

1.5kg haggis (MacSween's is very good)

4 celery sticks, thinly sliced

2–3 spring onions, thinly sliced

3 big pickled onions, thinly sliced

black pepper

● Preheat the oven to 200°C / 400°F / gas 6.

● Put the thyme in a 30cm x 30cm baking tray with high sides. Nestle in the haggis and pour in 500ml water. Cover with foil, ensuring it is not touching the haggis itself (because it will stick), and making sure that it is tightly wrapped around the edge of the baking dish. Cook for 40 minutes (or you can just blow it up in the box of nuclear radiation – the microwave).

● You can make the British Isles salsa by hand with a sharp knife and a chopping board (better), or by throwing it all into the food processor on pulse for a few seconds (less good in the texture department). Just mix your three ingredients together in a small bowl, add a crack of black pepper and leave to rest.

● Take the haggis out and pull off the foil. Leave to rest for a minute or 5.

● Serve the tender haggis with a good spoonful of the thoroughly British Isles salsa.

Shelf Life: 1–2 days (haggis makes a good fry-up for breakfast).
Best Kept: In the fridge.

swiss TART : their CHARD and their CHEESE

Chard and Swiss chard are both part of the *Chenopodiaceae* or beet family, and are closely related to spinach. Interestingly, spinach gets all the good press about iron but, in fact, because of its high levels of oxalic acid, most of the iron and calcium in it tends to be indigestible by us. So, even if the analysis states that spinach has a higher iron content, pound for pound chard is more useful.

At some point over the last 25 years, all the quiches became tarts. I am very happy to strut back to quiche – and do – but to me this has always been a tart.

serves 6

FOR THE PASTRY

260g plain flour

125g butter, cut into 8 pieces

1 tablespoon thyme leaves, picked off the branch

2 egg yolks

3 tablespoons milk

S & P

FOR THE FILLING

1 red onion (around 260g), sliced

2 garlic cloves, peeled and finely chopped

2 tablespoons olive oil

800g Swiss chard

6 eggs

150ml double cream

25g strong Gruyère cheese, cut into rough 1cm cubes

S & P

● Put the flour in a food processor, turn it on and drop in the butter pieces down the chute one by one. When the last piece has been incorporated, add the thyme and seasoning, then drop down the 2 egg yolks one at a time. Pour in the milk to bring the whole lot together. Wrap the pastry in clingfilm and rest in the freezer for 10–15 minutes.

● Meanwhile, sweat the onion and garlic in the olive oil in a large frying pan (lid on) over a medium heat.

● Cut off and throw away all but 10cm of the white stalk from the chard. Cut the leaf away from the remaining stalk, then split the white bit in half and slice into pieces 1cm thick. Wash these and then add to the onion mix and put a lid on. Now, very roughly chop and wash the green leaves and, once the stalks have had 5 minutes cooking time, add the leaves. Turn the heat down, take the lid off and keep cooking until all the liquid has evaporated, stirring occasionally – about 10 minutes. The stalks should now be translucent and the whole mixture should be a bit mushy.

● Line your tart case (24cm diameter) with pastry and rest in the freezer for 10 minutes before baking.

● Preheat the oven to 180°C/350°F/gas 4.

● Bake the pastry for 15 minutes, until golden brown, then take out and leave to cool.

● In a bowl, mix the eggs, cream, Gruyère pieces and S & P. Stir in the cooked veggies and transfer the whole lot to the pastry case. Cook the tart for 30–40 minutes, or until it has risen and browned on top. Serve warm, not hot, with a few great leaves.

Shelf Life: 3 days. **Best Kept:** In the larder.

gnocchi with artichoke

I don't know any cook who hasn't had at least one gnocchi gnightmare, but if you hadn't realised it by now, chefs are suckers for a hard time. Don't let that put you off as they are so worth it, especially with the company they keep in this dish: sage and artichokes are two of winter's finest. On the other hand, you could just sneak out and buy them.

serves 6

FOR THE GNOCCHI
500g floury potatoes, such
   as Maris Piper
a big handful of plain flour
S & P
or
800g ready-made gnocchi

FOR THE ARTICHOKE CRISPS
2 globe artichokes
juice of 1/2 lemon
about 1 litre vegetable oil
   for deep-frying
salt

FOR THE SAGE BUTTER
150g butter
15g sage (leaves and stalks)

TO SERVE:
50g Parmesan cheese,
   grated on the fluffy holes
S & P

● First make your mash in the time-honoured way: peel, quarter, cold water, simmer until cooked, drain thoroughly and mash.

● Meanwhile, prepare your artichokes. Trim the outer, tough leaves and cut straight across the top of the artichoke, just about an inch (2.5cm) above the widest part of the bulb. Put them cut-side down and halve from the top of the stems straight down through the middle. You can now see the hairy heart. Cut away any hard fibre around the stalks. Dip in lemon water. Using a teaspoon, scrape out all the hairy bits and discard. Put the hearts back in the lemon water to prevent them going brown. Depending on whether they are old or fresh, you will have to trim the stem. Like any flower, they dry from the cut stem end up. The longer it has been since they were cut, the drier and more fibrous the whole thing becomes. Slice the artichoke very thinly, the length of the cut-side, with a mandolin or other form of slicer, or in the worst case do your best with a knife.

● Back to the gnocchi. While the mash is still warm, mix in the flour and some S & P.

● Take a handful of gnocchi mixture the size of a tennis ball and begin rolling it out into a long snake on a well-floured tea towel. Carry on rolling with the palms of your hands until you have a thin sausage 2cm in diameter. Cut it at regular 3cm intervals.

● Now for the fun part. First dip your fork in a little bowl of flour. Place one of your mini-logs (the 3cm ones) in the dip of the fork at the base of the prongs; using your thumb, roll and press it against the tines, then flick it off the end. You're aiming for a cute, squashed C-shape with the marks of the tines around a little groove where your thumb was. The first one will be a disaster – a squashed sticky amoeba. It's all about a balance of pressures, and eventually it will become a satisfying procedure which involves a flick of the thumbs and wrist. It is better to aim for a squished roll than a boring barrel. Do it quickly, without stressing or obsessing, and then it's done.

● Back to the 'chokes: get the oil really hot and then drop a slice in to check it's hot enough – the artichokes should fizz a bit, then float to the surface. Do the rest in 2 batches for 8–10 minutes each, until the slices are the deeper side of golden brown. Take them out with a slotted spoon, drain immediately on kitchen paper and season with salt. Keep on a baking tray somewhere warm. If the artichokes have been properly cooked through, they will stay crisp for a few hours. If they start to get a bit soggy, then a quick flash in the hot oil should return them to crispness.

● Bring a big pan of salted water to the boil for the gnocchi, and remember that hot plates/shallow bowls are essential for something so delicate.

● In a small pan, melt the butter gently and then, without disturbing the milky solids, pour off the clarified into another small saucepan. Throw away the buttermilk.

● Pick the leaves off the sage and tie the stalks together. Infuse the stalks in the clarified butter for 10 minutes over a low heat. Remove the stalks and drop in the leaves. Keep the heat low as they fizzle and crisp – about 5 minutes. If it gets too hot, the sage will burn and destroy the flavour of the butter.

● Drop the gnocchi one at a time in quick succesion into the pan of furiously boiling water. When they float to the surface, count to 10 and take them out with a slotted spoon (if you have used bought ones, they will need a bit extra). Drain on a tea towel.

● Share the gnocchi between the plates and spoon over the sage butter. Give each a good crack of pepper and a liberal dusting of fluffy Parmesan. Finish with a tiara of artichoke crisps and a smattering of sea salt.

Shelf Life: I don't understand what you're asking me. **Best Kept:** This one isn't a keeper.

radicchio and sangiovese risotto

There is a group of winter leaves that shares what are called Bitter Principles (sounds more like an S&M club than a group of plant chemicals), which increase activity in the liver and help digestion. Handily in winter, they also facilitate the body in getting the most energy out of the food we put into it, and help prevent cholesterol build-up. Thus radicchio is so much more than the obligatory bit of colour in a load of mixed leaves. It is radically underused as a cooked vegetable in this country, and I have a sneaking suspicion that it's the very thing I love that puts others off – its bitterness. Every time we go to Italy, one of my recurring joys is forcing Susi, my other half, to have a sip of my Campari soda; the way her face contorts and grimaces with those bitter flavours cracks me up (in a slightly evil way) every time. She's very patient with me.

Sangiovese is the main grape in Chianti, the heart of risotto land. You can use any full-bodied red wine, but avoid real rubbish as the wine substitutes the stock. This special risotto is deep and rich – not for the faint-hearted.

serves 6 (as a starter, which is what risotto should be)

3 garlic cloves, peeled and smashed

90g butter

3 tablespoons extra virgin olive oil

1 red onion, finely diced

3 celery sticks, cut into small dice

a few sprigs of rosemary, roughly chopped

375g Arborio risotto rice

1 bottle (75cl) Sangiovese (or similar full-bodied red wine)

350g radicchio, washed and shredded

50g Parmesan cheese, grated

S & P

● In your favourite, heavy-bottomed saucepan, sweat the garlic in the butter and olive oil.

● Add the onion and celery along with the rosemary and a touch of seasoning. Cover with a lid and sweat over a low heat for 15 minutes.

● Pour in the rice and stir well. Add half a glassful of red wine and stir. Normally with a risotto your liquid would be hot, but this works fine straight from the bottle – it just takes a bit longer to cook. Allow the wine to be absorbed before adding half a glassful more.

● Carry on adding the wine, half a glassful at a time, stirring constantly until there is none left. Now stir in your radicchio, keeping a handful back for a last minute crunch. Finish cooking the risotto with warm water – around 250ml should be sufficient.

● When the rice is cooked al dente (just with a bit of bite), turn off the heat and check the seasoning. Let it rest for 5 minutes, then turn in the last handful of radicchio. There will be a very multi-layered rich sharpness, as some of the wine is well-cooked and some is quite fresh. Very interesting.

● Stir in the Parmesan and serve, resisting the urge to overkill on the Parmesan.

Shelf life: I never find reheated risotto worth the expense in natural resources.
Best kept: Out; it doesn't like the fridge.

gemelli with anchovy and BROCCOLI

Broccoli is our best friend. It tastes great steamed, roasted, blanched and braised, whilst also moonlighting as a Top 10 Superfood. My favourite reference book says it is: 'Anti-Cancer, Antioxidant, Anti-Stress and Energy Boosting', which is just about as good as it gets at this time of year. Just reading that amount of positivity has made me feel better already.

Assuming you can't get fresh anchovies, the ones you buy packed in salt are the best. They require boning and desalinating, but the taste makes the extra work a pleasure. You can use sardines instead for variation.

Gemelli are a great little pasta much liked in Sicily, where I first ate this dish. If you can't find them use fusilli – you want something with ridges for the bits to get into, rather than just letting the flavours slide off a flat-sided pasta.

serves 6

500g gemelli pasta, dried
1 large red onion, diced
4 garlic cloves, peeled and
    finely chopped
1 teaspoon fennel seeds,
    smashed with the back
    of a knife
18 good anchovy fillets (or
    6 sardine fillets), roughly
    chopped
2 tablespoons dried oregano
1 red chilli, finely chopped,
    (seeds in or out)
8 tablespoons extra virgin
    olive oil
1 head regular broccoli (or
    500g purple-sprouting
    broccoli)
60g raisins
60g pine nuts, toasted
juice of 1 lemon
S & P

● Boil a large pan of salted water with a splash of olive oil in it for the pasta. Once it is on a rolling boil, pour in the gemelli, stir, cover, cook to al dente (use the time guide on the packet) and drain.

● Meanwhile, in a separate pan, over a medium heat, sweat the onion, garlic, fennel seeds, anchovies (or sardines), oregano and chilli in half of the extra virgin, with the lid on, until soft – about 10 minutes, stirring along the way.

● Meanwhile, chop the broccoli, stalks and all, into 2cm pieces.

● Once everything is nice and soft, turn up the heat, take off the lid and throw in the broccoli and raisins with 200ml water. Put the lid back on just until the water is simmering, then take it off. As the water bubbles away it will cook the broccoli pieces, which you want to reach the tender stage – i.e. not crunchy. Stir in the pine nuts and season with pepper (the salt content will probably be OK).

● When the broccoli is beginning to break down, pull the pan off the heat, stir in the gemelli with the rest of the extra virgin olive oil and the lemon juice. Resist the urge to sprinkle with Parmesan: this would be most inappropriate, and you would simply be shot in Sicily.

Shelf Life: 1–2 days. **Best Kept:** In the fridge.

liver with SAGE and all the greens

Love the smell, love the soft, downy leaves, love the taste and love what happens when you fry it gently in butter. Sage is probably our nation's favourite winter herb, as synonymous with Christmas as basil and mint are to summer. The essential oil taken from it is strongly antiseptic, antibacterial and very good as a muscle relaxant. In classical times it was known as *Salvia salvatrix*, Sage the Saviour.

serves 6

6 rashers unsmoked bacon

4 tablespoons olive oil, not extra virgin

6 beautiful slices of calves' liver

300g winter greens, roughly chopped

600g whole leaf spinach

a squeeze of lemon

150g butter

25g sage leaves, roughly chopped

S & P

● Preheat the grill. Grill the bacon on both sides until crispy.

● Put a big pot for the greens and spinach onto the stove with a cup of water in it. Season and bring to the boil.

● Meanwhile, select a frying pan big enough to hold 3 of the liver slices flat (you'll need to cook them in 2 batches). Pour in a little olive oil and get it seriously hot – just below smoking; don't let it catch fire. Season the liver extensively on both sides, then gently lay down in the pan. Do not move the meat for the first couple of minutes to give it time to pick up some colour. Turn after 2–3 minutes, depending on how thickly cut your slices are; don't overcook them. They should definitely still be pink inside.

● Turn the oven on low to warm the plates. Put them in now – with this dish you really haven't got time to muck around with cold plates later. Keep the bacon in there just staying nice and warm, along with the first batch of livers. Add a slash more oil to the frying pan, and once it is really hot, cook the rest of the liver.

● Put the winter greens in the big pot, stir immediately, and add some seasoning. Put a lid on for the 3-ish minutes it takes them to wilt, then add the spinach. Move them all together, take the lid off, and keep jostling them until all the water has evaporated. Once that has happened, pull the pot off the heat, check the seasoning and add a squeeze of lemon. Put the lid back on to keep them hot. By this time, the liver, bacon and greens should all be cooked. Keep the liver pan on the heat while you take the last slices out to keep warm in the oven for a minute.

● Add the butter to the liver pan, now on a medium heat, and melt it in any residual juices. Roll it around as it sizzles, then add the sage leaves, taking care not to burn either the butter or the sage. (If you do, just chuck it out, dry-wipe the pan, heat it up again and add new butter.) Keep going until the sage is crisping and goes a bit see-through – a matter of a couple of minutes. Season it.

● Put the greens on the warm plate first, rest the liver up against them, bacon on top and plenty of sage butter spooned over at the last minute.

Shelf Life: Greens for a couple of days. If you have any sage butter left, that'll go for about a week. **Best Kept:** Meat not; fridge the greens.

saltimbocca SARNIE

Fred and I got very excited about this way to twist the classic, tried it out and it didn't work. Some seven goes later we absolutely nailed it, and it is now one of my favourite recipes in the book.

These are more delicious than you can imagine, and eating them sends me into a dreamlike state... all the juices of the ham, sage, veal and mozzarella are absorbed by the bread... crisp, crunchy, warm crust and soft, gooey, perfect inside. They make for great party food (everyone will swoon): you can do them up ahead of time and bang them in the oven when you need them.

This would qualify as one of those winter treats I may have mentioned before – an eating experience that takes you a couple of steps closer to enlightenment.

serves 6

2 tablespoons extra virgin
    olive oil
2 x 150g mozzarella balls
6 x 60g pieces of veal
    escalope
juice of ½ lemon
6 slices Parma ham
6 ciabatta rolls, or
    something similar with
    a bit of a crust
12 sage leaves
S & P

● Preheat the oven to 250°C/475°F/gas 9.

● Tear off 6 pieces of foil, roughly 50cm x 30cm. Drop a teaspoon of extra virgin in the middle of the dull side of each one and spread it out to within 4cm of the edges.

● Slice each of the mozzarella balls into 6.

● Season the escalopes with S & P and lemon juice.

● Lay out the slices of Parma ham in front of you. Put one escalope onto one half of a Parma ham slice. Fold the other half of the ham over the top, like a book. Repeat to give you 6 ham and veal cahiers (booklets).

● Cut the ciabatta rolls in half across the middle. On the bottom half, sit the veal and ham booklet topped with two sage leaves. Put two slices of mozzarella on top of the sage and season with black pepper. Top with the other half of the roll. Put the completed sandwich into the centre of the foil. Bring the foil edges up around the sandwich to the top and fold them over a few times to seal them. It doesn't need to be neat, but it must be sealed, and it must not be too tight. Make up 5 more sarnies in the same way and set them on a baking tray. Bake in the oven for 15 minutes.

● Carefully take them out of the oven and leave to rest for 5 minutes. They are damned hot!

● Cut them in half and serve with some serious napkinry or kitchen roll, as they can be deliciously dribbly.

Shelf Life: Wouldn't be doing them justice to let them go cold. That would be rude.
Best Kept: Wrapped and not cooked, in the fridge.

kale hotpot with COOL crab

Kale is another player in the Brassica All-Stars, and if you want to be on their team you have to be highly nutritious and rich in vitamins, minerals and protective phytochemicals, all of which will help you stave off illness and keep your body tickety-boo. Importantly, they also include glucosinolates, which increase the activity of enzymes that help the body to eliminate potential carcinogens. I find these kinds of statements slightly anxious-making: I don't believe that if you've got a carcinoma then any amount of curly kale will cure you, but equally it has been proven that eating the right fruit and veg can decrease your chance of ever getting one.

This recipe is a two-parter: the simple, warming and comforting hotpot, which then meets a cool crab crème fraîche on your plate. The contrasting textures, flavours and temperatures really work well together and make for a great, straightforward supper.

serves 6

FOR THE HOTPOT

1.75kg King Edward
   potatoes, peeled
1 litre chicken or veg stock
60g unsalted butter
120g smoked streaky bacon,
   thinly sliced
1 large red onion, cut into
   large dice
4 garlic cloves, peeled
   and chopped
1¹/₂ tablespoons chopped
   thyme
2 leeks, thinly sliced
400g kale, washed and very
   roughly chopped
3 bay leaves
¹/₂ teaspoon ground mace/
   nutmeg
S & P

FOR THE COOL CRAB

4 tablespoons crème fraîche
250g white crab meat
juice of ¹/₂ lemon
¹/₂ teaspoon smoked
   paprika (the sweet
   variety works
   best with the crab)
2 spring onions, thinly sliced
S & P

● Preheat the oven to 220°C/425°F/gas 7.

● Cut the spuds into slices 2cm thick and put into a bit of cold water so that they keep white.

● Get the chicken/veg stock on to warm up.

● We all have a favourite pot, and mine is perfect for this job. It's an old Le Creuset of my mum's, and boy has it taken a battering. It's a really good example of getting your money's worth out of a bit of kit, and I can't help thinking that M. Le Creuset would be pleased to see the way it has held up. It's 30cm across and 10 deep, with a massive scorch mark up the side. Find yourself something similar that can go on the hob and in the oven. Melt the butter in it and fry the bacon. Once it has browned a little, add the onions, garlic, thyme and leeks, mix well and leave to cook for a few minutes. Then stir the kale into the pot along with the bay and mace. Have quite a heavy seasoning moment – lots of pepper.

● Over a medium heat, sweat this lot together for a good 15 minutes with the lid on, stirring regularly. You want the onions and leeks to have softened and the kale to have collapsed a bit. Then tip them out into a bowl, but don't wash up the pot.

● Now start building everything back into the pot. Begin with a layer of potato on the bottom. Season with S & P, then a layer of bacon-kale-leek mix, laid as flat as you can. A touch more seasoning and push the layer down with the back of a spoon. Repeat until you finish with a layer of the mix, rather than the spuds, on top.

● Pour on the warm stock so that the top layer of potatoes is just covered. Put the lid on (or cover with foil) and bake in the oven for about 1 hour, or until the potatoes are super tender.

● When you are confident that the potatoes are cooked (the old stick-a-knife-in trick), take the lid off and put back in the oven for 10–15 minutes until you have a nice golden top.

● In a small bowl, mix together the ingredients for the crab. Check the seasoning.

● Take the hotpot out of the oven and leave to rest for 5 minutes. Serve a good scoop of the hotpot in warmed bowls with some of the cooking liquid, and top with a blob of crab crème. Stir it in and enjoy with a plume of watercress.

Shelf Life: Crab, a day or two, depending on how fresh it was when you got it; hotpot, 3-ish days. **Best Kept:** Try not to fridge the hotpot; just keep it out and you'll be amazed how it goes down. Crabby in the fridge.

parma ham, mozzarella and RADICCHIO lasagne

We all love lasagne. It's one of those dishes that goes in the magic book of foods that everyone adores: crispy duck pancakes, a good bacon sarnie, roast beef (sorry, I did try and think of a veggie one). But this isn't a lasagne like the one you're thinking of.

It's a soupier version of the classic, almost broth-like in its stock levels, but delicious in so many ways. Forget the mince, forget the tomato sauce and forget the béchamel – it's lighter, healthier, easier and quicker to make. And let's face it, you can get *that* lasagne almost anywhere in the world now, so try something different and see how it fits.

serves 6

250g radicchio

2 teaspoons dried oregano

4 tablespoons extra virgin olive oil

1.5 litres chicken stock (or 1½ stock cubes dissolved in 1.5 litres boiling water)

250g dried lasagne

250g Parma ham, thinly sliced

250g mozzarella, grated

140g Parmesan cheese, grated

S & P

● Split the radicchio down the middle and remove the core. Wash the leaves and drain well. Shred the radicchio into thin strips and put into a medium-sized bowl. Now dress it with the oregano, some salt and pepper and the extra virgin.

● Heat your chicken stock (or make the broth up with the stock cube and boiling water).

● Preheat the oven to 180°C/350°F/gas 4.

● Now it is simply a matter of assembling everything. Have your cheeses and ham ready, along with the dressed radicchio. My pack of lasagne has 12 sheets, so I figured 3 for each layer – 4 layers in total.

● Lay down 3 sheets of lasagne in the bottom of a deep lasagne dish (20 x 30 x 5 cm) and top these with a layer of Parma ham. Sprinkle on a quarter of the radicchio, followed by a quarter of the mozzarella and Parmesan. Season with salt and pepper. Now lay down another 3 sheets of lasagne and repeat so that you finish the top layer the same way.

● Gently pour over the stock, aiming for a thin stream around the sides. Cover with foil and bake in the oven for 45 minutes. The stock will cook the lasagne and keep it moist. This is a simple, but rich dish so serve with a big green salad. This lasagna *al forno* needs no excuses, just a bit of understanding.

Shelf Life: 2 days. **Best Kept:** Can be reheated from the fridge, but is at its best when just out the oven. It's a pasta thing.

fontina, cima di rape and toasted almond PIZZA

Cima di rape. I like to throw myself at those words in my best cheesy Italian accent as I storm around the kitchen. 'Chima di Rapay' is how you pronounce it, but you have to really say it with conviction and try and roll the 'r' a bit. It's a bit like purple-sprouting broccoli and, as a member of the brassica family, it displays all the usual vits and mins, as well as considerable amounts of folic acid and calcium. If you love a proper pizza, look no further; if you like Pizza Hut, look away.

serves 6

FOR THE PIZZA DOUGH
2 teaspoons dried yeast
a pinch of sugar
660g strong white flour
20ml extra virgin olive oil
a pinch of salt

FOR THE CIMA
2kg cima di rape, ends
    trimmed off, stalks
    chopped into 3cm pieces
    and leaves roughly
    chopped, all washed
120ml extra virgin olive oil
4 garlic cloves, peeled and
    chopped
1 red chilli, deseeded and
    finely chopped (or 1
    teaspoon Crema di
    Pepperoncini –
    see page 171)
S & P

FOR THE PIZZA TOPPING
350g fontina (or taleggio),
    cut into 1cm thick slices
40g flaked almonds
a drizzle of extra virgin
    olive oil
S & P

● In a small bowl, dissolve the yeast with the sugar in a little warm water. Leave in a warm place for 10-ish minutes to kick-start the fermentation process.

● Sieve the flour and salt into a mound in the centre of a big bowl. Make a well in the middle. Slowly fill up the well with the yeast mix and, using a wooden spoon, gently draw in the flour immediately surrounding it to make a paste. Keep working the flour in, and as it gets stiff slowly add about 320ml water until everything is incorporated.

● Tip onto a surface, ideally a lightly floured marble slab, and knead the dough for a few minutes until it is smooth and elastic – when you prod it the dough should bounce back a bit to close up the hole your finger just made. Put in an oiled bowl, cover with a lid or cling film and put somewhere warm. I use the airing cupboard.

● Heat the extra virgin in a saucepan large enough to hold the cima. Fry the garlic and chilli with a pinch of salt for a few minutes, until the garlic starts to go golden. Throw in the cima, roll it around in the infused oil and whack up the heat. Stir well so that it is all coated and beginning to wilt. Turn the heat down to half and cover with a lid.

● Cook the cima like this for 15 minutes, then take the the lid off and whack up the heat again, stir well and let all the excess water boil off for 5-ish minutes more, just until it begins to catch on the bottom. Give it a good crack of pepper.

● After an hour in a warm place, your dough should have risen nicely. Take it out of the bowl and knead for a few minutes, admiring your handiwork.

● Preheat the oven to 220°C / 425°F / gas 7.

● Divide the dough into 2 balls and roll one out so that it covers a lightly oiled baking tray that is as wide as your oven (approximately 30 x 35cm for mine). Roll out the other dough ball on a second baking tray.

● Spread the cima all over the 2 pizza bases. Dot with the pieces of fontina (or taleggio) and the almonds.

● A final drizzle of extra virgin olive oil and some S & P, then into the oven they go.

● Cook for about 20 minutes, until the base is golden brown and all is sizzling nicely. Swap your pizzas around halfway through to ensure proper even cooking.

Shelf Life: 1 – 2 days. **Best Kept:** We all know how good pizza is the next day, best if you cover but don't fridge it.

chicken KIEFF

This is a meeting of monarchs: can there be any more regal Russian dish than the classic Kieff, so overdue for a return to court favour? Here it is kept in good company with some of our own veg patch royalty, the January King cabbage. Our kieff is much more a herb assault than a cholesterol splurt. Feel free to make the kieffs up the day before.

serves 6

6 garlic cloves, peeled
200g butter (at room temperature)
40g flatleaf parsley, finely chopped
25g chives, finely chopped
zest and juice of 1¹/₂ lemons
6 big and lovely corn-fed chicken breasts, skinless
about 200g plain flour
a branch of rosemary, leaves chopped
5 eggs, lightly beaten with a tablespoon of water
300g breadcrumbs (NEVER buy breadcrumbs)
sunflower oil, for drizzling
1 head of January King cabbage
S & P

● First make the garlic butter. Smash the garlic cloves with the side of your knife, then finely chop them with a little salt. In a bowl, mix the butter with the parsley, chives, lemon zest and juice, then season with S & P. Stir in the garlic and divide the mixture into 6. Using clingfilm, roll each blob of garlic butter into a log roughly 2cm x 6cm and put into the freezer until hard – about 40 minutes.

● Using a knife with a narrow blade (a boning knife is perfect), and starting at the thin end, make a hole inside each breast the length of the fillet. As long as you have made a tunnel for the butter to go into, it will stretch to fit. Insert the hard butter into the soft breast. Roll the stuffed breast up in clingfilm and twist the ends tightly – just like a Christmas cracker. Put into the freezer for half an hour to allow everything to get hard, which will make the next stage much easier. Do this for them all.

● Set up your breadcrumbing station. This is a small conveyer-belt operation involving 3 shallow-wide bowls. In the first bowl, put the flour with a healthy crack of black pepper and a couple of pinches of salt; in the second, put the eggs; finally in the last bowl, the breadcrumbs and chopped rosemary.

● Take the chicken from the freezer and unwrap. It should be semi-solid. First, roll the chicken in flour, then in egg, then in breadcrumbs. Then go back to the egg and dip the breasts in it a second time, followed by a final roll in the breadcrumbs. This is to ensure that you have a thick, even coating, so all the goodness stays inside. Refrigerate for 1 hour.

● Preheat the oven to 180°C / 350°F / gas 4.

● Place a sheet of greaseproof paper on a 25 x 40cm baking tray. Put the breasts on the tray, evenly spaced. Drizzle over a little sunflower oil (about ¹/₂ tablespoon on each) and put in the oven for about 25 minutes – generally, when the breadcrumbs are a deep golden colour, the chicken is cooked and the butter melted.

● Trim the bottom of the cabbage stem and take off any manky leaves. Halve the head, through the core, then each half into three wedges, held together by a bit of the core.

● When the Kieffs have cooked for 15 minutes, bring a large pan of salted water to the boil. Drop in the wedges of cabbage, cover with a lid and cook for 4–6 minutes, or until just tender. Serve the Kieffs just nuzzling up to wedges of the King.

Shelf Life: Couple of days for the bubble-to-be. **Best Kept:** Cabbage in the fridge.

smashed brussels

There's a real bit of unfair mass-hysteria going on where Brussels are concerned. Lion cubs, party-pack cereals, bonsai trees, babies, miniature dachshunds and Celebrations! (mini chocolates) are all considered cute, but when it comes to these poor little baby cabbages, the world loses its maternal instincts and just talks about farts.

It helps that in this recipe they are not cooked for a cruel amount of time – just a quick steam to penetrate them with heat and moisture – which will do little damage to their very high nutritional content. The other thing that might help you sell them at the supper table is that the finished product looks nothing like Brussels, so you don't even have to tell anyone.

Here, in an effort to improve their image, is a recipe entirely designed to turn you, and your beloveds, into rampant Brussels lovers. It really is nothing like what you'd expect, and comes out more like a rich, rough mash than anything else.

Sublime with pork. Easy too.

serves 6

30g butter

140g smoked streaky
  bacon, thinly sliced

500g Brussels sprouts,
  trimmed

80g crème fraîche

1 tablespoon English
  mustard

3 spring onions, thinly
  sliced

S & P

● Melt the butter in a heavy-bottomed saucepan on a low heat, and cook the bacon gently so that the fat melts out and the bacon begins to brown.

● Toss the sprouts in and roll them around.

● Add 300ml water, turn the heat up to medium and cover with a lid. Cook for 5 minutes.

● Take the lid off and let the liquid reduce by half.

● Take the saucepan off the heat and mash roughly. The best consistency is achieved with a masher. This is hard work because the sprouts are still al dente, which is what we want. So if you have weak wrists or are in a hurry, pulse in a food processor for a few seconds to a chunky consistency.

● Stir in the crème fraîche, mustard and spring onions and season with S & P.

Shelf Life: 2–3 days. **Best Kept:** In the fridge.

little CHOCOLATE
tarts with a bit o'bling

These are richer than Midas and definitely as dazzling – only for the seriously choc-hearted. And then there's the gold leaf. Nearly everyone has internet access these days, and there's a great Italian company who get edible 23k gold leaf to you (via Wales) in a matter of days*. It's really not that expensive and goes a long way. I happen to have some left over from a party and have been known to have a quick leaf mid-afternoon, just for a frisson of decadence. There's no reason why you can't make one big tart (20cm x 6cm), I just never have; and obviously you should cook it for longer at a lower temperature.

Makes 4 or 8 depending on the size of your tart cases.

Either 4 individual spring-forms (10cm across and 4.5cm deep) or 8 regular individual tart cases (10cm across and 2cm deep)

A few leaves of gold (6 needed + more to play with)

FOR THE PASTRY
150g ground almonds
160g plain flour
70g caster sugar
120g unsalted butter
2 egg yolks

FOR THE FILLING
200ml double cream
3 tablespoons Amaretto
300g plain chocolate
3 egg yolks

Shelf Life: I dare you to not eat them all.....
Best Kept: At room temp.

*Fabbriche Riiunite Metallis in Foglie in Polvere f.p.a.
www.frm.it/food

Via per caselle 1
Morimondo (MI)
Italy 20081

● Whizz the ground almonds, flour and sugar together in a food processor, then drop the butter down the chute in knobs. This will make a kind of crumbly texture. Add the egg yolks and pulse until it all becomes one. Turn out onto a piece of clingfilm and press the pastry together tightly. Refrigerate for 20 minutes. This is a very soft pastry.

● Preheat the oven to 200°C/400°F/gas 6.

● When the pastry has had a good rest, line the tart cases with it but do not attempt to roll, just push it into place, trying to keep it even at 3-ish mm. Don't get too anal about it, though: each case should take only a minute or three. Allow them to firm up in the fridge for 15 minutes. Once the pastry has set to very hard, prick the bases with a fork, put your chilled tartlets into the oven and bake for 12 minutes for individual tart cases, 20 minutes for individual springforms and 30 minutes (but on 180°C) for one big tart. The pastry needs to be properly cooked and golden brown.

● Heat the cream and Amaretto for the filling in a metal bowl sitting above a saucepan of gently steaming water. Once it's warm, stir in the chocolate until melted. As soon as it is all smooth, turn off the heat. If the water underneath the pan was boiling furiously, there is a chance the chocolate will either seize or split. This is easily rectified by adding 1–2 tablespoons of warm water to it and whisking vigorously.

● Now add the yolks one by one, whisking them in energetically. If the mix appears to be splitting, add a drop or two of warm water and whisk with renewed vigour, which will bring it back. Keep the bowl on the pan of gently steaming water (no longer on the heat) until needed, so that the mixture stays at a pourable consistency.

● When the pastry shells come out, let them cool for a mo' before loading them up with molten chockie goo. Let them cool at room temperature, rather than fridging them, which would slightly spoil the sexiness of the chocolate experience.

● For the final act of decadence, crown with a sheet of gold leaf on top. Small word of warning: the gold is deeply magnetised, so handle it only with the bamboo tweezers that the company supplies. If you go at it with anything with a magnetic charge (which includes your fingers), you will have a sod of a time getting it off, and the next thing you know, there will be a thin veneer of gold leaf all over you.

portuguese custard TARTS

The winter months are drab for good fruit, so knocking back a taste of summer – and even better a taste of summer suspended in booze – is a great way to cheer things up. And that's only the half of it. Anyone who's ever had a Portuguese custard tart will be so pleased to learn how to make their own (unless you live above Lisboa on the Golborne Road in London, in which case I wouldn't bother).

If you're ever in Lisbon you can go to the shop where, legend has it, they were first made. It is called the Casa dos Pastéis de Belém, roughly translating as 'The House of the Custard Tarts', which is one address I really covet. There are many imitations (including mine) all over the world, but go to Belém for the religious experience. They really don't need the brandied cherries, but I think little moments of extravagance are the way to get through winter.

Makes 12 large or 24 small tarts

I made 2 x 12 muffin trays of wee ones, 4.5 cm in diameter, which were super-cute; alternatively, make 1 x 12 muffin tray of normal sized ones, 6.5 cm in diameter

250 g homemade rough puff pastry (or 1 packet of frozen puff pastry)
275 ml milk
zest of 1 orange
1 vanilla pod, split in half, seeds scraped out and kept separate
4 egg yolks
150 g white sugar
1^1/$_2$ tablespoons plain flour

TO SERVE
a few tablespoons of Brandied Cherries (see page 153)

● Grease your muffin tins with butter.

● Roll out the pastry to 3mm thick and use to line the moulds.

● Preheat the oven to 220°C/425°F/gas 7.

● Heat the milk in a non-stick pan with the orange zest and scraped out vanilla pod.

● In a separate bowl, beat the egg yolks with the sugar until pale, then stir in the flour and vanilla seeds.

● Just before the milk boils, pull it off the heat and strain through a fine sieve onto the egg mix, whisking all the time. Throw away the orange zest and pod.

● Fill each of the pastry cases right to the brim.

● Cook for 15 minutes if you've made weeny ones, and 25 for the regular size. You're looking for a bit of colouration on top, so it may be necessary to grill for a couple of minutes to achieve those delicious burnt spots on the surface.

● Warm the cherries in a saucepan and serve with the tarts.

Shelf Life: 2 days max. **Best Kept:** These are best not refrigerated.

the essential HOT toddy

We all know about the therapeutic qualities of a good toddy, but this mix, with essential oils of thyme, ginger and lemon, really does make the ultimate in winter soothers. Some plants, but by no means all, can produce essential oils, or volatile oils as they are sometimes known, which are so intense that they magnify any pharmacological properties that plant has.

The oil of *Thymus vulgaris linnaeus* is obtained from the little leaves and flowers, and has long been used for its antibacterial and antiviral effect. Ginger is a famous fighter of colds, and is never more potent than in this form.

Very good for the nerves as well, what with all that whisky...

serves 6

¹/₂ cinnamon stick

whisky, to taste (I would recommend quite a lot of good Irish)

2–3 tablespoons clear honey, to taste

5–8 drops essential oil of lemon, to taste

3–4 drops essential oil of thyme, to taste

5–8 drops essential oil of ginger, to taste

● Slowly heat 1.2 litres of water with the cinnamon stick in a small pan until it is just about to boil, then turn the heat off.

● Stir in the whisky, honey and essential oils. Depending on the brand used, these can vary in strength so I would taste the toddy after a couple of drops before whacking in all the suggested amounts in the recipe.

● Cover with a lid, and let stand for 5-ish minutes for the flavours to infuse and settle.

● Serve in glasses. Or mugs.

Shelf Life: The essential oils will keep for up to 2 years – that's 2 winters' worth.
Best Kept: Drink it whilst it's really hot and reap the maximum benefit from the aromas.

spring

Green means go, and that's what this season is all about. Like Olympic athletes, single-minded and unstoppable in their need to go faster, our veg patch is breaking for the skies. It's not surprising that spring is many people's favourite season: after so much winter inertia and drudgery, the joy of seeing some action in the garden and getting some colour in your life feels truly God-sent.

Let's look at those colours: we start our palette with a white-out, a divide between what has passed and what is to come. The easel has been painted over, ready for a new picture, and here it comes in the form of new life. As the young, yellow shoots push through the earth, whether you are a cook or an aesthete, or just bored with polonecks, it's an exciting time. So much to look forward to, the English asparagus season (which kicks off on May 1st) probably being my biggest treat. And if for some weird reason you aren't excited by these native spears, you have the choice of peas, broad beans, gooseberries and little courgettes (with their adorable flowers) all coming up and at'cha.

And that's just the first team. Also pressing for attention are mangetout, sugarsnaps, all the soft herbs, and most of the lettuce heads and leaves, including that No.1 year-round housewife's favourite – rocket – now's the real time to eat it.

When I was growing up, I wasn't too fond of May. For me it signalled only one thing: my sister's birthday. Not only was she the older ('I've had two and a half years more love, and you're never going to catch up' was a common taunt in my youth) but also she had picnic and rounders parties and 'pick-your-own' parties, whereas I, with my late November birthday, got to have videos and sleepovers. (This is a great example of humans and plants behaving identically.) It is only through cooking that I have learnt to love the month of May, if only for all that it signals.

Root veg lovers would point out that a robust swede lasts much longer than a couple of flimsy asparagus stalks, but the nature of that beast is that we have to boil it, mash it, soup it, or roast it. That's the deal through the autumn and winter, but come the warmer months we can do what's best for us – eat it raw, or near as, dammit.

Nutritionists recommend that a third of our diet should be raw – that's a whole lot of crunching. Some things in life were never meant to be cooked, such as avocados or, leaving the delicious petit pois Française aside for a minute, lettuce. The percentage of vitamins and minerals that are either heat-damaged, lost to boiling water or both is an unbelievable and little-known fact: it is generally agreed that most foods when eaten cooked have, on average, only 15 per cent of the original nutritional value, whereas eating them raw allows us to absorb 100 per cent of its nutrients. (Conversely, some foods respond well to cooking, allowing their micronutrients to become more accesible to us in the process.)

Chlorophyll (the atom that makes plants green) is truly a wonder cell: it's almost identical in molecular structure to haemoglobin – the building block of human red blood cells – and it does many of the same important jobs. Once eaten it is absorbed straight into the blood system and feeds oxygen to the brain and other fundamental parts. It helps to build a healthy immune system and de-toxifies our organs (especially the liver); it increases cell growth in the same way that haemoglobin does. Fruit and veg that contain a lot of chlorophyll are high in essential enzymes and rich in B vitamins. The only problem with chlorophyll is that it is destroyed at a fairly low heat (108°F). Spring is the right season to make the most of this natural, not to mention delicious, care-package. With all this young, vital veg around we are really spoilt for choice.

If the first word of this season's eulogy was green, let tender be the last, because there is not a better time in the year to appreciate England's green and tender land.

Asparagus – really hones its activity towards the blood and the digestive system by acting as a strong diuretic for the kidneys. Loads of vitamin B3 and high fibre make it good for your insides, perfect to help with that spring clean.

Baby leaves – contain potassium, essential for correct functioning of the cells. All lettuces should be served as starters for a good reason: their high fibre content aids digestion. They act as mild sedatives too; start your meal calmly.

Bean sprouts – help to maintain energy levels during times of crisis and keep our nervous systems well-oiled. They help lower cholesterol too.

Broad beans – loaded with potassium, phosphorus, iron, zinc and complex carbohydrates, are detoxifying and have protein too. And we moan when we have to pod them. This is one of nature's full nutrient packages.

Cauliflower – wind is a small price to pay for vitamins C, B3, B5 and B6, phosphorus and potassium. All of these help our skin to have a healthy glow and regulate blood-fat concentration.

Chervil – has plenty of vitamin C, to aid tissue repair. It also acts as an antiseptic for the lungs, to help with the elimination of phlegm. Clear lungs can help us to deal with all that pollen.

Chicory – a liver cleanser that will boost your immune system and help keep your energy levels buoyant. Chicory tea aids restfulness in colicky infants and agitated adults.

Chives – along with lowering cholesterol, help breathing and deter the formation of blood clots. They also assist in the elimination of urea which helps our bodies get rid of heavy minerals and waste products from the blood.

Coriander – is rich in folic acid, part of the vitamin B complex. It also helps cure wind and make blood cells.

Courgettes – are rich in phosphorus, which is necessary for our bodies to absorb nutrients. They are also gentle on the digestion and smooth all absorption and elimination systems.

Cucumber – is one of our wettest vegetables. It stimulates the urinary tract and, with its trace amounts of sulphur, works with the body as an anti-fungal and antibacterial agent.

Dandelion – has the active bitter principles which keep our liver and kidneys strong to maintain the elimination of waste at a balanced level. Bioflavonoid-rich dandelion ensures absorption of vitamin C.

Dill – is the feathery cousin of fennel and can help to sooth abdominal cramps, including those associated with period pains. It can also help to regulate the menstrual cycle.

Elderflowers – are our spring hedgerows, and some allergy sufferers' seasons, would not be complete without elderflowers. They enhance the body's natural resistance to disease and act as an expectorant (i.e. they clear the chest).

Fennel – has an instantly recognisable flavour which is exceptional when it is raw. A perfect starter, it eases the digestive tract, and then regulates blood-fat levels. Excellent for the mucous membranes and the nerves.

Garlic – was used by ancient races to ward off infection and they were right. The immune system works in tandem with the lymphatic system and its white blood cells; garlic stimulates the latter's production.

Gooseberries – contain the A, B and C of vitamins as well as natural sugars. They act as a diuretic and thus also stimulate liver function. Any inflammations in this region can be soothed with the help of gooseberries.

Green/French beans – contain chlorophyll, as their name suggests, but also folic acid and vitamin A, which help us to have healthy skin and a strong production line of white blood cells.

Jersey Royals – are the first of nature's harvest from within the earth. Potatoes contain copper, which is essential for the formation of connective tissue, and they help us to absorb the other essential metal, iron.

Mangetout – are rammed with all the beneficial Bs. They are kind to the glands, aid antibody production and help maintain energy levels.

Mint – purportedly has aphrodisiac properties, which might be because it stimulates the nervous system. Also calms aches of the head and stomach.

Peas – contain plenty of vitamin C, as well as good carbohydrate, fibre and protein. They also activate the immune system.

Spring onions – the necessary element in salads, are excellent for rheumatism and arthritis. The regulation of body fluids and the prevention of arteriosclerosis are all helped by this adolescent member of the allium family.

Tarragon – stimulates the digestion and also acts as a calming antispasmodic on the intestinal tract. Maybe the French know something by dressing their salads with tarragon vinegar...

GRILLED sardines with a blackened CORN salsa

The trouble with writing about food is that it's all been said, all the words have been used up. Words like delicious and yummy are meaningless and slightly irritating, but the language you would naturally use when you eat something great ('mmm... delicious' and 'yum') become so flat on paper, they're even annoying to type.

So to you – and I address every grilled sardine out there, wherever you are in the world – I say the only words left that have any meaning in them: I love you.

serves 6 as a main

4 ears of corn (precooked/
   frozen/tinned won't do)
12–18 scaled and gutted
   sardines, 2–3 per person,
   depending on their size
25g coriander, washed
   and rough-chopped
2 red chillies, teeny
   weeny dice
2–3 spring onions, finely
   sliced
3 garlic cloves, finely
   mashed
²/₃ cucumber, cut into
   small dice
1 avocado, ripe but firm
2 limes – depending on
   juiciness and your tangy
   needs, plus 1 cut
   into wedges for the
   sardines
6 tablespoons extra virgin
   olive oil
S & P

● If you have a griddle pan, it is going to get a workout with this one. If you don't have one, preheat the grill, and go and get a griddle pan really soon.

● Grill the corn, dry with no oil, until it is lightly, but erratically blackened – about 10–15 minutes. Turn the griddle down low, but keep the heat going through it.

● Lay out your sardines on a plate and season well with sea salt.

● When the corn has cooled, shuck the corn by standing it on its end and sawing down the length of the cob in vertical strokes as close to the core as you can, although too close and you cut through the tough membrane. The cob carcass makes an excellent stock, if you have time – a perfect chowder opportunity here.

● Put the shucked corn in a bowl and as it is cooling, go on a chopping mission with the coriander, chilli, spring onion, garlic and the cucumber. When your chopping is done, cut the avo in half, remove the stone and scoop it out in neat little curves with a teaspoon into the bowl with the rest of the salsa.

● Squeeze on the lime juice and season again – you may want some more lime. The flavours should be fresh and explosive on your palette. Now stir in the extra virgin. Whack the heat up on your griddle, or turn on the grill again. When it is smoking, lay on the sardines, as many as you can comfortably fit without jamming. If using the grill, smear a bit of water on the baking tray before you lay out the sardines on it. Cook the sardines for 6 minutes a side.

● I like to pile the sardines up, as if you were making a low wigwam, and scatter over the multi-coloured salsa, but serving the sardines on a big plate and then passing the salsa in a bowl works too. Lime pieces on the side.

Shelf Life: About 24 hours. **Best Kept:** You can make the salsa up a few hours ahead of time, but don't put the lime, avocado or oil in until 20 minutes before you serve. Cooked fish and salsa will last in the fridge.

chicken and preserved lemon BROTH with turnips

Only go for this if you have some lentils in your cupboard (but there are none in the recipe), a pair of beaten up sandals and the desire to be in the souks of Marrakech rather than in the concrete jungle. In other words, it's a bit authentically ethnic. The French love a turnip, and so maybe it was their colonial influence that introduced them to the Moroccans, who welcomed them into their tagines and soups. That slight bitterness works so well in a braising situation, and combined with the sharp saltiness of the preserved lemons it really does make for a whole bowl of interesting.

serves 6

FOR THE STOCK (can be made the day before)

4 chicken thighs, skin off, but bone still in

2 celery sticks

2 carrots, washed

1 red chilli

a few sprigs of thyme, tied together in a bunch

1 white onion, peeled and left whole

4cm piece of root ginger, peeled and thinly sliced

3 garlic cloves, peeled

2 bay leaves

S & P

FOR THE BROTH:

50g brown basmati rice

10g fresh coriander, chopped

10g preserved lemon, finely chopped

85g baby turnips (trimmed weight), scrubbed

6 mint leaves

S & P

● The best way to get a clear stock is by cooking it very, very slowly. I did mine on a very low heat so that it was just steaming, not even simmering. Put all the ingredients for the stock in a large saucepan with 2.5 litres water and set over a super-low heat until the chicken is cooked and the flesh comes away from the bone – about 2 hours.

● After 1½ hours, put the rice in a small saucepan and strain over 200ml of the chicken stock. Bring to the boil, cover with foil, then turn down to the lowest heat on the smallest burner and simmer gently for 25 minutes. Pull off the heat; even if there is some liquid left it can be added back into the soup.

● Use a slotted spoon to take the chicken out of the stock, along with the bay, carrots, celery and onion, and put them all onto a plate to cool down. Strain the stock into a clean saucepan and throw away all the little scrotty bits.

● When the chicken is cool enough to handle, pick the flesh off the bones and throw them away – they have done their fair share of work. Roughly chop the flesh into soup-sized pieces, which you can then put back into the strained stock. Transfer the bay leaves as well to the stock and then season with S & P.

● Chop the cooked onion, celery and carrot into nice 1cm square dice and add to the strained stock. Put the saucepan with the stock and chicken back onto the stove and bring up to a simmer. Add the cooked rice, coriander and preserved lemon.

● On a mandolin, or the slicer side of a grater, slice the turnips into 1mm thick discs.

● When the broth has come to the boil, throw in the turnip discs and cook for 2 minutes – they should still have some crunch. Check the seasoning and serve with a floating mint leaf.

Shelf Life: Good for a couple of days; you will lose crunch, but the flavours will keep on trucking. **Best Kept:** In the fridge.

gazpacho VERDE

This is a spring version of the summer classic – just as crunchy and delicious, but with a light spinach base to replace the tomatoes, because tomatoes don't really kick off in the flavour department until summer. What it lacks in protein, it makes up for in fresh, green goodness – an energy boosting lunch with all that raw veg keeping you perky throughout the afternoon or, it makes a perfect light starter.

serves 6

1 small white onion, roughly chopped

4 garlic cloves, peeled and roughly chopped

2 tablespoons olive oil

180g baby spinach

150g white bread (no crusts please)

3 tablespoons red wine vinegar

2 celery sticks

1 green pepper

1/3 cucumber

2 spring onions

3 tablespoons finely chopped mint

2 tablespoons finely chopped flatleaf parsley

1 green chilli, de-seeded and cut into tiny dice

4 tablespoons extra virgin olive oil

S & P

● In a saucepan on a medium heat, sweat the white onion and half of the garlic in the regular olive oil until soft. Pour in 800ml water, and whack the heat up. When it starts to boil, immediately turn the heat off and stir in the baby spinach until it wilts – literally seconds.

● Blend thoroughly (roughly 3 loads in a normal-sized blender), dropping in 5–6 ice cubes per load as you go. Season a bit, then put the super-green liquid into the freezer in a shallow, metal container to chill quickly, giving it a stir every 10 minutes or so. If you have a super-freeze button, hit it on for half an hour, but be careful to take your greenery out before it freezes.

● Tear the bread into small pieces in a bowl, pour on the vinegar and push it around a bit to make sure all the liquid is being soaked up.

● Now start your chopping. Split the celery lengthways into 3, then chop it the whole way along so it falls into tiny squares. Split the pepper in half, de-seed and chop it into like-sized chunks.

● If you have a mandolin, use it to cut the cucumber into thin slices first. There's no real need to peel it. Then stack the slices up and cut them into long matchsticks, then teensy cubes. If you don't have a mandolin, do the best and most logical job you can, knowing that you're aiming for tiny squares. The spring onions, including the green parts, just get thinly sliced. Have your chopped herbs ready as well, and give the bread a final squish with the back of a spoon.

● Take the chilled soup out of the freezer and tip the soaked bread into it, using a whisk to make sure it is properly dispersed. Stir in the chopped veg, herbs, chilli and remaining garlic. Then add nearly all of the extra virgin and some more S & P. Save a little extra virgin to drizzle over the top, and serve with a few pieces of crushed ice in it as well, if you're out to impress.

Shelf Life: 2 days. If you're eating it the next day, it may need reactivating with a splash of vinegar. **Best Kept:** In the fridge.

CHIVE vichyssoise

Chives are the babes in the great and large allium family, which as a collective boasts more antioxidants than practically any other. I'm sure if it wasn't for the breath factor, all doctors would preach a raw onion over an apple a day to keep you safe and well.

serves 6

1 leek

2 celery sticks

1 tablespoon butter

1 tablespoon light olive oil

2 large mashing potatoes, King Edwards, Maris Peer, Marfona

1 litre veg or light chicken stock

700g broad beans, in the pod (or 250g frozen)

150g baby spinach

200ml double cream

40g chives

1 lemon

S & P

● Cut the leek in half lengthways (keep any ropey outer leaves for your stock) and then slice thinly all the way along. Run under cold water until you're happy that they are properly clean.

● For this silkiest of soups you could be a bit prissy and peel the celery. But at the right time of year (now), you can find wonderfully crisp celery, so peeling may be unnecessary. Anywhichway, slice into similar-sized pieces as the leeks.

● Put a large saucepan on the stove with a tablespoon of butter and about the same amount of olive oil (preferably not a really overpowering, strong extra virgin). Add the leeks and celery and sweat very gently. Put on a lid and stir regularly for the 7-ish minutes it will take for the veg to soften. It is vital the veg don't brown at all, not even the tiniest bit.

● Meanwhile, peel the spuds and cut them into rough 2cm dice. When the veg is translucent, add the spuds, stir well and then pour in the stock. Turn the heat up and bring to the boil, skim and simmer for about 10 minutes until the spuds are cooked.

● Bring a small pan of salted water to a rolling boil. Throw in your podded broad beans, blanch them for 3 minutes, then run immediately under cold water. Once cooled, take them out of their shell and allow them to fall into their natural halves.

● When the potatoes are tender, turn off the heat and throw in the baby spinach. Blend immediately with a dozen ice cubes: you want your soup to be totally smooth. Tip into a large, flat dish so it cools down quickly and retains as much of the greenness as possible. Chuck in a couple of ice cubes just to speed the cooling.

● Stir in the cream and season well with plenty of salt and pepper (white, if you're feeling fancy). The thickness of the soup depends on the variety of the potato, so if it's a bit too thick, add a touch of milk to let it down. Store in the fridge until needed.

● When you're ready to go, slice the chives as thinly as you can. Stir most in and sprinkle the rest on top with the broad beans. Serve in chilled bowls. And maybe add a squeeze of lemon. A few croûtons wouldn't go amiss either.

Shelf Life: 2 days. **Best Kept:** In the fridge covered; if you throw in all the chives, the flavour will allium up a few notches the next day.

BERBER salad

In the land of camels, chebis (moving sand dunes) and a million stars, we ate this salad sitting in a tent on the edge of the Sahara with some very friendly but rough-looking men. One of them told me his name was Max Relax, but even though he seemed to be living as his name suggested, I wasn't convinced. Mind you, he thought my name was pretty funny too.

What a great combination of textures: chewy bulgar with crisp veg and herbage, as well as the nuttiness of the argan oil (see page 187 for more on this great oil) and low-level spice. This is my sister Floss' favourite recipe in the book – and by now she has eaten her way through most of them.

You can boost this from being a salad to a complete light lunch by serving it with warm flatbread and a couple of bowls of yogurt and olives, and we also think it would be great with grilled lamb chops.

serves 6

5 tablespoons argan oil
$1/2$ teaspoon ground cumin
180g bulgar wheat
180g tomatoes, roughly
    chopped
1 medium green pepper,
    diced small
4 spring onions, thinly
    sliced
30g flatleaf parsley,
    roughly chopped
30g mint, roughly chopped
1 green chilli, seeds removed
    and cut into small dice
450g broad beans in the
    pod (or 150g frozen)
juice of 1 lemon
S & P

● Gently heat the argan oil over a low heat and fry the cumin in it for a minute or two to release the aroma.

● Stir in the bulgar and keep frying for a couple of minutes more until all the grains are well coated.

● Season the bulgar with S & P and pour over 200ml water.

● Cover, then simmer for 20 minutes until all the liquid is gone.

● Bring a small pan of salted water to a furious boil. Blanch the podded broad beans for 3 minutes, then refresh under cold water.

● Turn the heat off and let the bulgar cool like that with the lid on (unless you are in a hurry, at which point you could spread it out on a tray so it cools slightly faster).

● When the bulgar is cool, mix it with all the other ingredients in a bowl, finish with the lemon juice and check the seasoning.

Shelf Life: Not going to be so great tomorrow. **Best Kept:** Room temp for a short while; fridge if for more than an hour.

scallops with asparagus

At the height of the season, I try to have asparagus at least three or four times a week, and it still feels like a treat every time – especially when you put it with a few scallops and a load of seasonal greenery. The dark green leaves of the garlic plant come into season around the same time as asparagus. Carrying those famous healing garlic properties, it is found for only a couple of weeks in good greengrocers and farmers' markets. Use baby spinach if there's no garlic leaves, but do try to hunt them down as they are a whole new kind of fabulous.

serves 6

100ml extra virgin olive oil

2 garlic cloves

2 bunches asparagus
  (allow 3–6 spears each)

1 tablespoon chopped mint

1 tablespoon chopped dill

1 tablespoon chopped basil

1 tablespoon chopped
  chervil

1 lemon

12–18 scallops (allow 2–3
  per person, depending
  on their size), cleaned
  and keep the rounded
  half of the shells

1 tablespoon olive oil

150g garlic leaves, cut into
  3cm lengths, or
  baby spinach

S & P

● Get your griddle pan very hot or preheat the grill and place a rack sitting over a foiled baking tray on the highest shelf.

● In a small saucepan, heat the extra virgin and the garlic cloves very gently. Be careful not to let everything get too hot or the flavour of the oil will change. Hold it like this for 5–7 minutes.

● Slice the asparagus stalks on the diagonal into 3–4cm lengths, keeping the tips whole.

● Turn off the heat on the garlic oil, cool to room temperature, then fish out the garlic and chuck it. Once the infused garlic oil is completely cool, stir in the chopped herbs, a squeeze of lemon and some seasoning. You have to wait until it's cool or the herbs will discolour; even the smallest amount of heat will ruin the bright greenness we're after.

● Pat the scallops dry, roll them in olive oil and season them well.

● Put a wide-bottomed pan on the stove on a high heat with about 150ml of water. Bring to the boil and then add the asparagus. Cover with a lid and steam for 2 minutes.

● Take the hot rack out from under the grill. Quickly, but carefully, place the scallops (not touching) on the rack and stick it back under the grill. Alternatively, just place them on the griddle – they will take 2–4 minutes each side depending on size; if you are grilling them you won't need to turn them at all unless they're whoppers.

● Now take the lid off the asparagus pot and add the garlic leaves or baby spinach. Shake it all about for a couple of minutes – the idea is that the greens are just wilted as all the water evaporates away.

● Check the scallops are cooked (opaque with a small amount of resistance when you squeeze them round the middle).

● Add two thirds of the soft herb dressing into the pan with the greens and toss well.

● Divide the greens between the shells or small plates and top with the scallops. Finish with a generous napé of the last bit of the herb drizzle.

Shelf Life: N/A **Best Kept:** I'd be very surprised if there is any left.

CHICORY sails with crab and dilly CHILLI

Cleopatra supposedly strewed chicory upon Mark Antony's bed to induce calm, restful sleep... all the easier to take advantage, my dear. The knowledge has been passed down and folk now make a tea out of it to give to colicky babies or stressed-out adults.

Get hand-picked crab meat from a decent fishmonger if you can. The others have been factory-produced and/or tinned and thus chemically processed, pasteurised or homogenised. These processes impart a nasty taste, one that will far outshine the natural oceanic flavour of fresh crab. It's just about worth doing with pasteurised, but forget about tinned.

This is a cool little canapé, or pile 'em up four per person for a starter. The sail bit is just a romantic felucca image I had whilst dreaming about pottering down the Nile.

makes 24: 4 per person for 6

180g picked white crab meat
1 red chilli, de-seeded and then finely chopped into 2mm squares
10g dill, roughly chopped
juice and zest of 2 limes
1 tablespoon best extra virgin olive oil
2 heads of chicory
S & P

● In a small bowl, mix the crab meat, chilli, chopped dill, lime juice and zest, a touch of salt and the extra virgin olive oil.

● Cut the leaves off the chicory: you'll find as you work towards the centre of the bulb you need to cut higher up to detach them from the core. They also look nice if you trim the stem end of each leaf into a point. Wash the chicory in icy cold water and leave to drain well in a colander.

● Correct the seasoning of the crab mixture – it may need a touch more salt – and spoon a blob into the centre of each of the sails.

Shelf Life: 1–2 days for the crab mix depending on how fresh the crab was when you got it. **Best Kept:** Fridge, but I'd rather you ate it all on the night.

With a bit of wistful imagination on your side, the chicory leaves look like wind-filled sails...

salad of LIFE - seeds, sprouts, SHOOTS and leaves

This is what we should eat every day in the spring, the best time of year to celebrate new life. This salad sums up all the joy in this book by telling the life story of a plant, with all the different stages present at the same time.

If anything causes you trouble in this recipe, it will be finding the sprouts (not Brussels), which are available in punnets of mixed sprouting pulses. These are wonderfood and bring an awful lot to the party that is your body.

The quantity of roasted seeds is enough for the recipe but, as they are good to have around, I'd make a bigger batch and keep some for snacking on.

serves 6

FOR THE ROASTED SEEDS
20g each of sesame, pumpkin and sunflower seeds

FOR THE SALAD
2 tablespoons red wine vinegar
4 tablespoons extra virgin olive oil
240g baby salad leaves, washed
180g bean or pea shoots
90g sprouting pulses
S & P

● Preheat the oven to 200°C/400°F/gas 6.

● Spread the seeds out on a baking tray and pop into the oven for 8–10 minutes until toasted. Then take them out of the oven and leave to cool.

● Make the dressing by mixing together the vinegar with the extra virgin olive oil and a bit of S & P.

● I like to build this salad layer on layer – all the parts are so delicate and their little voices need to be heard. So it is just a matter of dividing the ingredients amongst your 6 plates with the leaves on the bottom, then the shoots, the sprouts and then finally the seeds. Drizzle the dressing over the top and have a bite of life.

Shelf Life: Leaves, etc. in the fridge for 3 days as long as they're not dressed. Seeds, a week or two – same for the dressing. **Best Kept:** All the parts will keep in the fridge. Seeds you can keep in a dish on the table for munching and dressing in a jar on the side.

chariots of fire - best of the
BRITISH runners

Runner beans were first brought to Europe from South America a couple of hundred years ago, not for their edible seed pods but for their fantastic flora – different varieties produce dazzling scarlet, white and vermillion flowers. Since then, they have become an allotment classic, but for some reason they seem to have remained on small-scale production rather than hitting the big time like their French bean cousins. I have two theories for this:

One is that they involve a bit more prep time. Generally, by the time they reach us they are a bit big and old and need peeling down the stringy sides. All you lucky folk with allotments or veg patches know this is not the case when freshly picked off the stalk. As an aside, it is both encouraging and a bit depressing that the current waiting list for an allotment in Hackney is two and a half years. People are keen; there just ain't enough green bits to go round.

The second is that being a big old climber, The Great British Runner is harder to harvest mechanically than its cousins. Sad but true.

**serves 6 as a side
or part of a mezze**

500g runner beans
2 garlic cloves, peeled and
    thinly sliced
1 red chilli, thinly sliced,
    seeds and all
1 courgette, cut into quarter
    lengths and then into
    1cm thick chunks
juice of 1 lemon
80ml extra virgin olive oil
20g chives, cut into 4cm
    lengths (or thin slices
    of spring onion)
S & P

● Top, tail and peel off the strip down the sides of the runner beans, then cut into 2–3cm diamond-shaped rhomboids.

● Bring a pot of water with 1 teaspoon of salt to a rapid boil. Blanch the beans, garlic, chilli and courgette for 6–8 minutes.

● Strain the veg and tip into a bowl.

● Toss well with the lemon juice, extra virgin, chives and seasoning. Then cover with foil for 5–10 minutes to let the flavours develop.

● Eat warm.

Shelf Life: 2 days. **Best Kept:** At room temp, as long as your room isn't too hot.

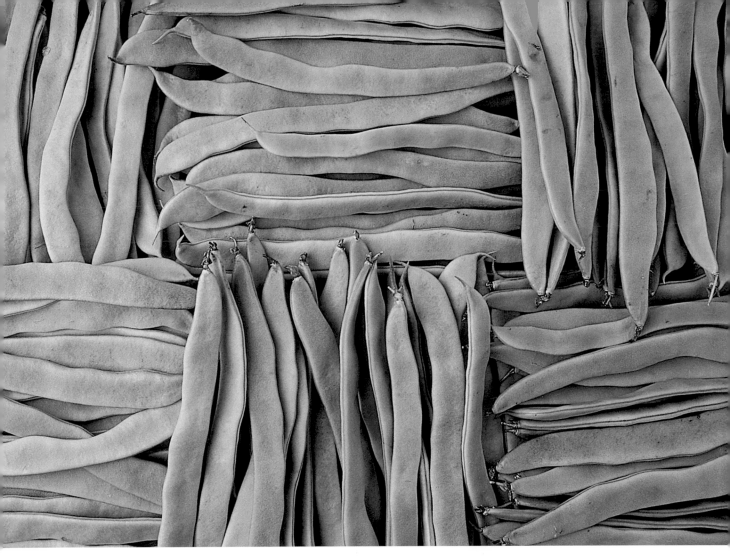

lemon - blanched French beans with sauce REMOULADE

French beans are used prolifically as a supporting veg, but rarely are they given a starring role. In season, however, they are little superstars: tender and sweet, crisp and flavourful, not to mention the fact that they are good for our kidneys and stimulate the production of white blood cells, which help fight infections.

This is the simplest of dishes and the simplest of recipes, nicking the creamy-mustardy remoulade dressing from its usual dance partner, the celeriac.

I kind of meant this to be a starter, but if you fancy it as a side veg, give it a whirl. I have a sneaking suspicion it might be rather good with fish and some boiled new potatoes.

serves 6

3 tablespoons extra virgin
   olive oil
1 lemon, cut into quarters
1 teaspoon grain mustard
3 tablespoons crème fraîche
juice of $1/2$ lemon
400g French beans
1 tablespoon sultanas
S & P

● Put 1cm of water, half the extra virgin, the lemon quarters and $1/2$ teaspoon of salt into a large saucepan, put the lid on and bring to the boil.

● In a small bowl, mix the grain mustard, crème fraîche and the rest of the extra virgin olive oil. Add a good crack of black pepper, the lemon juice and a touch of salt.

● When the water has come to a rolling boil, tip in the beans and sultanas. Cover with a lid and cook for 2 minutes.

● Take the lid off and continue to cook until the water has evaporated, 4–6 minutes. Shake occasionally to prevent the beans from catching.

● When the water has evaporated and the beans are coated in the oil, throw away the lemon wedges – they will make things bitter now. Serve the beans in a great pile, with a small dish of sauce remoulade on the side. Eat like asparagus and hollandaise.

Shelf Life: Remoulade, 3 days; beans, a day, then they do that nasty shrivelly thing.
Best Kept: In the fridge.

goat's CHEESE, parmesan and CHIVE soufflé

My mum used to make an anglicised version of this called Mrs Johnson's Cheese Pudding, and although I didn't realise that when I came up with this recipe, the minute I tasted it I was straight back at our kitchen table with my parents looking very young on either side of me. Funny how tastes can do that to you, but I guess Proust covered that one with his Madeleines.

Foodie purists might claim that this is not a true soufflé, but the upside is that it always rises and has none of the stress factor associated with the classic.

It's a bit of a bloke's dish, combining the two things blokes like best in the kitchen: minimal work with a showy result. You'll need 6 individual soufflé dishes or ramekins, 7–8cm across.

serves 6

55g unsalted butter
55g plain flour
100ml milk
1 teaspoon Dijon mustard
a little extra butter, for greasing
15g Parmesan cheese, grated on the spikey side that makes the fluff or, failing that, on the small holes
100g goat's cheese, crumbled
4 egg yolks
15g chives, finely chopped
6 egg whites
juice of ¹/₂ a lemon
S & P

● Melt the butter gently in a small pan and then stir in the flour to make a roux. Cook the roux over a low heat for a couple of minutes, then slowly add the milk, stirring constantly. Once you have a smooth paste, pull the pan off the heat, add the mustard and allow to cool.

● Grease the insides of the soufflé dishes with a little butter, then dust with a small amount of the grated Parmesan. The best way to do this is to toss a handful into the greased dish and shake it about so it sticks to the butter. Tip out any excess into the next ramekin.

● Once the paste is cooled, stir in the rest of the Parmesan with the crumbled goat's cheese, egg yolks, chives and plenty of black pepper.

● Preheat the oven to 200°C/400°F/gas 6.

● In a separate big bowl or mixer, whisk the egg whites with the lemon juice and a pinch of salt. Keep whisking until you are at the firm peak stage – this is essential to make your soufflés rise. Fold the whites gently into the cheesy mixture in 3 loads. The first load you can stir in quite forcefully, as this will loosen the mixture for the next 2 loads which can be folded in more gently. Once everything is gently combined, divide the mixture between the prepared dishes.

● Bake for 12-ish minutes, dropping the temperature a little if the tops seem to be going too brown, but don't open the oven. Serve immediately – the middle should still be a bit gooey, but not too liquid. Serve with a few sharply dressed rocket leaves to contrast with the richness of the soufflé.

Shelf Life: 10 minutes max. **Best Kept:** No, you can't keep this.

dandelion salad, GOAT'S cheese POLENTA croûtons

Yellow is by definition the sunniest colour. This is a triple-yellow special. Dandelion is one of the first early leaves to push its way through the soil in spring, similar in colour, flavour and natural attributes to chicory but the leaves are longer and narrower with yellow, jaggedy edges. Try to find them for your pleasure, but if all else fails use rocket.

serves 6

FOR THE CROÛTONS
180g polenta
15g Parmesan cheese, grated
1 tablespoon extra virgin
    olive oil
100g goat's cheese
S & P

FOR THE DRESSING
30g flatleaf parsley, finely
    chopped
2 tablespoons capers,
    drained and chopped
10 anchovies, chopped
2 garlic cloves, peeled and
    finely chopped
juice of 1 lemon
4 tablespoons extra virgin
    olive oil

FOR THE SALAD
350g yellow wax beans,
    trimmed, but if you can't
    get hold of them do a
    French exchange
250g dandelion leaves

● Cook the polenta as per the packet. When it is done, add the Parmesan, the oil and some seasoning, but hold back on the salt, because of the upcoming goat's cheese. Crumble in the goat's cheese and fold it in gently. We want there to be lumps and chunks of white. Turn the whole lot onto your very generously oiled baking tray (15cm x 15cm) to set for about 40 minutes.

● Put a small pan of salted water on the stove for the beans. Preheat the oven to super hot: 240°C/475°F/gas 9.

● In a small bowl, mix together the parsley, capers, anchovies and garlic. Pour over the lemon juice and the extra virgin and stir well.

● Turn the set polenta onto a chopping board and cut it into neat 2cm cubes. Place the cubes, not touching, on a lightly oiled baking tray. Drizzle a little bit more oil on top of each one, just a drop, and pop into the oven.

● After 20 minutes, check the polenta, it should be getting a good colour. Using a palette knife, turn each cube over, then put back in the oven for a further 5–10 minutes. You are looking for a golden-brown crust on the edges of the croûtons and a hot, gooey, cheesy inside.

● Blanch the beans in the boiling water for 4 minutes and refresh in a sink full of very cold water. Drain.

● Prepare the dandelion leaves. It should be a simple matter of washing, cutting off the heavy, thick stump from the end and chopping into 8–10cm lengths.

● Dress the beans and dandelion with a third of the ancho dressing. Divide the mix between 6 plates.

● Take the polenta croûtons from the oven and allow to cool for a minute. Give each person a big portion of super-crunchy, golden croûtons for their spring yellows salad, and finish by drizzling over the rest of the dressing.

Shelf Life: Polenta and ancho dressing, 2 days. **Best Kept:** The salad won't keep once it's assembled, but the polenta could be made and cubed the day before, as could the ancho dressing. Both can be kept in the fridge.

yellow courgette, broad bean and fresh PEA QUICHES

Somewhere round about 1980 the word quiche became deeply naff and suburban. Towards the end of that decade the rise of the gastropub heralded the entry of the tart, and everything that was once a quiche became tart like. Same recipe, different name. Now it's time to call a spade a spade and allow these rich, eggy classics to reclaim their true identity.

This is spring in a pastry case: the colours and flavours sing of it, and the joy of being able to use fresh peas and broad beans makes all that shelling a pleasure not a chore. And whilst you've got that time on your hands, take a minute to appreciate the nutritional value that comes with all that freshness: plenty of vitamin B5 (the one that's good for your immune system) and C.

Obviously, if you can't get yellow courgettes, green works fine – you just lose a few colour points. I've done little ones for the cutesy factor, but a big one would be equally delicious. You would have to cook it on a lower temp for longer, until the custard in the centre is just set.

serves 6
6 individual tart tins, 10cm in diameter and 4cm deep, or whatever shape and size you fancy

FOR THE PASTRY
200g plain flour
100g unsalted butter
1 egg yolk
40g Parmesan cheese, grated
a drop of milk
S & P

FOR THE FILLING
650g broad beans in the pod (or 220g frozen)
200g courgettes, preferably yellow, cut into 1cm dice
400g fresh peas (120g podded weight)
6 egg yolks
150ml double cream
1 tablespoon chopped mint
S & P

● Preheat the oven to 170°C/350°F/gas 4.

● In a food processor, spin the flour for a minute, and then drop the butter down the chute in small knobs. Once incorporated, add the egg yolk, Parmesan and some seasoning. Tip out onto your workbench and bring the pastry together with a little milk. Wrap in clingfilm and rest in the fridge until needed, minimum time 30 minutes.

● Bring a saucepan of salted water to the boil and drop in the broad beans. Blanch them for 3-ish minutes, then drain under cold, running water and shell the lot.

● Grease your mini tart tins with butter and then dust with flour; line with pastry then chill in the fridge for 10 minutes. Blind bake (no beans necessary) for 8 minutes. Cool and then fill with your 3 kinds of veg.

● Mix together the egg yolks and cream, add the chopped mint and some S & P and pour over the tarts, right up to the top. Bake for 25 mins, or until the custard has just set. Let it stand for 5 minutes before serving with a few dressed mixed leaves.

Shelf Life: 24 hours. **Best Kept:** Out and about.

salt COD fritters (balls of bacalao)

Salt cod (bacalao) is big in all sorts of places, from Spain to the Caribbean, France to South America. It has a truly special taste and texture, quite different from fresh cod and not at all inferior. In this recipe, the spuds balance the saltiness equation. I put these fritters on the menu at the ICA with the grim determination that chefs get when they know it's a great dish but equally know it won't sell. It turned out I couldn't have been more wrong. These crunchy little balls of Iberian love flew out the door faster than Casanova to a virgin. Great party food, especially with Chipotle Ketchup (see page 170).

serves 6 and a bit

750g salt cod (dried weight)

1.2kg mashing potatoes, peeled and cut into 3cm chunks

5 eggs

200g plain flour

1/2 teaspoon cayenne

4 tablespoons roughly chopped flatleaf parsley

2 corns on the cob, raw and shucked

4 garlic cloves, smashed

4 tablespoons chopped chives (or you could use thinly sliced spring onions)

juice of 1–2 lemons

vegetable oil, for deep-frying

black pepper

● Soak the cod for 24 hours (preferably under running cold water for at least some of that time).

● The next day, preheat the oven to 160°C/320°F/gas 3.

● Put the cod into a roasting tray that is large enough to hold it, with sides that are at least 4cm deep. Pour over enough fresh water to half cover it. Cover with foil and bake in the oven for 30 minutes.

● Take the cod out of the oven, chuck the foil and leave to cool in the cooking liquor.

● Put the spuds into a saucepan and carefully pour over the cooled cooking liquor, adding more water, if necessary, to cover. Don't add any salt. Bring to the boil and cook until the spuds are soft.

● Now turn to the cod. Do not let it go stone cold: much easier to handle when she's still warm. Pick the flesh off and put in a food processor. Throw the skin and bones away. Pulse the picked cod until you have a fibrous/hairy consistency – you'll see what I mean. Scrape all the cod out of the food processor into a large bowl.

● Drain the spuds and mash them. Put them in the bowl with the cod and throw in the rest of the ingredients, except the veg oil. Mix everything together, then give it a couple of cranks of the pepper grinder and put into the fridge to rest for an hour or so.

● When you are ready to go, heat 8cm veg oil in a wide saucepan over a low heat. You do not want the oil to be smoking. To check it is the right temperature, drop in a little bit of the mixture: it should fizzle and float.

● Divide the mixture into golf-ball-sized fritters and cook in the hot fat, about 8 at a time, for 4–6 minutes each, or until golden brown on the outside and hot and steamy in the middle. Drain on kitchen roll and keep hot in the oven.

Shelf Life: In the fridge, 3 days; raw mix in the freezer for a month.
Best Kept: Raw, in the fridge; cooked, on the table.

CHICORY TARTE tartin

Cooked chicory has the most amazing, sensuous texture and eating it involves a bit of chew and a whole lot of suck. Some of the slightly bitter flavour of the raw leaf is carried through the cooking, but this is counterbalanced by the sweetness that comes from the caramelisation necessary for a tatin. There's something a bit Roman about braised chicory.

serves 6

a non-stick pan, 25cm
across and 6cm deep

4 chicory bulbs
60g unsalted butter
2 tablespoons honey
30g pine nuts
5g marjoram, leaves
   picked off
200g puff pastry
S & P

● Trim the bases (the root end) of the chicory by millimetres. Then cut each bulb in half lengthways through the core and then in half again, so that you have 4 quarters held together by a bit of stem.

● Put your pan on a medium heat and melt the butter in it. As it starts to bubble, pour in the honey and swirl the pan until the butter and honey are amalgamated. Put in half the chicory and roll it around until all is coated. Now carefully add the rest of the chicory (there will be way too much volume of chicory to start with, but it will wilt down) and roll it around again.

● Cover and cook for 15 minutes over a low/medium heat, stirring from time to time so the wilted leaves come to the top and the raw to the bottom.

● Now take the lid off and turn the heat up. Keeping an eye on it, let the chicory caramelise for 10 minutes until it is soft and completely floppy; the hearts or stems should be soft too. If at any time the caramel seems to be darkening faster than the chicory is cooking, add a splash of water. Stir in the pine nuts and marjoram with some S & P. Wait for the nuts to get some colour on them – 5 minutes.

● Preheat the oven to 200°C/400°F/gas 6.

● Tip the whole lot onto a plate and then rearrange the chicory back in the pan like spokes in a wheel but closely packed, not forgetting the pine nuts and marjoram.

● Roll out the puff pastry into a circle that is just slightly larger than the top of the frying pan. Lay the pastry on top of the arranged chicory, and use your fingertips to press down all round the edge, thus pushing the excess pastry up the sides of the pan. This will allow for shrinkage during cooking.

● Bake for 25 minutes. When the pastry is cooked to golden brown, take it out of the oven and leave it to cool for a few minutes. Loosen the pastry by running a knife around the edge, give it a bit of a shake and turn upside down onto your serving plate. This is a perfect slice of caramelised goo. Doesn't need anything, perhaps a few leaves of rocket if you fancy, or maybe a dormouse.

Shelf Life: Can be reheated the next day, but please don't mike it: pastry and microwaves are sworn enemies. **Best Kept:** At room temp.

new season's garlic,
roast on toast

The new season's garlic is a joy to look at, to work with and above all to eat. The bulbs are sold with a few inches of stalk still attached, and are the purest of whites with beautiful purple and green tinges, as opposed to the yellowish-white that develops with age. The skin that separates the cloves is fresh and edible, and hasn't dried out like that of the regular garlic we are used to.

There are two reasons why this dish of essentially pure garlic won't make you honk: firstly, the fresh bulb is milder than the dried; and secondly, the process of roasting mellows it further, so don't be scared off by the quantity involved.

If you are a true garlic head, then you will be pleased to hear that I have done this recipe out of season with just regular bulbs and it's still ace.

serves 6 as a starter

15g thyme on the branch
6 fresh garlic bulbs, 1 per
    person
2 tablespoons extra virgin
    olive oil
1 tablespoon sherry vinegar
6 slices crusty bread
    (brown, white or
    sourdough)
1 lemon, cut into 6 wedges
S & P

● Preheat the oven to 190°C / 375°F / gas 5.

● Lay the thyme branches on a flat black tray. Slice each bulb of garlic in half, through the root, and sit them on top of the thyme, cut-side down.

● Drizzle over the oil and vinegar, add some seasoning, cover with foil and bake in the oven for around 1 hour (whether young or old), or until the garlic has gone mushy when you squeeze it.

● Once the garlic is ready, toast the bread.

● Serve each person an entire bulb – 2 halves – on toast with a little drizzle of olive oil on top for good measure, a pinch of sea salt and a good crack of pepper. A squeeze of lemon and away you go….

Shelf Life: Roasted garlic is good for days, especially if you squeeze the cloves out of their skins and submerge it in extra virgin. **Best Kept:** Eat it hot.

BISTEK chimmichurri

Chimmichurri is not only a great word, but a great sauce. It's a herb-driven Argentinean salsa, good for marinades, dipping bread into and accompanying the world-class beef that the Argies are famous for.

When compared to a salsa verde it has more bite and depth of flavour, and it does so much more for the meat than a fat-driven béarnaise. Have it with a few simple, oven-roasted chunks of spud, or just a great tomato salad. I wouldn't go down the mash route as it's a bit dairy heavy for this uplifting little salsa.

Obviously, it's at its best with a piece of beef to match its class: very good quality, very rare, wobbling flesh.

serves 6 with a bit of chimmichurri for later

6 x 180g rump steaks
2 tablespoons good dried
   oregano (wild, preferably)
8 tablespoons extra virgin
   olive oil
3 red chillies, de-seeded
   and chopped
8 garlic cloves, peeled and
   smashed
75g flatleaf parsley, chopped
1¹/₂ tablespoons sherry
   vinegar
juice of 1 lemon
S & P

● Season the steak with sea salt and sprinkle with half the oregano. Roll in enough olive oil to coat (1–2 tablespoons), and some black pepper. Leave for about half an hour or so at room temperature so as to absorb the marinade.

● By hand on a chopping board (or in a food processor), combine the rest of the oregano with the chilli. Next add the garlic, then the rest of the ingredients along with some S & P and enough olive oil to give you a smooth paste. If possible, set aside for an hour to allow the flavours to mingle.

● Make your griddle pan very hot, then cook the steaks according to your taste – roughly 3–4 minutes on each side, but it's really hard to say without seeing your beef. Rest the steaks for a minute, then hit them with a healthy dollop of chimmichurri.

Shelf Life: Steaks, eat within a day or two; chimmichuri is good for 1 week in a sealed container, but hold on to your hat as the heat will increase impressively.
Best Kept: Steaks and chimmichurri are both fine in the fridge.

Khaukswe chicken

We all have a pestle and mortar. It's either on top of the cupboard, or right at the back of it, or maybe it's in the loo brimming with potpourri. If you only use it once a year, make sure it's now, because textually the blender just doesn't do the same job. If you do, I promise that you will find it physically satisfying and gastronomically rewarding. This is a seed-driven version of a great dish from Burma. The gremolata (a herby, zingy sprinkle) brings the whole thing up a notch. Serve the chicken with rice and salad if you fancy it. Great buffet food.

serves 6

1¹/₂ teaspoons cumin seeds

2 tablespoons pumpkin seeds

2 tablespoons sunflower
   seeds

2 tablespoons sesame seeds

6 garlic cloves, peeled

2 red chillies, chopped

2 tablespoons vegetable oil

1 teaspoon turmeric

1 teaspoon paprika

2 tablespoons tamarind
   paste

1 teaspoon dried shrimp
   paste, dissolved in
   1 tablespoon hot water

juice of 2 limes

50ml coconut milk

6 tablespoons plain yogurt

1.3kg free-range chicken,
   jointed to give you 12 pieces

S & P

FOR THE GREMOLATA

50g coriander, chopped

2 red chillies, de-seeded
   and finely chopped

zest of 4 limes

2 garlic cloves, peeled and
   finely chopped

salt

● Preheat the oven to 160°C/320°F/gas 3.

● Tip the cumin seeds, pumpkin seeds, sunflower seeds and sesame seeds onto a baking tray and mix together.

● Sprinkle over some salt. Bake in the oven for 20 minutes, taking them out halfway through and moving them around a bit. All ovens are different – some hotter at the back, some around the edges – but the aim of the shuffle is to swap the brownest seeds geographically for the palest. Take out, shuffle again and cool completely.

● In a pestle and mortar (or blender/grinder), smash the garlic and chillies with a little salt and oil. Add the turmeric, paprika and toasted seeds and pound to a crude, golden paste. Stir in the tamarind paste and the shrimp paste. Finish with the lime juice, a lot of black pepper, a serious whack of salt, and the coconut milk and yogurt.

● Use your hands to smear this mixture all over the chicken pieces (a dirty job) and leave to marinate for at least 3 hours in the fridge.

● Preheat the oven to 180°C/350°F/gas 4.

● Knock up the gremolata by mixing everything lightly together in a little bowl. Keep it dry and sprinkleable.

● Spread the chicken out on a rack placed over a foiled baking tray – these ladies are a bit drippy and messy. Roast in the oven for 35 minutes, or until the juices run clear.

● Pile up the chicken on a pretty plate and sprinkle with the gremolata.

Shelf Life: The gremolata will be alright – but not so punchy – the next day; it's all about freshness. Cooked chicken is good for 2 days. **Best Kept:** Chicken, whether raw or cooked, lives in the fridge. Please make the gremolata just a couple of hours before serving.

poached chicken, juvenile veg and dragoncella

Admittedly, it was the name that first attracted me to dragoncella, but then I tasted her and our love was sealed. Think of a salsa verde, then whack in a bit of tarragon with a chopped-up, hard-boiled egg for richness.

The relationships of the flavours in this dish are lent from the great *bollito misto*, the classic from the north of Italy with a name that just doesn't translate at all well: mixed boiled meats. Nevertheless, it is a great dish of bits of animal (tongue, beef flank, stuffed pig's trotter, a big boiling hen, and so on), which are all slowly, slowly boiled up together for hours, then served with salsa verde (for a bit of fresh and sharp) and Mostarda di Cremona (fruits cooked in a mustardy syrup, for a bit of sweet and hot). So this is a spring version of that – chicken for your meat, dragoncella where the salsa verde once stood, and some tender young veg for a bit of light relief.

Fred always gets a bit freaked out when chicken and egg meet in the same dish, but I think it's all right really, maybe just a little confusing for the chicken.

serves 6

FOR THE DRAGONCELLA

20g white bread (no crust please, torn into small chunks)

1¹/₂ tablespoons red wine vinegar

1 garlic clove, peeled

15g tarragon

40g flatleaf parsley,

1 hard-boiled egg, peeled and grated on the big holes

80ml extra virgin olive oil

S & P

● First get your stock on: put the chicken carcass in a saucepan along with the other stock ingredients. Cover with about 2 litres cold water, making sure everybody is submerged, then put over a medium heat and bring it up to a very gentle simmer.

● Turn the heat down so that the water is just steaming – no bubbles – and leave it to cook oh-so-gently like this for about an hour.

● Meanwhile start the dragoncella: soak the bread in the vinegar, making sure you give it a good mushing, then leave for 5 minutes to really soak up the vinegar. Smash and finely mince the garlic; finely chop the tarragon and parsley too.

● Scrape the garlic and herbs into the bread and mix them all together with a fork. Add the grated egg, stir in the extra virgin olive oil and season well with S & P.

● When the stock is ready, strain it into a big pan and ditch the bones and veg. Bring back up to steaming, season it with salt and lower in the two thighs and drumsticks, along with the spuds and fennel.

FOR THE STOCK

1.5 kg free-range chicken,
  legs off and split into
  thighs and drumsticks;
  breasts off too, also cut
  in half – you need the
  carcass to make the stock
1 large carrot, cut in half
1 onion, cut in half
2 sticks celery, cut in half
1 head garlic, cut in half
2 bay leaves
few peppercorns

FOR THE VEG

650 g new potatoes, washed
  and any big ones cut in
  half (I used Yukon gold
  – small and buttery)
1 tablespoon extra virgin
  olive oil
400 g baby fennel, tops
  chopped off
420 g baby turnips*
300 g baby carrots
  (chop off the ferny leaves
  5 cm above the carrot)
400 g baby courgettes
S & P

● After 20 minutes add the four bits of breast, the carrots and the courgettes to the stock. This will immediately drop the temperature, but once the stock has come back to steaming cook it for about a further 15 minutes.

● By now the chicken should be cooked (firm to the touch) but as all birds are different you can check by pulling back the fillet that sits under the breast and if the flesh is still pink, poach for a further 5-ish minutes. Whilst you're there you might as well stick a knife in a spud to make sure they're cooked too.

● When you are happy that the chicken and veg are all done, turn off the heat and leave to settle for a few minutes just to let things cool down a bit in there. Taste the broth very carefully for seasoning, then use a slotted spoon to serve your supper, finishing with a ladle of stock and the dragoncella on the side.

*Do use the turnip leaves as they are good for your liver and pancreas. Take off and throw away any that are yellow and manky. Any young, green and good ones should be roughly chopped and thrown in at the last minute.

Shelf Life: Really good for another 2-3 days. Good stock is always welcome in my fridge. **Best Kept:** A la frigo, amore..

roast leg of LAMB

It's time to celebrate New Season English Lamb, backed up here by some friends from the field and some rather superior baked beans. This is Roast Dinner Primavera.

serves 6

FOR THE BEANS

350g haricot beans, dried

3 garlic cloves, peeled and
    thinly sliced

10g rosemary, chopped

3 bay leaves

3 red onions, quartered

600ml chicken stock

80ml sherry vinegar

3 tablespoons extra virgin
    olive oil

20g flatleaf parsley, roughly
    chopped

4 rounded tablespoons
    Nut Pesto (see page 228)

S & P

FOR THE LAMB

1 x 2.5kg leg of lamb (ask
the butcher to remove the
notoriously tricky 'H' bone

extra virgin olive oil, to drizzle

S & P

FOR THE TURNIPS AND SPINACH

a big knob of butter (40g)

600g baby turnips, tops
    trimmed off but still leaving
    a green plume

1/2 tablespoon picked fresh
    thyme leaves

600g whole leaf spinach,
    drained

juice of 1/2 lemon

S & P

● Soak the beans overnight in plenty of water. The next day change the water, bring the beans up to a gentle simmer and keep them there until just cooked, for 1–2 hours, depending on their freshness.

● Preheat the oven to 220°C/425°F/ gas 7.

● Put the cooked and drained beans in a roasting tray and stir the garlic, rosemary and bay into them. Nestle the red onions in the beans and pour in the stock, vinegar and extra virgin.

● Brush or rub your lamb with olive oil and season extensively with sea salt and black pepper. Set a rack on the roasting tray on top of the beans, put the lamb on it and cook for 1 hour.

● When the meat has about 10 minutes left, heat the butter in a heavy-based saucepan and fry the turnips gently, without colouring them. Add the thyme, 200ml water, some S & P and simmer furiously for 5 minutes, giving them the odd shake.

● Take the lamb and beans out of the oven and rest the meat on its warmed serving dish for 10–15 minutes, covered in foil.

● Throw the spinach in with the turnips and roll it around in the pan until it is just wilted. Finish by checking the seasoning and adding a squeeze of lemon.

● Stir the chopped parsley and Nut Pesto, (if you have some, but don't worry if you don't) into the beans, and have a last look at the seasoning.

● Your work is done, your turn to sit down. Somebody else can carve.

Shelf Life: 2–3 days. **Best Kept:** The beans will only get better with time. The spinach and turnips less so. Keep them all in the fridge.

bake in the bag monkfish with preserved lemon COUSCOUS

This is just about the healthiest and easiest supper or light lunch in the book. It's an all-in-one, steam in the bag number, which lets the flavours just hang out and party together without getting busted. The real joy of this is what happens to the couscous, which cooks in the fish juices and greedily absorbs all the aromatics.

If you can't get monk, any fresh, white fish will do – I've done this with halibut and turbot before. The bags can be made up a few hours ahead of time and kept in the fridge.

serves 6

250g couscous

2 teaspoons ground cumin

1 teaspoon cumin seeds

6 spring onions, thinly sliced

2 preserved lemons,
  golf-ball sized, sliced
  and roughly chopped
  (about 75g)

10g coriander, roughly
  chopped

18 cherry tomatoes,
  quartered

1.2kg monkfish fillet

6 tablespoons extra virgin
  olive oil

1 teaspoon saffron

1 large or 2 small fennel
  bulbs, cut in half, core
  removed and sliced into
  5mm slices

S & P

● Preheat the oven to 200°C/400°F/gas 6.

● Mix all the ingredients, except the monkfish, extra virgin, saffron and fennel, in a bowl and add some seasoning. This is essentially a raw couscous salad that will be the base of your parcel.

● Now turn your attention to the monk. Lay the fillet(s) out on a chopping board and cut into 1cm thick, obliquely angled slices. You might be lucky enough to have a big fillet, as these fish do grow quite large. If so, slice it a bit thinner. The idea is to have around 2–3 nice monk medallions for each person.

● Put a small saucepan with 180ml water onto the stove to boil. When it does, add the saffron, then pull off the heat.

● Clear your work space. Tear off six 60cm sheets of foil – my roll is 30cm wide. Lay them out, with the short side towards you.

● Pour 2 tablespoons of extra virgin into the couscous and mix well so that all the grains are well coated in oil, then add the saffron water and stir.

● Spread a little extra virgin in the centre of the front half of the foil, closest to you, and put one sixth of the sliced fennel on the oil. Repeat for all. Divide the couscous mix equally over the fennel in neat little piles.

● Top the couscous with your slices of monkfish. Drizzle the rest of the extra virgin over the monk and add a touch of S & P. Take a few moments to see how pretty it looks – at times like this, Fred usually likes to take a photo with one of the hundreds of disposable cameras that are always hanging round our house leftover from parties.

● Bring the top edge of foil over the fish to meet the bottom edge. Turn the parcel 90° and line up the side edges. Seal the side edge closest to you by folding it over 3 times and secure by pressing down firmly with your fingertips. Turn the parcel 180° and do the same to the opposite side edge. Repeat for all the parcels.

● Now your parcels should be well-sealed on 3 sides, with just the top open. Rest them all lined up at a 45° angle so that you are not mucking up the arrangements inside, but you are able to pour 3 tablespoons of water into each bag without it all dribbling out. Seal the top edge of each parcel with the same neat folds. Split the 6 parcels between 2 baking trays. Pop them into the oven for 15–20 minutes, swapping the shelves halfway through – they should be puffing up nicely now.

● Take your little pillows out the oven and serve straight onto warm plates. Let your guests unfold the front end and tear back. Be there for the first burst of flavour, but mind the very hot steam. Eat off the foil – very little washing up!

Shelf Life: 1 day. **Best Kept:** Once cooked, not designed for keeping.

chilli-miso POACHED salmon
with eastern GREENS

Go to any Asian shop and there's a dazzling array of loose-headed cabbages and stunning leaves. Bok choi, choi sum, tat soi and pe-tsai. This recipe is a one-pot wonder, so easy and fresh. Use basmati, brown or wild rice or even a combo – in which case they will need cooking separately. The only potential hard part is getting the miso, which must be paste, not dried. You can buy fresh from the fridge in Oriental shops, but even easier is getting packets of good-quality instant miso soup from a regular supermarket. Especially good at lowering blood fats, it also helps the liver, muscles and nerves.

serves 6

240g mixed rice (basmati, brown or wild)

400g Oriental greens

20g coriander, roughly chopped (stalks and leaves)

2 garlic cloves, peeled and thinly sliced

6cm piece of root ginger, peeled and finely grated

2 green chillies, thinly sliced at an angle (seeds and all)

100g sugar snap peas

6 asparagus spears, trimmed

3 spring onions, sliced as long and as thinly as you can

2 teaspoons chopped red chilli (or 1 teaspoon Crema di Pepperoncini, see page 169)

1 tablespoon miso paste

6 x 150g slices of salmon fillet, skin on

a drizzle of sesame oil

1 teaspoon fish sauce

3 teaspoons shoyu (a thinner soy sauce aged in cedar casks) or light soy sauce

juice of 2 limes

● Get the rice going as per the instructions on the packets.

● Wash the greens. Cut the bok choi in half through the root and then into quarters.

● Choose a saucepan with a lid that is large enough to hold all of the ingredients. Put the thickest greens in first, and then the next thickest lying on top of them. As you layer, sprinkle in the coriander, garlic, grated ginger and green chilli. Finish with the lightest of the greens, the sugar snaps, asparagus spears and the spring onions.

● Mix the miso paste with the chopped red chilli and spread on one side of each salmon piece. Lay the salmon on top, miso-side up, and drizzle on the sesame oil, fish sauce and soy. Pour in 500ml water around the salmon and cover with a lid.

● Turn the heat onto high and when it comes to the boil, turn down to steam for 3–5 minutes, after which time the fish should be cooked – it's easy enough to test, just pull at one of the natural flakes. You want it still to be a bit pink in the middle.

● Liberally squeeze the lime juice all over the salmon and greens. With a fish slice or your best special flipper, carefully take the fish off the now wilted greens and set aside. Put the rice and the greens onto plates and top with a piece of salmon, miso-side up, and serve with a ladle of the broth.

Shelf Life: Can be resteamed the next day, but don't you just hate overcooked salmon. **Best Kept:** Eat this hot – it's all about freshness.

turbot baked in SALT with cockles and leeks

This is the purest way I know of cooking fish. The rock salt literally forms a crust over the body of the fish and falls away in huge slabs once it is cooked to reveal the magic that's happened inside. At this point, you should always take a deep breath in of the first released aromas; the flesh has cooked solely in its own juices. Any fine flat white fish – halibut or brill – will do.

The cockle and leek mixture makes a great stand-alone fish soupy dish. Leeks, like all the alliums, have good things going for them, but less so than garlic and onions, because the active ingredients are in proportion to the ferocity of their taste.

Despite the length of the method, this is a very easy recipe; it just needed to be explained properly. If you can't get cockles, use mussels instead.

serves 6

2–2.5kg turbot,
   gutted and cleaned
4 fresh bay leaves
20g parsley (leaves roughly
   chopped, stalks whole)
20g thyme (1/2 on the branch
   and 1/2 picked)
4 garlic cloves, peeled,
   2 sliced and 2 chopped
3kg coarse rock salt
600g leeks, sliced thinly (or
   you can use baby ones)
70g unsalted butter (at
   room temperature)
2 glasses white wine
500g fresh cockles (in the
   shell) or mussels
600ml fish stock (beg
   some bones from
   the fishmonger)
100ml double cream
black pepper

● Preheat the oven to 220°C / 425°F / gas 7.

● Fill the roe cavity of the fish with the bay leaves, parsley stalks, sprigs of thyme and sliced garlic.

● Find a roasting tin large enough to hold the fish and spread 750g salt on the bottom. Lay the fish on top and cover with the rest of the salt. The salt crust must be intact, around 1cm thick all over.

● Sprinkle on a little water – this helps create a total seal when it goes in the oven. Whack in the oven for 35–40 minutes, depending on the size of the fish.

● If you are using baby leeks, trim them at the top and bottom and wash thoroughly.

● In a large, deep saucepan melt two thirds of the butter and gently fry the leeks, the rest of the garlic and the picked thyme for 10-ish minutes with a lid on. Add the fish stock and reduce by two thirds. Then add the wine and cockles and, with the lid on again, bring back to simmering point.

● Transfer the leeks, cockles, thyme and garlic to a clean pan, using a slotted spoon, and then strain over the stock to get rid of any grit. Stir in the cream and parsley leaves. Turn the heat off and put the lid back on to keep warm.

● Take your fish out of the oven. Using the back of a wooden spoon, tap the middle of the mound firmly to break the salt crust. Go gingerly at first, but you may need to increase your force to crack it. Peel, brush and gently sweep away the salt to the edges of the roasting tin with your best fish slice (mine is called Special Flipper). Much of the salt will be compacted. Clear away as much as possible from the surface of the fish and ditch it. Then carefully remove the skin – it should just peel off – and throw it away. Don't try and eat it.

● Lightly score along the backbone with a fish slice or palette knife. Scrape away the fin bones, which run all around the edges of the fish, leaving just the clean and boneless fillets. Carefully lift off the white flesh in portions. The fillets on the top are much thicker than the ones at the bottom, so don't be caught out and not have enough for yourself.

● Whisk in the remaining butter in knobs into the cockle mix. Season with black pepper (it should not need any salt).

● Serve the beautiful slabs of white fish with the cockles and leeks ladled around.

Shelf Life: The fish will be alright for 2 days, but the cockles shouldn't sit around. You know what they say: 3 days for fish and guests... **Best Kept:** Any fish leftover, give it a generous drizzle of extra virgin olive oil and keep in the fridge. Same for the cockles (but without the olive oil).

elderflower sorbet

As a rule, cordials work well as sorbets. A few springs ago, two of my best friends (Rose & Tom) got married. One church service, a long lunch and several buckets of champagne later, I was totally wasted and the only thing that whipped me back into shape for the evening session was a Martini infused with elderflowers from their garden. Perfectly light and restorative. Thus started a small elderflower obsession: you name it, I've elderflowered it. However, I've now gone full circle and decided that this most English of flowers is so special that it's best not mucked around with. This recipe is simple, a total winner. Try the Martinis, too, next time you need a pick-me-up.

If you want to use other seasonal fruits, general rules for sorbet-making are as follows: if you are infusing (for lavender, elderflower, green tea, etc.), do this when the syrup is cooking, then strain. For really fresh, fruity sorbets (raspberry, lychee, pink grapefruit, for example), wait for the sugar syrup to cool, then add your puréed or juiced fruit, so that the sorbet retains a fresh, not cooked look and flavour. It is essentially impossible to make a smooth sorbet without an ice-cream machine, but regular stirring by hand works just as well, and gives it a charmingly crunchy texture.

serves 6

125g caster sugar
1 large sprig of elderflowers
   (or 2 tablespoons
   elderflower cordial)
a squeeze of lemon, lime
   or pink grapefruit, to taste
1 egg white
a few redcurrants and/or
   elderflowers, to garnish

● Put the sugar and 500ml water in a heavy-based saucepan and set over a low heat until the sugar has dissolved. Throw in the elderflowers, bring to the boil and cook for 5 minutes. Allow to cool to room temperature and strain through a fine sieve.

● Once the sugar syrup is at room temperature, add cordial if using, and adjust the taste with a squeeze of citrus juice (bear in mind that everything tastes less sweet once it's frozen). In a separate clean bowl, lightly whisk the egg white until smooth and frothy and then mix well with the syrup. Then either put it in an ice-cream machine and let it do the work, or into a suitable container in the freezer, whisking every half hour until set (2 hours or so).

● Taste when it is crystallised. It might want a touch more citrus, in which case serve a wedge on the side.

● Pile up in Martini glasses, wine glasses, tumblers or whatever. Finish with a sprig of something colourful such as redcurrants and/or a few elderflowers. I personally take great umbridge at superfluous sprigs of mint.

Shelf Life: 2 weeks, but it will get kind of gnarly in there. **Best Kept:** In the freezer.

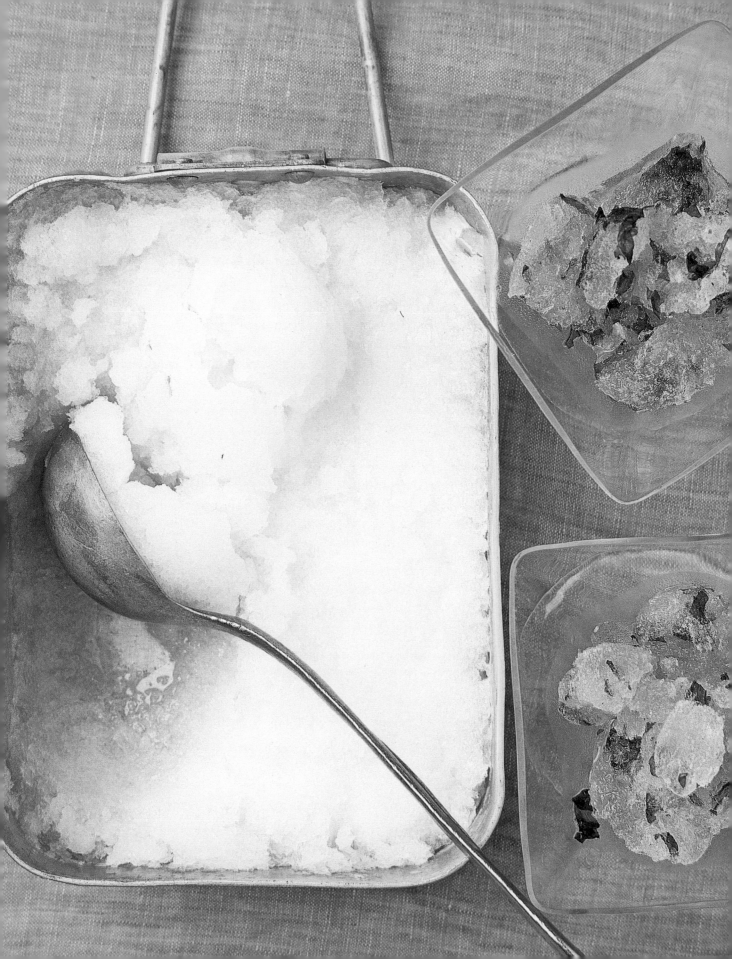

green TEA and spearmint granita

My sister said no one would make this because granitas sound difficult. As part of my lifelong mission not to be put down by my big sister, I have given a full explanation of why they are EASY and DELICIOUS on page 216, where you'll find the recipe for Cox Granita. Younger siblings of the world unite.

Green tea comes from the same bush as black tea, so it still contains caffeine, but since it is unfermented, it lacks the tannins in regular tea; it is the tannins which make our bodies unable to absorb the micronutrients in the leaves. There are many reasons why green tea enjoys such a senior place in the health hierarchy: lowering blood pressure (what with being chunky with bioflavonoids) is high on the list, as is being a powerful antioxidant.

This is all about clean flavours and spearmint has a particularly fresh taste. Obviously if you can't get it, use regular mint. I wouldn't like to say what variety you get in those plastic packs in the supermarket. I'm always astounded by the balance of plastic used in the packaging and the money spent on it, versus the few strands of leaves inside. Just to give you a tip so you can pick the right occasion for your granita, herbalists reckon that as well as being good for digestion, mint is also an aphrodisiac.

serves 6

3 heaped teaspoons loose
  green tea leaves
  (or 8 green tea bags)
10g fresh spearmint, stalks
  and leaves
100g caster sugar

● Pour 400ml boiling water over the leaves or bags and spearmint stalks. Add the sugar and stir until dissolved. Leave to steep for 10 minutes, then take out the bags (if using) and strain out the tea leaves and stalks. Leave to cool completely.

● Pour into a shallow tray, one with a depth of at least 4cm that can sit flat in the freezer, and put it in there for an initial 30 minutes.

● After this time, the granita should start to frost and crystallize around the edges. Stir the solid outside into the still liquid middle, along with the chopped mint. Put it back into the freezer and it'll be ready after another 20–30 minutes.

● Granitas, being essentially frozen water, have a tendency to go rock hard, which is not right: they should be stratas of refreshing crystals and look a bit like kryptonite. So if it does go rock hard, leave it out to de-frost a bit, then break it up with a fork and return to the freezer until needed.

Shelf Life: Best within 12 hours, but will be fine for up to 3 weeks.
Best Kept: In the freezer.

yogurt JELLY with boozy gooseberries

I realise that this may sound like an odd idea, but it works 100 per cent as a pretty, delicious, light and low-fat pud. There's something about the wobble of a jelly that is particularly satisfying, funny and sometimes downright rude.

Gooseberries are an old English classic, mentioned in recipe books as far back as William Turner's *Herball* – written around the middle of the 16th century. They are ideal for the British climate, loving the cold and damp. The short gooseberry season is easily missed, and as they freeze well I usually stock up at the right time of year. Gooseberries contain the A, B and C of vitamins, natural sugars (though it doesn't always taste like it) and help digestion – read 'are a laxative'. Takes seconds to make.

serves 6

FOR THE JELLIES
450 ml milk
a vanilla pod, seeds scraped
1^1/$_2$ level tablespoons powdered gelatine (or 6 leaves)
330 ml nice plain yogurt
zest of 3 limes
45 g icing sugar

FOR THE BOOZY GOOSEBERRIES
200 g gooseberries, fresh or frozen, but defrosted
40 g golden granulated sugar
100 ml Curaçao or Grand Marnier (the clear stuff makes a nicer colour)

● In a pan, gently warm the milk with the scraped seeds and the vanilla pod.

● Presoak the gelatine leaves, if using, following the instructions on the box.

● Put the yogurt, lime zest and icing sugar into a bowl and mix well. Once the milk is just below boiling, take out the vanilla pod and whisk in the gelatine, making sure any lumps are dissolved as you stir.

● Slowly pour the milk onto the yogurt mix, whisking all the time until fully incorporated. Transfer straightaway into the individual moulds – mine are 6 cm across and 5 cm high, but use whatever you have. I suppose you could make one big one, but little ones are somehow much more pleasurable. Chill in the fridge until set, preferably overnight.

● Put the gooseberries, 2 tablespoons of water and the sugar in a small saucepan with a lid and set over a low, low heat for about 15 minutes – or until the gooseberries have popped and are broken down a bit.

● Turn the heat off and stir in the Curaçao or Grand Marnier. Your sauce should be nice and loose. Leave to cool completely to room temperature.

● When it comes to serving, spoon a pool of the goozies into the middle of each plate. Dip the bottom of the moulds into hot water for a second just to loosen them up, and use your fingers to gently pull the jelly away from the edge of the mould before turning onto small plates. These really are something special.

Shelf Life: Jellies good for 3 days; gooseberries for 1 week. **Best Kept:** Jellies and gooseberries in the fridge.

poppy seed snaps
filled with LEMON curd

This poppy seed version of the brandy snap is a triumph with the lemon curd filling. If you ever need to impress a visiting Great Aunt at tea time, these would definitely secure your inheritance. For more common use, they also make a fabulous and beautiful pud.

This seems like as good a place as any to talk about lemons: they are a star fruit with natural disinfectant properties and a powerful antioxidant function. Loaded with vitamin C, they help to boost the immune system and prevent infection and disease. They are also one of my ten desert island ingredients (my favourite game on long car journeys).

You can make the snaps into whatever shapes you want: thick tubes (like that favourite Mafia *dolci* from Sicily, the *cannoli*) or a delicate British curl.

**makes 12 snaps and
240g lemon curd**

FOR THE LEMON CURD
115g butter
230g caster sugar
juice and zest of 3 lemons
1 egg yolk
3 eggs

FOR THE SNAPS
70g butter
2 tablespoons demerara
   sugar
2 tablespoons golden syrup
4 tablespoons plain flour
1 teaspoon poppy seeds

FOR THE FILLING
3 tablespoons thick double
   cream
3 tablespoons lemon curd

● First make your curd. Warm the butter, sugar, lemon juice and zest in a heavy-based saucepan over a very low heat until all is smooth and translucent. Add the egg yolk, then the eggs one by one and whisk until thick – about 5 minutes. Take off the heat and cool.

● Now for the snaps. Heat the butter, sugar and golden syrup in a medium saucepan over a low heat until the sugar has dissolved and it looks a bit like toffee. Turn off the heat and stir in the flour and poppy seeds with a wooden spoon. You should end up with a gloopy dough. If the butter starts to leech out, don't worry. Leave to cool for 15–20 minutes, stirring occasionally.

● Preheat the oven to 150°C/300°F/gas 2.

● Divide the dough into 12 little balls. Put 4 balls evenly spaced a good 12ish cm apart onto a baking tray and press down. Repeat with the other 4 balls on another baking tray and then again with the other 4. Cook in the oven for 12–15 minutes or until flat, golden and honeycombed. No need to cook them all at once, because you must let them cool for a minute when they come out. Just one. At that moment they are only molten butter and sugar, but as your snaps cool they go from floppy to crackled-fragile in about 4 minutes, and your job is to catch them at the malleable stage.

● Carefully remove one snap with a pallet knife and shape around any kind of rod-shaped thing you have lying around (a broom handle balanced between the backs of two chairs works quite well) until you have a good long curl, sealed along the bottom. Here's a secret: these little buggers can be re-warmed to a bendable temperature until you get the right shape, so if you don't like the lilt of your curve you can just pop it in the oven for a minute or less and do it again. What you don't want to do is either break them or overcook them; they won't go back together and burnt butter and sugar is just not very nice.

● When all the snaps are shaped, leave them to cool completely on a wire rack while you make the filling.

● Whisk the double cream until half whipped, then fold in 3 tablespoons of lemon curd. Whenever you're adding anything to thickened cream, you should whip the cream to about halfway – the thicker the other component, the less you whip the cream – to achieve a smooth, un-split filling.

● Using a teaspoon, drop blobs of the lemon-curd cream into your curls until just full, not packed. Once filled, they will only hold together for about an hour – they go soggy pretty quickly – but for that hour, my God they're on the money.

Shelf Life: Unfilled, they will keep for 2 days. Filled, only about an hour. Lemon curd in the fridge – 2 weeks. **Best Kept:** Unfilled, in a dry, sealed container – humidity plays a devastating role, so not in the fridge. Leftover lemon curd in the fridge.

Alfie's christening cake

The basis for this cake is a recipe called Never Fail Victoria Sponge, which, aged nine, was my first memorable cooking experience (unless you count grabbing a frying pan off the stove some 5 years earlier and ending up in A & E, which was also memorable). I re-found the recipe in the tattiest of cookbooks after my mum died, gave it a bit of a spring clean in terms of the flavours and then let it loose on a whole new generation of cake-baking kids by doing it for my nephew's christening.

serves 6

FOR THE CAKE

2 tablespoons milk

4 eggs

1 teaspoon vanilla extract (not flavouring)

225g self-raising flour, sifted

150g caster sugar

a pinch of salt

1 teaspoon baking powder

100g unsalted butter, melted

FOR THE ELDERFLOWER SYRUP

80g caster sugar

a big handful of elderflowers (or 4 tablespoons elderflower cordial)

zest and juice of 3 unwaxed lemons (use a zester or slice thinly, don't grate)

FOR THE ICING

15g unsalted butter

1 tablespoon milk

juice of 1/2 a lemon

70g icing sugar

1 tablespoon elderflower cordial

● Preheat the oven to 170°C / 325°F / gas 3.

● Cake time. In a bowl or mixer, whisk together the milk, eggs and vanilla. Mix all the dry ingredients into another bowl. Add half of the dry ingredients to the egg/milk mixture and really work hard with a wooden spoon to stir it all up, or let the mixer do the work for you. Once the batter starts to come together, pour in the other half of the dry ingredients and beat again until smooth. Now very gently work the melted butter into the mix.

● Grease and then lightly flour the inside of a cake tin about 20cm across and more than 8cm high. Pour the cake batter into the tin and put in the oven for 45 minutes. Turn the oven down to 160°C / 320°F / gas 3 if it's browning too quickly.

● In 150ml water, boil up the ingredients for the syrup, except for 1 tablespoon elderflower cordial and the lemon juice, in a heavy-bottomed saucepan. After it comes to the boil, simmer very slowly for about 20 minutes. When it has reduced down to about 4 tablespoons, take it off the heat. Once cooled, add the lemon juice and 1 tablespoon elderflower cordial.

● Use a toothpick or small knife to test that the cake is cooked before taking it out. Rest in the tin on a wire rack for 10 minutes.

● While the cake is still steaming in the tin, on the cooling rack, slowly drizzle the elderflower syrup into it, letting the candied zest sit nicely on top. Give it 5 minutes to absorb, then take the cake out of the tin to finish cooling.

● Now make the icing by melting together the butter and milk in a small saucepan. Turn the heat off and add the lemon juice, then sieve the icing sugar into the pan and beat until smooth. This is a proper drizzle icing. Lightly ice the cake, then decorate with flowers and foliage from the garden (preferably elderflowers) and dust the whole thing extensively with icing sugar.

Shelf Life: 3 days. **Best Kept:** Wrapped in foil to keep it moist.

garlic JELLY (for roast meats)

In 2,600 BC at the building of the pyramids, garlic was given to the workers to make them strong. The Ancient Greeks used it to ward off infection and in sixteenth-century Britain, monks ate it to keep away the plague. Swinging through to the nineteenth century it was taken to stop the advancement of cholera epidemics. Either it's one of the longest lies in history, or garlic is good for you. This recipe is one for real garlic lovers, people who have fortitude and those who want to eat to stay well. In other words, it's pretty intense.

There are two dishes in this book devoted purely to garlic, though being a kitchen staple it probably features in about 80 per cent of the savoury recipes. To understand where I'm coming from, think about redcurrant jelly for a second and then let that thought go. Now briefly allow horseradish to run through your mind... and release. Devote no more than a quarter of a second to English mustard before moving on. Now somewhere in your mind you have a fierce, slightly sweet condiment to enjoy with all your roast meats.

Fortune favours the brave.

makes a jam jar

4 leaves of gelatine
40g garlic cloves, peeled
2 tablespoons caster sugar
5g tarragon, leaves picked
    and left whole
zest of 1 lemon
salt and lots of coarsely
    ground black pepper

● Soak the gelatine in warm water until it softens.

● Bring a small pan of water to a rapid boil. Drop in the garlic and cook for 2 minutes. Take the garlic out, save 300ml of the water and lose the rest.

● When the garlic is cool enough to handle, grate it on the finest holes.

● Bring the 300ml water to the boil with the sugar, then turn off the heat and stir in the tarragon, lemon zest and garlic. Leave to infuse for 5 minutes.

● Stir in the gelatine until dissolved, along with some salt and plenty of black pepper. Pour into a sterilised jam jar.

Shelf Life: Should be good for 2 weeks.
Best Kept: In the fridge. Near the front so you don't forget about it.

onion seed TWISTS with green coconut chutney

You are more familiar with black onion seeds than you know – they are the black teardrop seeds that are sprinkled on naan bread. Also known as Nigella (no relation) or Kalonji, they are a staple of Indian cookery and an essential part of the wonderful Bengali spice mix, Panch Poran. They have a distinct earthy, nutty, onion taste and carry some of the allium family's nutritional properties: namely, cleansing of the blood and liver stimulation. I was amazed that my nearest chain supermarket now carries them.

makes plenty for 10

FOR THE CHUTNEY
250ml coconut milk

70g desiccated coconut

45g mint, chopped

60g coriander, chopped

2 green chillies, de-seeded and finely chopped

30g root ginger, peeled and finely grated

zest and juice of 2 limes

4 spring onions, thinly sliced

6 garlic cloves, peeled and finely chopped

S & P

FOR THE FLATBREADS
500g pizza dough (see page 48)

a sprinkling of flour, for dusting

6 tablespoons black onion seeds (or cumin seeds and black sesame seeds)

a drizzle of olive oil

● Start with the chutney. Pour the coconut milk over the desiccated coconut and stir well. Leave to soak for 30 minutes. Mix all the other ingredients together, then stir in the coconut mixture. Chill in the fridge for at least 1 hour.

● Preheat the oven to 200°C/400°F/gas 6.

● Now for the flatbread. Put the dough onto a lightly floured surface. Give it a good knead for a couple of minutes, then cut it in half. Using a rolling pin, roll the first dough ball out to a thickness of 3 mm in the shape of a rectangle, roughly 20 cm long on the long side, and whatever length it works out to be on the shorter.

● Liberally sprinkle half of the black onion seeds onto the rolled out dough as evenly as you can. Give the seeds a once or twice over with the rolling pin to secure them into the dough.

● Cut the rectangle into strips 1cm wide and the length of the dough. Lift each strip and give it 6–8 twists with a little pull – this will stretch it out a bit and add roughly another 10cm to the final length. Don't worry if the first ones break – practise makes perfect and there's enough dough to allow for mistakes.

● Lay them evenly onto a greased baking tray and, using your thumbs, push the ends into the baking tray a bit so they don't unravel. When one tray is done, drizzle them with a bit of olive oil for sheen and put into the oven for about 8–10 minutes. As they are cooked, move them onto a wire rack to cool but try to hand them out whilst they are still warm. Continue cutting the rest – you may need up to 4 baking sheets. They look good standing up in pint glasses, with the chutney in a bowl next to them, or served in half a coconut.

Shelf Life: 2 days for the sticks; chutney, 5 days in the fridge. **Best Kept:** OK in an airtight container, but they're best when still a bit warm.

summer

This is all about the fruit. And the sun.

You may have noticed that, in this book, each season has a varying number of starters, mains, puds and what I loosely call 'others'. I didn't mean it to be like that, but when you look at what's available and peaking, the produce lends itself to certain types of dishes. This is clearly reflected in what our bodies tell us that they want – hearty, warming soups in winter and, in summer, an altogether lighter touch. Summer is really all about fruit, cramming the natural sugars into our mouths whilst we can, which is why I'm a little pudding-heavy right now.

The story of our summer colours is a pleasure to tell: she starts a little shy, coy and blushing the pink of innocence. Then, as the sun warms her up, she gets a little hot under the collar and begins to get a bit rosy. As the rays fall on her skin she reaches the height of her hue, and the same sun that makes us red (or me anyway, being of fair complexion) has the matching effect on our lady fruit. Come the end of what is really everybody's favourite season, she is swollen with colour, having been drenched for months in summer sun and ripened to within an inch of her life. She is mature and developed.

This is not a story about one particular fruit, but a passage through what peaks when during the hottest months of the year.

The two real Superstars are the entire berry family, and the tomato.

Berries are the real deal, the way nature intended for us to cram our bodies full of oracs. Whether they are strawbs or raspberries, black or blue, the intake of vitamins that berries provide is a great way to top ourselves up. Leading the berry field in terms of goodness – it's not the first to ripen – is the blueberry, strong with bioflavonoids (which aid the absorption of vitamin C) and anthocyanosides. These sound dodgy to me, but in the way that free radicals sound cool and clearly aren't, so anthocyanosides sound like trouble but are actually great fighters against bad bacteria.

The other fruit we are really excited about now is the tomato, and there can be no better way of illustrating why eating by colour by season is the way forward. As the fruit ripens, a pigment called lycopene in their skin becomes more potent, which is better than good as it has been linked to the prevention of cancer. The joy of a ripe tomato is unbounded. It puts the pale and cotton woolly specimens that flood our supermarkets during the rest of the year to shame. It's just a different beast; it smells of summer, it's juicy, flavourful and red, red, red. Do what you will with it, or do nothing and eat it as it comes.

Staying on the subjects of red and hot, there's a feisty little fellow that I need to mention. This morning we had a run in and he did me up like a kipper. Some might say it's unwise to combine the two activities of making your first cup of morning tea, dressing-gowned and blinky-eyed, with cleaning a kilo of chillies. But there they were, in a bowl exactly where they had been for the last two weeks, and this morning I realised they were going to die unless they got prepped. Stupid, foolish girl decides to wash the morning crust out of her eyes, just like every morning. It was a full hour before I could open both eyes, fully at the same time. And I resent the amount of morning energy that was taken up with writhing and cursing like that. Still, I got the last laugh as I chopped them up into tiny weeny pieces.

But you have to admire their cheeky little sense of humour, and the way they consistently come up with the goods. We've all had crap tomatoes, tasteless avocados, juice-free limes, and strawberries that in a blindfolded taste test (one up from a blind tasting) you wouldn't be able to identify. But it's super-rarely that a chilli disappoints with a 'phut' not a bang. A clue to my extreme esteem is the 4 chilli sauces on pages 168–172: a quartet of chilli sauces from different parts of the world (Italy, Mexico, Thailand and Morocco) that I think demonstrate their global importance. My advice is to make all of them, and admire their differences, but don't start 'til after breakfast.

Aubergines – are rich in the micronutrients glycoalkaloids. Low in calories and high in minerals, with soothing influences on the liver and pancreas, aubergines are also antibacterial and work as a mild diuretic (keeping the waterworks clear and flowing).

Beetroot – is loaded with folic acid, iron and potassium. By increasing the cellular uptake of oxygen, raw or roasted, beetroot is a powerful blood builder. The huge amount of potassium looks after your heart and blood, and the very pigment that makes it purple, betanin, is thought to do some good preventative work against cancer.

Blackberries – are full of vitamin C that stops bad bacteria from growing and building up in our guts. All berries with high pectin tend to maintain their goodness in the preserving process, so jams and jellies are orac power in a jar.

Blackcurrants – have a very stable form of vitamin C, so even after a year of preserving, whether in syrup form or jam, the vitamin C will only decrease by about 15 per cent. Of the total British annual crop of blackcurrants, ninety five per cent go to making Ribena. Shocking.

Black grapes – have a skin which is high in quercitin and has one of the highest orac counts. Grapes in their natural state, with seed, contain a good type HDL cholesterol. Grapes, as part of your regular diet are good for your hair, skin and nails – all the encouragement I need to drink a glass of red wine a day.

Blueberries – reduce blood sugar, enhance circulation and stop our blood from clotting when it shouldn't. They contain all the oracs we need, and one of the micronutrients inside them enhances the capillaries in the eye. Also, being in the same family as cranberries, blueberries are good for cystitis, too.

Borlotti beans – help to maintain healthy hair, skin and bone marrow, along with promoting normal function of the immune and nervous systems. Another great thing about them is that when they are dried they hold their nutrients.

Cherries – are the fruits of love and lovers. They contain a lot of folic acid and iron. Good for removing catarrh and clearing the lungs, cherry syrups have been made for centuries to treat bronchial complaints. Asthma sufferers indulge...

Chillies – gain their power by their heat, which is good for the blood and circulation. They also control wind, while the mucokinetic agents that they contain help us cough up (well you guessed it) excess mucus.

Crab apples – are bright red and with a blush of purple, and packed with pectin, they make impeccable jewel-like jellies. Their active ingredients drive down cholesterol.

Damsons – which rate high purple in the orac spectrum, contain a lot of pectin and naturally hold cell membranes together, so they are good for cell growth, development and repair. Perfect for keeping the free radicals at bay.

Figs – food of the gods, have all the minerals we need for strong bones and blood and improve gingivitis. They ease constipation and remain potent when dried.

Peaches – contain micronutrients from which the reproductive system benefits, thus making peaches the sexiest of summer's fruits. Natural sugars will keep you going through the lazy, summer days and their zinc content also helps promote good night vision, so load up for when the day/night ratio is reversed come winter.

Pink grapefruits – have strong antioxidant properties and help balance cholesterol levels in the blood. The essential oil in grapefruit cleans out the liver.

Plums – our favourite purple, are good for the bones and joints and they have a laxative effect with their bumper load of fibre. Minerals are here in abundance: magnesium, phosphorus, potassium, calcium and iron.

Raspberries – have a particular strength which helps activate the body's natural self-cleansing ability, so they are a thorough tonic for every organ, including the skin and glands as well as bone marrow. Not only that, but they encourage the right metabolism of fats and proteins.

Radishes – are our fiery, crunchy friends. Although they contain very few nutrients, radishes have raphanol, which promotes the emptying of the gall bladder, so they are helpful for passing gall stones.

Red peppers – are at the optimum level of ripeness and are packed with antioxidants. Capsaicin is the flavour we all love in the pepper/chilli family and this is the substance that is beneficial for the heart and circulatory system.

Rhubarb – is filled with iron. It also induces a regular flow of bile, so it works as a tonic to the digestive system, preventing bad bacteria from growing in our insides.

Runner beans – are full of antioxidants and lower cholesterol. This is done by strengthening the liver functions, essential for keeping your energy up.

Sloe berries – Culpeper (the 17th century herbalist) recommended: 'the distilled water of the flowers is a most certaine remedy, tried and approved, to ease all manner of gnawing in the stomach, the sides and bowels'. Bring on those sloe G&Ts!

Strawberries – like pretty much all the berries, contain all the summer micronutrients, but they also encourage iron absorption for the formation of strong blood and a good immune system.

Tomatoes – have powerful antioxidant and antiviral properties, helping the body to maintain the constant production of all immune system requirements. They are packed with vitamins and are my lypocene superstar and orac hero.

Watermelons – are rich in vitamins A and C, which work to eliminate free radicals before they can do damage. They are also cooling to the system and calming to the digestion.

roast TOMATO soup with cottage cheese and astro-pesto

Although roasting the tomatoes means one loses a bit of colour freshness, it's well worth it for the added depth of flavour. I use the term 'astro' to mean really quick. Pesto is a real no-brainer to make, so I don't understand why so much is bought in – the UK is the biggest buyer of pesto in the world. Pine nuts are excellent energy providers; flavour-wise, the good ones come from Spain, not China, are a more teardrop shape and, if you're lucky, actually have a touch of the real masticky-pine taste.

serves 6

FOR THE SOUP

1.5 kg vine-ripened tomatoes, cut in half

2 small red onions, finely diced

1 red chilli, de-seeded and roughly chopped

6 garlic cloves, peeled and thickly sliced

5 tablespoons olive oil

1¹/₂ tablespoons caster sugar

500ml chicken or veg stock

S & P

FOR THE PESTO

1¹/₂ tablespoons pine nuts

80g basil, roughly chopped

25g Parmesan cheese, grated

¹/₂ garlic clove, peeled and minced

4 tablespoons extra virgin olive oil

S & P

TO SERVE

300g cottage cheese

● Preheat the oven to 180°C/350°F/gas 4.

● Cut the spigot out of the tomatoes and throw it away. Put the tomato halves cut-side up in a roasting tray and sprinkle on the chopped onion, chilli and garlic. Pour over 5 tablespoons olive oil and distribute the sugar over the open faces of the tomatoes. Season well and roast in the oven on the middle shelf for 30–40 minutes.

● Now for the pesto. Put the pine nuts in a dry, ovenproof frying pan and pop them into the oven on the top shelf. Shake them every few minutes or so until they take on some colour. It is not necessary to totally toast them – heating them up quickly releases their aroma and makes them more nutty tasting. Just be careful not to burn them. The whole operation should take no more than 5 minutes. Once your minor nut stress is over, tip them onto a chopping board to cool down and roughly chop.

● Put the basil, Parmesan, pine nuts and garlic in a small bowl and season. Slowly pour over the 4 tablespoons olive oil and stir so everything is evenly coated.

● Take the tray of roasted tomatoes out of the oven and cool for 5 minutes

● Throw the tomatoes into a blender and whizz until smooth. Pass the soup through a fine sieve using the back of a wooden spoon to push it through.

● Gently warm up the stock and add it to the sieved soup reasonably slowly as you may not need it all. Stop when the consistency is thick-ish. Not that far from Heinz. Load up your warmed bowls with soup, spoon in a good dollop of cottage cheese and finish with some pesto.

Shelf Life: Pesto will keep for a few weeks, as long the solids are kept covered by oil. The soup is good for 3 days. **Best Kept:** Keep pesto and soup in the fridge.

grated BEETROOT salad

The first time I made this it was so voluminous that I had quite a lot left over. Grabbed by huge morning hunger pangs the next day, I fried it up rösti-style and had it with bacon and eggs. So good.

Beetroot is always served boiled or roasted, pickled or in those nasty vac-packs of little, round balls with an everlasting expiry date. When I was first given my juicer, I was astounded by the length of time it took to clean and also by the amount of fibrous waste from the beetroot. Fibre is good for you, and with a vegetable that has such a dynamic and invigorating colour, the pleasure of the whole vegetable chilled and grated is supreme.

A swirl of Greek yogurt before serving softens the colour and flavour from passionate crimson to girly pink, but in a not unpleasing way.

Whether you have a latex fetish or not, I strongly recommend wearing gloves for the start of this procedure.

serves 6

350 g raw beetroot, washed
4 tablespoons extra virgin
  olive oil
juice of $1/2$ lemon
2 spring onions, finely
  sliced
1–2 garlic cloves, peeled
  and minced
1 teaspoon dill seeds or
  $1/2$ teaspoon caraway
  seeds
1 teaspoon grain mustard
15 g flatleaf parsley,
  chopped
1 tablespoon yogurt
  (optional)
S & P

● First peel the beetroot with a peeler or sharp knife (the skin is very thin). Then grate the beetroot on the big holes of your grater. This can be done in the food processor with a grater blade if a larger quantity is required, but there is a lot of loving and flavour to be had from a hand job.

● You will inevitably have a few colour stains. The colour is verdant and fun, but it is natural food colour so will wash out with a helpful dose of the wonderful Bio-Tex (thanks Floss). Thus this can be turned into a white T-shirt colouring party with the kids, young and old – not to mention pink clown's cheeks.

● Mix the grated beetroot with the olive oil and lemon juice and season with S & P. Stir in the spring onions, garlic, seeds, mustard and parsley. If you want some creaminess, swirl yogurt in just before serving, but I sometimes prefer mine *au naturel*.

Shelf Life: Should last 2 days. **Best Kept:** In a covered bowl in the fridge.

beetroot and GOAT'S cheese filos

Beetroot is the new black. At Leon, the healthy fast food group of restaurants I co-founded and develop the menus for, we are big on Superfoods, a category of ingredients all noted for doing something particularly great for our bodies. To name but a few, grapefruit, avocado, kale, Brazil nuts, garlic, beetroot and broccoli, but the Top Ten changes depending on who you're talking to. Beetroot is always in there, and usually in the top three. It truly has amazing properties. Associated with both Apollo and Aphrodite (apparently it was the secret of how she kept her looks), it is known to have been eaten for over a thousand years.

serves 6 (2 each)

500g raw beetroot

a drizzle of olive oil

40g chives, chopped

3 garlic cloves, peeled and
   finely chopped

25g flatleaf parsley,
   roughly chopped

220g goat's cheese,
   crumbled

2–3 spring onions, thinly
   sliced

juice of ½ lemon

8 sheets filo pastry
   (30cm x 20cm)

90g unsalted butter, melted

S & P

● Preheat the oven to 200°C/400°F/gas 6.

● Wash the beetroot, but do not peel, and put in a small roasting tray with a drizzle of oil, some S & P and about 3cm water. Cover with foil and bake for 45 minutes, or until a knife penetrates the beetroot without much resistance. Take out of the oven and let them cool a bit. Slip into your latex gloves.

● Whilst the beets are still warm, squish the skins off with your hands – they should just slide away in a satisfying way. Cut them into small dice – about 1cm squared. Put your beetroot in a bowl with the chives, garlic, parsley, goat's cheese, spring onions, lemon juice and some seasoning. Mix together properly with your hands.

● Lay out the filo sheets, keeping the ones you are not working with under a damp tea towel to stop them drying out. Put one sheet out on a clean surface and brush with melted butter. Put another sheet on top and brush with melted butter again. Cut the sheet lengthways into 3 strips approximately 10cm wide; this will make 3 filos.

● Somewhere round about now preheat the oven to 180°C/350°F/gas 4.

● Put a blob (about 1 heaped tablespoon) of the beetroot on to the lower right hand corner of the bottom 8cm of your first strip, leaving a 2cm edge of pastry below it. Now fold this edge over the beetroot, so the bottom is closed. Take the right corner and roll the blob over the diagonal, so your folded edge is now facing left and you have a triangle. Flip the triangle up and then to the right and up again until you reach the top. Wrap the excess around, brush with butter and pop on to a baking tray. Repeat until you have 12 parcels. Bake in the oven for 15 minutes. You can now slip out of your latex.

Shelf Life: After cooking, you want to eat them within 12 hours. **Best Kept:** You might want to make them up a day ahead and keep them in the fridge.

pink GRAPEFRUIT, watermelon and avocado salad

I'm usually a bit funny about using fruit in salads, a bit too San Fran for me, but this triple fruit and herb number – sharp and fragrant, light and aromatic – is pure hippy love.

Pink grapefruits are higher in vitamin A than the yellow ones, and as melons are one of the top five sources of it too, this salad is limbering up to be a supple skin special. The other big jobs retinol (vitamin A) takes care of are stopping colds and sore throats, as well as increasing night vision – this is fast shaping up to be a salad for sickly, cigar-smoking models who work in the dark.

**serves 6 as a starter
or 3 as a light lunch**

2–3 ripe avocados
2 pink grapefruits
50g flatleaf parsley, finely
    chopped
50g mint, finely chopped
800g watermelon, de-seeded
    and cut into 3cm chunks
70ml extra virgin olive oil
1¹/₂ teaspoons pink pepper-
    corns, crushed with the
    back of a knife and then
    finely chopped
handful of edible flowers;
    I used purple and yellow
    pansies, but nasturtiums
    add a butch pepperiness
S & P

● Peel and cut the avocados into wedgelettes and put in a bowl.

● With a small, sharp knife, cut the top and bottom off the grapefruits, then slice off the skin working vertically from top to bottom (make sure you get rid of all the pith).

● Holding the grapefruit above the avocado bowl (this is so you catch all the juice), cut out the segments of fruit with a small, sharp knife. This is done by coming in on either side of the tough white membranes and working towards the centre. Allow the segments to fall into the bowl.

● Toss in the herbs and the chunks of watermelon.

● Pour in the extra virgin and stir in the peppercorns. Season with a little S & P and serve straightaway, with a sprinkling of petals if you are feeling flowery.

Shelf Life: Non-existent. **Best Kept:** Not.

greek DAKOS

Cheese and Tomato, one of the best combos in the world. This is the Greeks' answer to *bruschetta con pomodoro e mozzarella*, and I have to say it deserves to be as well known. The trouble with the Italian classic is that the mozzarella just doesn't travel well. Something happens as it gets to the airport in its super-chill boxes, leaving a not-very-special, white, boingy ball to be picked up at the other end. The Greeks, on the other hand, developed a cheese that can travel. Feta brings a sharp, saline, creamy flavour to the party, which complements the tomatoes beautifully – especially if they're ripe.

I don't buy any big tomatoes during the winter months – just vine-ripened cherry ones – it literally is not worth it. Late summer is a different story, when the lycopene in their skins, which is the antioxidant part, is at its best. The redder the tomato the better it is for you, and to crown it off, lycopene is better absorbed into our bodies with a bit of oil around, so bring on the Extra Virgin (but I'm not quite sure what happened to the first one).

serves 6

400g rye bread

300g tomatoes, vine-ripened or cherry – just use whatever's best on the day

100g feta cheese

2 large garlic cloves, peeled and roughly chopped

1 teaspoon dried oregano

1 tablespoon extra virgin olive oil, plus extra for drizzling

a splash of red wine vinegar

S & P

● Preheat the oven to 200°C/400°F/gas 6.

● Tear the loaf into 6 hunks, put them on a baking tray and pop into the oven for 10 minutes, until crunchy and golden brown.

● Meanwhile, quarter the tomatoes and put them in a mixing bowl. Crumble in the feta, add the garlic, oregano, extra virgin and red wine vinegar and season with S & P. Mix well until the feta breaks down a bit.

● Take the hot bread out of the oven, drizzle with a touch more extra virgin and pile the cheese and tomatoes on top.

Shelf Life: At room temperature for no more than an hour. **Best Kept:** Eat this fresh.

A bit of a messy eat, but worth it for the flavours.

cuban CORN

This is a rocking bit of street food from the streets of Havana, but the closest I've ever been to Castro is a fab and funky little café on Spring St. in New York's Nolita called, weirdly, Café Habana.

Radiocarbon dating has found that maize has been eaten in the Americas for over 3000 years. As it was the only grain used by the Incas, the Mayans and the Aztecs, this multitalented foodstuff clearly makes you want to build tall things.

serves 6

1¹/₂ teaspoons smoked paprika
1¹/₂ teaspoons chilli powder
zest of 1 lime
1¹/₂ tablespoons sea salt
90g Parmesan cheese, grated
6 raw ears of corn
2–3 tablespoons sour cream
3 limes

● Get your griddle pan fired up or preheat your grill.

● Mix the smoked paprika, chilli powder, lime zest, sea salt and Parmesan together and spread out thinly on a big plate.

● Cook the corn on all sides until some of the kernels are nicely blackened – about 12–15 minutes.

● Cool for a minute, then brush the corn with sour cream and finish by giving it a good roll in the cheesy spice mix.

● Squeeze on a bit of lime juice and serve with a wedge on the side.

Shelf Life: N/A **Best Kept:** In your hands.

LOBSTER summer rolls

Summer rolls are of Vietnamese extraction and are a raw, fresh and, in my opinion, much nicer version of a spring roll – a bit of Asian cuisine that has been utterly murdered in this country. The last time I saw a good spring roll in these parts was in my junior school gym displays.

serves 6

FOR THE ROLLS

1kg lobster, cooked

12 rice wrappers

1 head soft lettuce, washed, drained and separated into leaves (cut the thick stems as they break through the wrapper)

$^1/_3$ cucumber, peeled and cut into matchsticks

1 bunch spring onions, cut into matchsticks

1 large carrot, peeled and cut into matchsticks

1 ripe but firm avocado, peeled, halved and cut into long, thin strips

a few mint leaves

$^1/_2$ punnet mustard cress, snipped off

juice of 1 lime

FOR THE DIPPING SAUCE

2 heaped teaspoons wasabi powder

50g crème fraîche

light soy sauce

● Break the tail section off the lobster and, using scissors, cut through the shell on the underside. Remove the tail meat and carefully slice lengthways into 4 beautiful pieces. Now cut each of these pieces into 3 long batons, so you have 12 pieces in all. Put them into the fridge.

● Crack open the large claws, remove that meat and roughly chop. Put with the other lobster in the fridge. If you are lucky enough to have a lobster with eggs, scrape them out and add to the rest. Suck or chew the little claws, or save for a lobster stock.

● Make up the wasabi cream for the dipping sauce. Mix the wasabi powder with a teaspoon of water – this brings the inert powder to full bloom. Stir into the crème fraîche and put in the fridge.

● Prepare all your veg and other bits for the inside of the rolls.

● Now to the wrappers. These strange beasts are made of rice flour, look like plastic, but after a few seconds in warm water, they are pure satin. We know we are going to make 12 rolls, so you might want to roughly divide each of your ingredients into 4, thus you make 3 rolls out of each pile and you won't run out.

● Soak your wrappers in warm water one at a time, but don't leave them in it for more than a minute or your rolling life will be made a lot trickier. Lay a soaked rice wrapper on your board. Put a lettuce leaf down in a north-south direction on the wrapper and then follow with the matchsticked cucumber, spring onion and carrot, then the avocado, a leaf of mint torn up, some mustard cress, the lobster (tail and claw meat) and finally a squeeze of lime juice.

● Fold the top and bottom up onto your veggie lobster pile. Then fold the long right hand side over and roll the whole lot snugly to the left. As you complete them, put them on a plate and cover with a damp, light tea towel. Keep going until you've done the lot.

● When you are ready to serve, choose 6 dainty little dishes for your dipping sauce. Make a high pile of wasabi cream in the centre of each one and then flood around this green island a placid lake of soy. Serve with the rolls.

Shelf Life: Eat within 2–3 hours. **Best Kept:** Under a cool, damp cloth in the fridge.

squid with HARISSA

Many moons ago, the River Café put Grilled Squid with Rocket and Chilli on the menu. Five changes of government and four degrees of global warming later, and it still never misses a service. As I always say to anyone who will listen: 'there's a reason why the classics are classics', and the squid-chilli partnership is proof of that.

Doing it with harissa instead of chilli adds a depth of flavour – and, after all, it is only a small hop from Fez to Taranto.

Eat plenty of rocket, such a flavourful leaf, for healthy skin, improved immunity and happy blood fat levels.

serves 6

800g cleaned squid
4 tablespoons olive oil
250g rocket
1 lemon
$^1/_2$ recipe quantity Harissa,
    (see page 166)
2 tablespoons extra virgin
    olive oil
S & P

● First prepare the squid. Split the tubes of squid down the middle so that you have flat triangle-like things. Score with short, shallow, cross-hatches on the inside. Cut into rough, bite-sized triangles and wedges. If you have the tentacles, chop them in half lengthways and put them with the scored squid pieces. Season well with S & P.

● Get 2 pans nice and hot, each with 2 tablespoons of olive oil, and sauté the squid for 3−4 minutes. Splitting the squid like this helps it pick up some colour and cooks it faster, which is good for the squid.

● When it is just about cooked, put 2 tablespoons of harissa into each pan and pull them off the heat. Really coat the squid with the harissa.

● Dress the rocket with 2 tablespoons of harissa, the extra virgin and the juice of half a lemon and divide between the plates.

● Squeeze a little lemon juice into the pans and give them a quick swirl around, then spoon the squid and saucy bits over the rocket. Serve with a wedge of lemon.

Shelf Life: Harissa, 2 weeks. **Best Kept:** The squid, once cooked, needs to be eaten straightaway. The harissa is good in the fridge.

thai-ger PRAWN cocktail

Whether you admit it or not, we all love a good prawn cocktail – the trouble is that we rarely get a good prawn cocktail. This Southeast-Asian-influenced version wins in so many ways. It calls for good-quality, large prawns with flavour, as opposed to the watery ones that usually sit on the limp iceberg down the social club. The dish borrows the bit of having chilli mixed with raw French beans from my favourite Thai salad, Som Tum. Even the traditional Marie Rose sauce gets a lesson from the Siamese. It looks smashingly gay in Martini glasses, tastes great out of any kind of glassware – the only drawback being the dodgy recipe title. Use half tarragon, half mint if you can't find Thai basil.

serves 6

120g Chinese leaf or white cabbage, finely shredded

60g Thai basil, chopped

18 raw tiger prawns, peeled and de-veined (but leave the tail fan on 6 of them)

120g French beans, topped, and tailed, cut into 1cm pieces

200g cherry tomatoes, cut in half

FOR THE SAUCE

6 tablespoons mayo

2 tablespoons Sweet Chilli Sauce (see page 168)

2 tablespoons chopped fresh red chilli (optional)

2 teaspoons fish sauce

juice of 1 lime

TO SERVE

1 lime, cut into 6 slices or wedges

pinch of cayenne pepper/ paprika

● Mix the cabbage and nearly all the chopped basil together and put in the bottom of 6 martini glasses.

● Bring a small saucepan of salted water to the boil. Plunge the prawns into the water, turn the heat down and poach gently for 4 minutes.

● Take the prawns out and leave to cool on a plate; either throw away the water or save it for a light broth-style soup for later.

● Scatter the French beans and cherry tomatoes on top of the cabbage in the glasses.

● Mix together the ingredients for the sauce.

● Roughly chop 12 of the prawns (the ones without the pretty tail bits) and stir into the sauce.

● Divide the prawn and chilli sauce mix between the glasses, then scatter on the last of the chopped basil.

● Top each glass with your presentation prawn. Hit it with the compulsory sprinkle of cayenne. Cut halfway through the lime slices or wedges and fit them onto the edge of the glass. A cocktail umbrella is completely necessary.

Shelf Life: This isn't really a keeper, as it will go a bit soggy… a day at the most.
Best Kept: In the fridge.

chicken and aubergine special

Aubergines have come a long way since they were first spotted in downtown Delhi in the fifteenth century. Every generic cuisine has naturalised them into their national culture. Melanzana (It), eggplant (US), bringal (Ind), bademjan (Iran) or Obo (Aus), aubergines win all the prizes. A steamed aubergine may not sound impressive, but I assure you it has truly hidden depths.

serves 6

3 Thai aubergines (or 2 regular)
6 skinless chicken breasts
   (about 150g each)
2 bay leaves
2 garlic cloves, smashed
4cm piece of ginger, halved
2 star anise
6 Chinese leaves
3 spring onions
1 big carrot, shaved thinly
2 red peppers, cut in half,
   de-seeded and each half
   cut into 5 or 6 wedges
1 lime, cut into wedges
salt

FOR THE DRESSING

3 tablespoons rice wine
   vinegar
2¹/₂ tablespoons good
   peanut butter
2 red chillies, finely diced
1 teaspoon caster sugar
2 teaspoons sesame seeds,
   toasted
1 teaspoon black sesame
   seeds
juice of 1 lime
3 tablespoons light soy sauce
2 garlic cloves, chopped
4cm piece of ginger, grated
2¹/₂ tablespoons sesame oil
25g coriander, chopped

● Trim the tops and bottoms of the obos, then cut each one across the middle. Stand each half on end lengthways and cut down in half again. Then cut each quarter into 3 long wedges and sprinkle with a good teaspoon of salt. Put into a colander. Leave to weep those bitter tears for 30 minutes, then pat dry with kitchen paper.

● Get a deep saucepan, about 25cm across, big enough to hold all the breasts closely together in one layer, but not too crammed. Put about 8cm water in it with the bay, garlic, ginger, star anise and a teaspoon of salt and bring up to just simmering.

● Whisk all the ingredients for the dressing in a mixing bowl, adding enough sesame oil at the end to bring it all together.

● Once the water is up to speed, sit a sieve on top, put the obos in it and cover with a lid. If the lid no longer fits tightly, wrap a tea towel round it to make sure you have a good seal. Steam gently for 10 minutes.

● Once the time is up, lift the sieve up and gently lay the chicken in, checking the water level is just covering the flesh and, if not, topping it up with some hot from the tap. Turn the obos over so the ones at the top are now at the bottom and vice versa. Check the water is back to a simmer and replace your turban-lid.

● After another 10 minutes, tip the steamed obos into the dressing. Give them a wiggle and a turn so that every side of each aubergine is seeing dressing. Cover the bowl to keep them warm. Use a slotted spoon to get the chicken out and rest on a chopping board. Keep the stock simmering gently.

● Tear the Chinese leaves into large pieces and cut the spring onions into 5cm slices. Put the thin carrot slices, red pepper wedges, Chinese leaves and pieces of spring onion into the sieve. Steam as before for 3-ish minutes.

● Meanwhile, keep turning the obos in the dressing, urging them to absorb as much of it as possible.

● Cut each chicken breast into 3, and put in shallow bowls with drooping carrot, juiced up aubergines and assorted steamed veg. Finish with a healthy drizzle of any leftover dressing, a wedge of lime and a ladleful of the stock. Serve with a spoon.

Shelf Life: 4 days in the fridge. **Best Kept:** This is fine in the fridge.

beaujolais BEEF fondue with
chilli aïoli and CHRAIN

Cooking beef in a red wine stock is so much nicer than cooking it the usual version of a fondue – in hot oil. The best part is that at the end of the meal the beef-infused stock can be reduced down and drunk as a broth. *Really* good.

I've done it with a loose chilli aïoli (for added zoom factor) and a walloping Jewish condiment of beetroot and horseradish called Chrain. So you cook your beef, and elevate with chrain. Boom boom. Try and get fresh horseradish if you can – impressively ferocious.

Beaujolais Nouveau is good for nothing except cooking, and in a really dreadful year not even that, but any vin rouge will do.

You'll need 36 metal or bamboo skewers about 30 cm long and a fondue pan.

**makes 36 skewers
(6 each for 6 people)**

FOR THE FONDUE

2 bay leaves

1/2 beef bouillon cube

a couple of sprigs of rosemary

1 bottle Beaujolais Nouveau

2 tablespoons sherry vinegar

1/2 onion, thinly sliced

2 garlic cloves, peeled and
    smashed

FOR THE SKEWERS

4 thick slices of white bread,
    cut into 2cm cubes

a drizzle of extra virgin
    olive oil

500g beef fillet

6 spring onions, cut into
    4cm sticks

200g button mushrooms,
    trimmed and washed but
    left whole

S & P

FOR THE CHRAIN

65g beetroot, raw

25g horseradish root, raw
    (or 3 tablespoons creamed
    horseradish)

juice of 1/2 lemon

1/4 teaspoon caster sugar

2 tablespoons crème fraîche

salt

FOR THE AÏOLI

3 garlic cloves, peeled and
    finely minced

1 red chilli, finely minced

10g breadcrumbs, toasted

1 egg yolk

juice of 1/2 lemon

6 tablespoons extra virgin
    olive oil

S & P

● If you are using bamboo skewers, put them into a tray or container that will hold them flat. Pour boiling water over them so that they are submerged. This will keep them malleable and hinder splinters.

● In the fondue pan, heat the bay leaves, bouillon, rosemary, wine, vinegar, onion and garlic to a low simmer. Cook this as slowly as possible for about 30 minutes, and in the meantime get on with your other jobs.

● Preheat the oven to 180°C / 350°F / gas 4.

● Put the cubed bread onto a baking tray and drizzle with some extra virgin olive oil. Give it a good crack of black pepper and some salt and bake in the oven until golden brown – say 12–15 minutes.

● Cut the fillet into 1cm x 4cm rectangles, about 5mm thick. Make up the skewers by sandwiching 1 square of spring onion between 2 pieces of steak. Repeat for all.

● Chrain is simply grated beetroot and horseradish. Grate them on the small holes. Mix them together with the lemon juice, a touch of salt and the sugar. Finish the chrain by stirring in the crème fraîche.

● Now to the matter of the aïoli. Mash the minced garlic and chilli with the bread-crumbs in a small bowl, using a fork. Whisk in the egg yolk whilst adding a splash of lemon juice – the emulsion should now go pale. Add a sprinkling of salt and begin adding the oil slowly – it should become emulsified, thicken and go smooth. When all the oil is in, you can taste, season and relax. Watch out for a consistency change as the bread thickens the aïoli.

● Once the skewers, mushrooms, croûtons, chrain and aïoli are finished, it is time to taste and season the broth – you want it to be quite acidic to bring out the flavour of the meat.

● When you are ready to fondue, bring the broth up to a gentle simmer and give your guests their share of beefed-up skewers, and a pile of mushrooms and croûtons to play with as they will. Put the beef in for between 3–4 seconds and 30 seconds, depending on how you like your beef and how thickly you've cut it. The 'shrooms will take longer. Just remember if anyone pulls out an empty skewer they have to do a dare or kiss the person on their left. Perfect – spin the bottle for grown-ups.

● Your dippers are the meat, the 'shrooms and the croûtons, and you know who your sauces are. Try the aïoli, and all hail the chrain, but mostly just enjoy the flavour of the beef. Keep a dish of sea salt on the table as the emerging meat could do with a touch of seasoning. Once all the meat has been cooked, reduce the stock by half, adding a splash of sherry along the way, then pour into cups or bowls and drink.

Shelf Life: 1–2 days. **Best Kept:** The whole lot could be done a day ahead, except for the bread cubes. Once cooked, well there are too many components to dispatch to different parts of the house...use common sense.

FRED'S roast PORK, grapes and SLOE gin

Fred is my best foreign friend in a culinary and family category. He came from the land of Green Gables, pigs and hay (Prince Edward Island, off the coast of Nova Scotia) many years ago and we've been cooking, laughing and causing trouble together for some 15 years now. He is my culinary muse and this book could not have been written without him.

Soaking the pork in brine is so easy and makes such a difference. Try it once and you'll never go back: the flavour, the colour, the succulence and oh my God the crackling. This is skin-crisp, wafer thin, and so, so good.

serves 6 (plus a night-time raid, and a lunch sarnie or two)

FOR THE PORK BRINE
800ml cider vinegar
250g salt
200g brown sugar
1 carrot, chopped
1 stick of celery, chopped
1 onion, sliced
4 bay leaves
10 peppercorns

1 x 2kg loin of pork, boned and rolled (but try and get the bones too)

FOR THE GRAPES AND SLOE GIN
500g dark red grapes (on the stalk weight), plucked
250ml sloe gin

● Take a saucepan that is large enough to hold the brining ingredients and 1.6 litres water. Put them all in (except for the pork), bring to the boil and take off the heat. Leave to cool completely.

● Submerge the pork in the cold brine, using a small plate with some tins on it to hold it down. Put in the fridge for about 30 hours.

● When your 30 hours are up, preheat the oven to 160°C / 320°F / gas 3.

● Take out the pork and throw the brine away. Cover the base of a large roasting tray with the rib bones you got from the butcher. Lay the pork on the bones, skin-side up. Put into the oven and cook for about 20 minutes, at which point you should have a good look and a thorough basting. Continue basting the pork until it is cooked – should be a further 40–45 minutes. The more often you baste (every 15 minutes is about right), the cracklier your crackling. Do not fret if the crackling seems to be getting very dark; the sugar absorbed by the pork from the brine is caramelising and the skin eventually comes out a stunning dark reddish-brown.

● While the pork is cooking, put the grapes and sloe gin in a small saucepan. Cover and cook on a high heat for 15 minutes. Lift the cover, turn down the heat and simmer to reduce the sauce a bit – about 30 minutes. This is a light, juicy sauce, not thick and gloopy – you will see why this works when you taste it with the pork.

● When the pig is done, take it out and let it rest for 10 minutes. Carve and serve with the sloe gin and grapes. Boiled new potatoes would be great with this, to keep it summery, and a few English peas.

Shelf Life: They will both keep in the fridge. **Best Kept:** The pork is good for 4–5 days. You must try it cold with Chipotle Ketchup (see page 170). That is special in itself, and well worth cooking the pork and letting it go cold for... The grapes are good for 5 days.

duck and baked PLUMS

Plums are one of late summer's finest fruits, and we should all make a concerted effort to eat as many of them as we can whilst they are bountiful. Star anise is a member of the magnolia family; the under-ripe fruits are picked and dried, resulting in this very special spice.

serves 6

6 plums (the purple variety have the best colour, but the yellowy-red ones are also good)

a drizzle of extra virgin olive oil

a dozen sprigs of thyme

6 pieces of star anise

120ml Madeira (or port or cherry brandy, or sloe gin – something boozy and fruity)

4 large duck breasts (the bigger they are the better they cook)

1 tablespoon sherry vinegar

15g unsalted butter

S & P

● Preheat the oven to 200°C/400°F/gas 6.

● Tear off 6 squares of foil large enough to wrap around the plums. Lay the squares dull-side up and drizzle with extra virgin. Sprinkle on a little sea salt and put a plum in the middle of each one with a couple of sprigs of thyme and a star anise on top. Gather up the sides of the foil and pour a tablespoon of Madeira in the hole at the top before squishing it loosely together. Put in a pan in the oven and cook for 25 minutes.

● Use a small, sharp knife to score the duck fat. The scores should be about $1/2$ cm apart, run the length of the fat and not go so far through it that the flesh underneath is visible. This opens up the solid fat for easier melting, which makes for a crispier skin.

● Heat a heavy-based frying pan big enough to hold all 4 breasts. Don't do this on the largest ring of your hob. As it gets properly hot, season the duck breasts heavily with sea salt on the skin side, and lightly on the flesh side. Pepper the flesh side only. Lay the breasts skin-side down in the hot pan and cook for about 3 minutes. Then using the back of a fish slice to hold the duck, drain the fat into a small bowl. Check that the skin side is a good golden brown colour and then turn the heat right down to the lowest setting. Cook for a further 12 minutes and, depending on how fatty your duck is, drain off more fat (you never want to have more than the thinnest layer in the pan). Flip it over for about 3 minutes to seal the flesh side. Take the breasts from the pan and put on a warm plate and rest for a few minutes, skin-side up.

● Put the duck pan back onto a low heat with just a thin film of fat. Pour in the last of the Madeira with the sherry vinegar and throw in the rest of the thyme sprigs. Let it reduce down to a saucy consistency and then turn off the heat. Sit the duck breasts on a board with a rim or channel around it – lots of precious, bloody juice will come out when you slice them and you will need to add it to the Madeira reduction in the duck pan. Carve the breasts into 1cm-thick slices, making them perpendicular to the cuts in the fat. I've allowed for two thirds of a breast or 4–5 slices per person.

● Reheat the Madeira sauce, adding the duck juices. Whisk in the butter and season. Take the plums out of the oven and give them a quick squish through the foil to make sure they're soft. I like to serve them wrapped in their foil like little presents for my friends, but if preferred, take them out. Don't lose the juice, though, which is special.

Shelf Life: 3 days. **Best Kept:** In a cold larder, or fridge if it's an Indian summer.

fish POT-AU-FEU with borlottis

Pot-au-Feu means nothing more than that you make it in a pot on the fire – so as long as you do it on the hob, it qualifies. Borlottis are Italy's favourite bean. The fresh ones are a joy in season, but even dried they still have a chalky magic to them. They are a good carb and a strong source of minerals. But really this recipe is all about the fish – the finest ambassadors of the sea – invited to impart their own special flavour to the cooking.

serves 6

400g fresh borlotti beans,
   podded (or 150g dried)

FOR THE STOCK

125g fish bones
1 large, white onion, diced
1 bay leaf
50g parsley, chopped
1/2 carrot
1 celery stick, cut into
   big chunks
400g tin of plum tomatoes
1 glass of white wine

FOR THE FISH

1.5kg cooked lobster
6 king prawns, raw
300g salmon, filleted and
   pin-boned
300g red mullet, filleted
   and pin-boned
300g mussels
300g palourdes or small clams
1 leek, cut into thin rounds
a pinch of saffron
6 scallops, shelled (not
   monster ones)
20g flatleaf parsley, chopped
S & P

● If using dried borlottis, soak them overnight in cold water. The following day, bring them to the boil in fresh water and simmer gently for 1 hour, or until cooked.

● Put all the fish bones and the rest of the stock ingredients into a 2-litre saucepan and cover with water (at least 1 litre). Bring the stock slowly to a simmer, skimming off all the scum. Turn right down for a total cooking time of 30 minutes.

● Get the meat out of the lobster tail and large claws; keep the claws whole, but slice the tail into 6 discs and put in the fridge. Roughly chop and smash the remaining bits of lobster shell, give the stock a skim and sweep the whole mess into the pot.

● Peel and de-vein the tails of the prawns and put in the fridge with the lobster. Plunge their shells and heads into the stock.

● Turn the heat off the stock to let it cool and settle a bit with everything in it.

● Slice the salmon into 6 slices and add to the fish in the fridge.

● Now cut the red mullet into 6 perfect shapes, whether they are long triangles or thin strips. Put with the rest of the fish.

● Clean the mussels of their beards and rinse with the palourdes in running water.

● Give the stock a final skim and then pass it through a colander (big holes are best) into a wide-based, low-sided pan. Bring the stock to a slow simmer, add the fresh borlottis (if using) and cook for 15 minutes. Now add the leeks and saffron.

● Carefully place all the raw fish, shellfish (including the scallops) and cooked lobster into the stock, trying to keep it in one layer and divided into creed. If using dried (and now cooked) borlottis, add them to the pan. Cover and allow everything to simmer gently for 3–5 minutes, then turn off the heat.

● Taste the stock (now a broth). It should need just a crack of pepper and a bit of salt. Use a slotted spoon to gently divide the fish and shellfish between bowls. Top up with a good amount of hot broth and sprinkle over the parsley. What a joy.

Shelf Life: The stock will be good for 2–3 days after it has been cooked.
Best Kept: The stock and fish could be prepped and made the day before.

SPANISH tortilla with chorizo and clam kicker

So I had something like this in a truck stop in Catalunya – we were the only women in there, and the only ones who didn't have a truck. I just don't understand where we went so wrong and the Spaniards so right; they get home-made, cheap grub on the go and we get faceless, tasteless franchises. If it had been up to me, I just might have let the Armada land....

serves 6

FOR THE TORTILLA

450g onion, finely diced

4 tablespoons extra virgin olive oil

1kg King Edward potatoes, peeled and diced into 1cm chunks

10 eggs

S & P

FOR THE KICKER

2 red chillies, or 1 tablespoon crema di pepperoncini (see page 169)

4 tablespoons extra virgin olive oil

180g chorizo, the kind in a whole sausage (not sliced), cut into 5mm dice

1kg clams (palourdes are good), or mussels

3 garlic cloves, roughly chopped

180ml white wine

35g coriander (leaves and stalks), roughly chopped

S & P

● Preheat the oven to 150°C/300°F/gas 2.

● Sweat the onion and spuds in the extra virgin on a low heat in an ovenproof frying pan (25 cm diameter and 6cm deep). Do this with the lid on for 10 minutes, stirring halfway through. Once the onion is translucent and soft, tip the whole thing into a bowl and season.

● Do not wash the pan, but tear off a 35cm square of greaseproof paper and line the pan with it, using the oil in the pan to grease it well on both sides. Pack the spuds and onions back into the paper-lined pan; they should pretty much fill it.

● Beat the eggs with a little seasoning and pour in. Put the pan into the oven on the middle shelf and let the tortilla cook for 50–60 minutes.

● When the tortilla is set around the outside but a tiny bit runny in the very middle, pull it out and let it cool completely. This is an exercise in not browning.

● Now for the kicker. Finely chop or blend the chillies (tops off, seeds in) with a shot of salt. Take it to a purée, adding a few drops of water if necessary to bring together.

● Heat half of the extra virgin in a pan and over a medium heat fry the chorizo for 3–5 minutes, until just beginning to pick up a bit of colour. Then add the clams (or mussels) and garlic. Sauté for a second and then pour in the wine (listen for that satisfying sizzle) and let it reduce by two thirds. Turn off the heat and stir in the puréed chilli and the chopped coriander. Finish with the rest of the extra virgin.

● Once the molluscs are cooked, shell 80 per cent of them, chucking any that didn't open. Doing this for your guests is very kind and will add to their overall enjoyment. Eat everything at room temperature. The idea is that you have a fat slice of tortilla and spoon some of the kicker over it with a sharply dressed green salad on the side.

Shelf Life: Kicker not more than a day or two. Probably the same for the tortilla.
Best Kept: Tortilla, out – it's the ideal snack to take a little wedge of as you're passing. Kicker in the fridge.

summer BERRY lollies

Sadly, lollies tend to be relegated to the under 10s, but with a shot of Kirsch as an optional extra, these can be served with pride to an audience of any age. Grown-ups actually love a lolly too.

Very low stress, as long as you make them a day ahead so they can freeze properly overnight, and you don't even need to have lolly moulds. Fred found that you can do them with equipment accessible to all...

serves 6

6 lolly moulds (or 6 lolly sticks and 6 plastic take away cups with lids)
125g raspberries
125g blueberries
200ml cranberry juice
caster sugar (optional, depending on your berries; they can be wildly sweet or sour as the season progresses)
a shot of Kirsch (optional)

● Put both berries in the food processor and whizz for a couple of minutes. Personally, I prefer to leave in the seeds because of their looks and texture, but if you want a smoother finish pass through a fine sieve.

● Add the cranberry juice, caster sugar, if the fruit needs sweetening and Kirsch (if you desire) and stir.

● Pour into the moulds, push the stick down to the correct depth and shove in the freezer.

Shelf Life: 1 month. **Best Kept:** In the freezer.

strawberries with orange BLOSSOM and pine nuts

I had this in Morocco a couple of New Years' ago with wild strawberries; truly delicious and truly different. The nuts, honey and orange blossom are all so good together, supported by the bulgar and led by the strawberries.

Wild strawberries are, of course, the best of all. Wild anything is better than its confined counterpart: in shops and on menus you regularly see it as a prefix to some ingredients, and it's always worth getting excited about – wild salmon, garlic, mushrooms (and sex) all being good examples.

Pretty much all the berries share some common attributes in matters of the body: good for circulation and blood pressure, helpful to the liver and thoughtful to the bladder. Bulgar is very digestible and energy-boosting, as are pine nuts, which also contain the good unsaturated fats.

serves 6

3 tablespoon sugar

120g bulgar, cracked wheat or couscous

1 green tea bag

a few sprigs of mint

60g pine nuts, lightly toasted

a splash of orange blossom water

500g strawberries, halved

3 tablespoons runny honey

● Mix the sugar with the bulgar or couscous in a small saucepan, add the tea bag and the mint and pour on the boiling water so that the level is about 2cm above the bulgar or just enough to cover the couscous.

● Then cover the saucepan with a tight-fitting lid or with clingfilm and leave on top of the oven (i.e. in a warm place) for 20 minutes until all the liquid is absorbed. If you are using bulgar you may actually want to cook it on a low heat for the 20 minutes depending on the size of the wheat grains. Leave to cool, then take out the teabag. Pick out the mint and put on one side.

● Mix the pine nuts, orange blossom water and bulgar together, and then carefully stir in the halved strawberries. Bind with the honey and leave to rest for 20 minutes at room temperature so that the flavours mingle.

● Spoon onto a large plate, and drape the cooked mint over and around the dish for a bit of fun decor. When I had this up a mountain in Maroc it was served in one big dish and we all picked and shared it. It was lovely like that.

Shelf Life: The strawberries will really turn to mush after a few hours.
Best Kept: In front of you.

blackberry and apple kaiserschmarm

I was recently asked to do a party at my old school for a friend of the family's sixtieth and did this for the pudding. It was weird enough being asked to take a leap back in time some eighteen years, but it was made even more so by the fact that the said Seriously Posh Girls' School had, in fact, expelled me for behaving unspeakably when I was seventeen.

This Austrian answer to crumble is truly delicious, dead easy, cheap as chips and comes out like a cross between a bread-and-butter pudding and a clafoutis. Delicious with cream, maple syrup or both. There is nothing here about either colour or seasonality, but the old blackberry and apple thing is so familiar and deservedly well-documented that I've taken it as a given.

serves 6

4 eggs

180g self-raising flour

300ml milk

110g golden granulated
  sugar

1kg great seasonal apples

100g butter

1/2 teaspoon cinnamon

250g blackberries (pick
  your own, if you can – it
  does make a massive
  difference; or try using
  lingonberries instead)

1/2 lemon

icing sugar, to dust

● First make your batter: beat the eggs well with the flour, then whisk in the milk and 80g of the sugar. Leave to stand at room temp for a couple of hours with a tea towel over it.

● Next peel, core and cut the apples into eighths.

● Select your cooking vessel: a deep frying pan is ideal, just make sure it's ovenproof. Heat the butter until bubbling and just beginning to brown. Tip in the apple pieces, then toss and sauté for about 10 minutes on a reasonable heat so they pick up a touch of colour. Sprinkle on the remaining sugar and cinnamon and keep cooking until the apples are soft but not breaking up – some 5–10 minutes, depending on the size of the apples.

● Preheat the oven to 190°C/375°F/gas 5.

● Just before you are about to eat the course before this one, give the apples a quick shuffle on the hob to get the heat back into them and have them all sitting nicely on the bottom of the pan.

● Scatter on the berries, tip in the batter and put the whole thing in the oven for an initial 15 minutes. Then squeeze over the lemon juice and dust well with icing sugar – this helps to make a nice crust – and put back in the oven for a further 10 minutes.

● Just before serving, dust over another load of snow (icing sugar) and put on the table immediately. Eat with your favourite creamy topping. Kaiserschmarmmmmm....

Shelf Life: She's not really a laster. **Best Kept:** In your tummy.

BRANDIED cherries

Buying an extra kilo of cherries in summer to make this recipe is the kind of investment that pays off heartily mid-winter (see page 56, Portuguese Custard Tarts) and takes care of all your needs for a bit of sun and something special on those shortest and darkest of days. We also found that floating one in a glass of champagne made for a very superior Kir Royale; however, due to the surfaces of the cherry drawing the bubbles out, it goes flat faster, which means you have to drink quicker, which is no bad thing.

Sarah, my mother-in-law, who comes from the land of brandied peaches, the Deep South, says these are great stirred into a bowl of Greek yogurt to kickstart the mornings, or over ice cream in the evening to finish the day!

makes about 500ml

820g cherries (750g stoned weight)

350ml cooking brandy

250g golden granulated sugar

● Wash your cherries before you stone them. Take this time to throw away any that are not absolutely perfect; even a bit of soft or a brown stain means they must be chucked – you can't use any damaged fruit at all when making a preserve.

● Now settle in and stone your cherries, whilst having a taste of the brandy: one part brandy to 2 parts ginger ale, over lots of ice and a squeeze of lemon for instance. Choose your tool wisely: a hairpin works, as do your fingernails, as does a stoner.

● Mix two thirds of the brandy with the granulated sugar in a large bowl and stir until the sugar begins to dissolve a bit. Add the stoned cherries, cover with clingfilm and leave somewhere cool for 24 hours.

● The next day, put the cherries and liquid into a heavy-bottomed pan 20cm across. You might need to scrape the undissolved sugar from the bottom of the bowl.

● Bring the whole lot to the boil on the smaller of your rings. You do not want to boil the merde out of them, but you do need a rolling boil. As the boiling begins, you will need to keep an eye, and a ladle, nearby. An eye to watch that the boil does not overflow and a ladle to remove the grey scum that will rise to the centre of the bubbles.

● Continue to cook like this for 15 minutes or so. A strange thing will happen. The liquids will evaporate, concentrating the flavour, and the sugar will increase the temperature (this aids the preservation and is the fruit jamming) and the bubbles will actually get higher than the liquid you started with. After this time, you should have a clear, dark red, boiling pot, and the amount of scum rising will have decreased. Take off the heat and pour in the rest of the brandy. Put into a sterilized jar and pop on the lid whilst still hot.

Shelf Life: 4–6 months. **Best Kept:** In a cool larder.

ROSE absolute pancakes
with rose PETAL sauce

Rose Absolute is known as the Queen of Oils, and according to the blurb that came with the teensy, potent bottle it is not only an aphrodisiac, but also has 'an affinity with female sexuality'. I am not sure exactly what that means, but I can tell you that these crêpes definitely made me feel good and rosy.

At the risk of harming a lot of people out there (and people I personally care about because they bought my book), there are some essential oils that say they are for external use only, and others that say they are alright for cooking. I have merrily used both kinds for years without suffering any ill effects. I'm not saying that you should do it, but just that I have and have lived to pancake another day.

The sauce is useless with Dutch hothouse roses, just not worth making. Hopefully you'll be able to grab a few petals from the garden for the sauce – from your fine array of old English varieties. If not, go and talk to your local florist about fragrance – I ended up doing a petal tasting in mine. If you can't get hold of the essential oil (easily ordered on the net), then substitute with 1 tablespoon of rose water.

Make this for your lover, but please resist the temptation to do it on Valentine's Day as the roses around then won't do it justice. Save it for a balmy, midsummer love-in.

serves 2

FOR THE PANCAKES
90g plain flour
1 tablespoon caster sugar
1 egg, beaten
a small pinch of salt
100ml milk
2 drops Rose Absolute
    (or ¹/₂ tablespoon
    rose water)
20g melted butter
a little butter, for frying

FOR THE ROSE PETAL SAUCE
75g caster sugar
petals from 3 fragrant roses
juice of ¹/₂ lemon

● Make the batter: in a bowl, beat the flour with the sugar, egg and salt. Mix together the milk and the Rose Absolute and gradually stir into the other ingredients. When it is smooth, add the melted butter and leave to stand for 2 hours.

● To make your rose petal sauce, bring the caster sugar with 225ml water to a simmer in a small pan. Sprinkle in the rose petals and stir them around to keep them bathed and submerged for the next 10 minutes.

● Bring the sauce up to a busy boil and reduce to a third of the original amount – I did this on the smallest ring of the hob and it took me 10–15 minutes.

● When the syrup is reduced and the petals are floppy and slightly translucent, turn off the heat. Add the lemon juice, a few drops at a time, and taste. You can always add more, but you can't take it out – you will know by tasting when it is right. Leave to cool to room temperature.

● Just before you use the batter, let it down with 30–40ml water to get it to the right consistency. It has to be loose enough to run round the pan as you swirl it.

● Heat a thin, flat frying pan over a medium/high heat, and melt a little butter in it, so that it coats the inside of the pan to grease it. Once the butter starts to violently sizzle, ladle in some batter and then immediately tip the pan so that the batter is spread in a thin layer all over it (it'll take you at least one practice go to get the thickness and the heat right).

● Cook the pancake for a couple of minutes on the first side, then as you see the edges begin to brown, use a palette knife to flip it over. The second side takes less time to cook, 1–2 minutes. When it is done, flip it onto a plate, fold it over once and then a second time and spoon over a bit of the sauce, petals and all. These are best eaten as they are made, they really are.

Shelf Life: Pancakes 5 minutes; sauce ages. **Best Kept:** Pancakes can be made ahead of time, stored between layers of greaseproof in the fridge and reheated in the oven, but where's the romance in that? The rose petal sauce will keep in the fridge; the colour may fade, but a rose is a rose is a rose.

PLUM cobbler or cobbled plums

This is roughly speaking an American crumble, but the top is a bit more scone-ish, and less crunchy-crumbly. You dollop it on, letting small pools of the fruit show through, so the top gets its name from the passing resemblance it has to a cobbled street. Having been to Cobbler Country (the Southern States) and been won over by them, I now always think twice about whether to crumble or cobble: Home or Away?

Plums are full of good fibre, and being the precursor to prunes are a great laxative, which is handy with all that fried chicken around.

serves 6

FOR THE COBBLES
225g butter (at room temperature)
75g caster sugar
460g self-raising flour
4 tablespoons milk

FOR THE PLUMS
1kg plums, stoned and quartered
100g demerara sugar

- Preheat the oven to 170°C/325°F/gas 3.

- In a bowl beat together the butter and sugar, incorporate the flour and as it gets thick, add the milk. You should have quite a smooth, shortbread-like dough.

- Take a bite of plum and, if you think they are tart, add another 50g sugar.

- Toss the plums with the sugar in a shallow, ovenproof dish. Tear off apricot-sized blobs of dough and rest on top of the plums – they don't need to be totally even.

- Bake in the oven for 40 minutes. Serve with double cream or vanilla ice cream.

Shelf Life: 3–4 days. **Best Kept:** Keep this one out, but covered with a plate. Good for a passing snack.

blueberry scones with raspberry BUTTER

Blueberries are among the top sources of antioxidant in the fruit world. Their list of beneficial properties is so long that if we all gave them the kind of attention they deserve, we would be a nation of Violet Beauregardes. They decrease blood sugar, enhance circulation, stop our blood from clotting when it shouldn't (someone should speak to Richard Branson about free blueberries on long-haul flights), are good for stomach ulcers, bones and joints. They have a powerful antibacterial action, and contain tannin and compounds that enhance the capillaries in the eye.

Despite the Englishness of scones, this deliciousness reminds me of my time in NYC. Whenever you had a proper brunch, a supply of muffins and strawberry butter would appear, and this recipe just plays with that idea a little.

makes 6–8

FOR THE SCONES
300g plain flour
3 heaped teaspoons baking
   powder
3 heaped teaspoons sugar
¼ teaspoon salt
40g unsalted butter (at
   room temperature)
about 150ml milk
50g blueberries
1 egg yolk mixed with
   1 tablespoon milk,
   to glaze

FOR THE BUTTER
125g unsalted butter (at
   room temperature)
35g icing sugar
90g raspberries

● Preheat the oven to 200°C / 400°F / gas 6.

● Make the scones: sift together the dry ingredients and then rub in the butter until you have a sandy texture. Use a wooden spoon to add enough milk so as to make a soft dough. You may want to do the last stage of the bringing together by hand.

● Once the milk has been added, move quickly to maximise the potential of the baking powder. Hanging around will lose height.

● Roll out the dough to 1.5cm thick and use a 7cm pastry cutter to make your scones. Push half a dozen bluebs deeply into the top of each scone and put on a lightly floured baking tray. Glaze with beaten egg yolk and milk and bake for about 15 minutes. Have a peek after they've had 5 minutes in the oven, and if your bluebs have popped up and are sitting on top of the scone, just push them down again with the back of a teaspoon – it doesn't matter if they explode. Cool on a wire rack.

● Now for the raspberry butter. Put the butter in a food processor or soften it with a fork. Incorporate the icing sugar 'til smooth, then mash in the raspberries, leaving them chunky or smooth depending on your preference. For the best consistency, put the butter in the fridge for 15 minutes before using.

Shelf Life: Scones are never the same once they cool down – 2 days at a push. Raspberry butter, 1 week. **Best Kept:** Scones in an airtight container. Raspberry butter in the fridge.

melted chocolate PEACHY pud

Summer is the time to get out of town, back to nature and go camping. Cooking and camping are not a particularly easy alliance and, even if you have a trendy Trangia, after a few meals your repertoire will be exhausted. The secret is to take a load of gas – I made a great Boeuf Bourguignon from local cows up in Scotland once, but I did have to cook it for about 10 hours, which used up three and a half canisters.

Puddings that convert to camping puddings are not that easy to come by, in general – I find the *Ile Flottantes* always blow away – but this one is a real find; it's easy and delicious and will keep the kids happy. Fred came up with this when I put him in the garden with a tin of peaches, a bar of chocolate, a packet of scone mix and an instant barbecue. All power to him – this is a total winner, which goes to show (yet again) that Necessity truly is the Mother of Invention.

serves 6

8 fresh peaches

120g golden caster sugar

480g instant scone mix, or make your own (see Blueberry Scones with Raspberry Butter, page 157)

milk, to make up the scone mix

160g dark chocolate

clotted cream or double cream, to serve

● First light the BBQ, or, if you're doing this at home, preheat the oven to 180°C/350°F/gas 4.

● Peel the peaches. I know it is fiddly, but if like me you have a problem with that fur in your mouth, it's a necessity. Cut them into biggish chunks, put them in a bowl and sprinkle on the sugar – this macerates them and helps them to soften. Leave for 30 minutes or so.

● Make 6 double-thickness 30cm squares of foil and divide the fruit between them.

● Make up the scone mix according to the directions on the side of the box (or make your own) and split into 6 balls.

● Divide the chocolate into 6 and push it into the centre of the scone dough balls, so it's no longer visible. Put one scone ball on each fruit pile, and then pull the foil up around it. Twist the foil at the top so it looks like a giant Hershey's Kiss, and then pop on the barbie or in the oven.

● Cover the whole thing (i.e. BBQ and foil 'kisses') loosely in foil, or close the lid if you've got a big gas one. This helps to keep the heat in and ensures even cooking.

● After half an hour or so (or if you smell burning) take the foil parcels, open them up, drop in a dollop of clotted cream or a sea of double and eat straight out of the foil. Totally piggy, and makes for added cushioning in the night.

Shelf Life: I really wouldn't know **Best Kept:** Sing it Elvis: 'It's now or never...'

frozen GREEK yogurt with pistachio filo biscuits and figs

Even before freezing, this makes a delicious syllabubesque pudding. The theory is Hellenic, the biscuits are staggeringly simple and the result is fantastic – an ice-cream sandwich for grown-ups with sophisticated tastes. The yogurt freezes to harder than diamonds, so only make enough for the night.

serves 6

FOR THE FROZEN YOGURT
500g Greek strained yogurt
zest of 2 lemons
80ml double cream
60g clear honey
50g halva, flavoured if you
    fancy it
6 figs, juicy and fresh, cut
    into quarters

FOR THE FILO BISCUITS
12 sheets filo pastry,
    30cm x 20cm
60g unsalted butter, melted
golden granulated sugar,
    to sprinkle
60g pistachios, lightly
    toasted in the oven and
    finely ground
ground cinnamon, to
    sprinkle

● Tip the yogurt into a mixing bowl and stir in the lemon zest, double cream and honey. Crumble in the halva, keeping the pieces about the size of a penny – it is a little bitter, interestingly so – but definitely enough that you don't want the pieces to be too big.

● Tip the mix into a suitable dish so the yogurt has a depth of about 5cm. Cover with foil and stick it in the freezer. It will take 3–5 hours to freeze. Because there are no eggs in it, the frozen yogurt can have an almost crumbly texture that I like very much, very rustic, not at all Mr Whippy.

● Preheat the oven to 180°C/350°F/gas 4.

● Now for the filo: keep 6 sheets under a slightly damp cloth to stop them drying out whilst you work on the first lot. Take one sheet, brush it with melted butter and sprinkle on a little sugar, some ground pistachios and a pinch of cinnamon. Lay another sheet on top, give it a light roll with a rolling pin and then repeat the melted butter, sugar, cinnamon and nut thing again. Keep going until you have a stack of layered filo sheets 6 high, then give it a final roll over. Repeat with the other 6 sheets of filo to make another sugary/nutty stack.

● To finish, mix the leftover sprinkles together, brush the tops with butter and sprinkle away. Save a tiny scattering of sugar, nuts and cinnamon for the edges of the serving plates.

● Using a round pastry cutter 8–10cm across, cut out 6 biscuits from each filo stack and lay them on a lightly buttered baking tray. You should have 12 in total.

● When all are done, put them in the oven and bake for around 10–15 minutes, or until the tops are golden brown. Take the filos out of the oven and leave to cool. This can be done ahead of time, before the yogurt goes into the freezer, if you want.

● To serve, build the sandwiches by putting a biscuit on the bottom, then a ball of frozen yogurt (run your scoop under very hot water for a minute), then another biscuit. To finish, pretty up the plate with the last of the sprinkly bits and put the fig quarters wherever you fancy.

Shelf Life: Frozen yogurt is best on the night; biscuits for 1 week. **Best Kept:** Frozen yogurt in the freezer; biscuits in an airtight container.

the magic RHUBARB trick

Too often rhubarb is just boiled to buggery, becoming a stringy compote. But not so here, hence the title. Load the batons side by side in a roasting tray and cook it in a low oven, covered; over time the rhubarb morphs into rows of pink, silky soldiers, who are keen fighters in the battle for flavour. The colour is so delightful, the method so simple and the pleasure of having shape and form to your rhubarb is boundless.

serves 6

FOR THE RHUBARB

675g rhubarb, washed and
   cut into 10cm batons
450g caster sugar
1 vanilla pod, split and
   scraped
juice of 1 orange, plus
   3 thin slices of zest

FOR THE SHORTBREAD

2 cardamom pods
80g unsalted butter (at
   room temperature)
80g plain flour
30g icing sugar
30g cornflour
a drop of vanilla essence

FOR THE CHOCOLATE SAUCE
AND WHIPPED CREAM

300ml double cream
1 tablespoon caster sugar
200g best dark chocolate

● First get the rhubarb in, as the magic can't be rushed. Preheat the oven to 110°C/ 225°F/gas $1/4$. Lay the rhubarb out on a tray in military fashion. You are aiming for a single layer. Sprinkle the sugar over and add the scraped vanilla pod. Splash on the orange juice and slices of rind. Cover tightly with foil and pop into the oven on the middle shelf to bake slowly for $2^1/_2$–3 hours. Have a peek after $1^1/_2$ hours.

● Now have a go at the shortbread. Preheat your other oven to 180°C/350°F/gas 4. Gently break open the cardamom pods, scrape out the seeds and carefully chop them with a knife and then squash them down. Discard the husks (or bury them in a little sugar to make cardamom sugar for a rainy day). Either in a mixer (not a food processor) or by hand, cream the butter until pale and fluffy. Sift in the flour, icing sugar and cornflour and beat again until fully incorporated. Stir in the vanilla and ground cardamom. Put squash-ball sized lumps of the mix onto a greased baking tray, about 2cm apart (they don't spread). Bake in the oven for 12–15 minutes, until the shortbreads are just golden. Take them out and leave to cool for a few minutes. Then carefully lift them off the tray onto a wire rack to cool completely.

● Take the rhubarb out of the oven once it has done its bit. You will see the sugar is totally dissolved and the rhubarb is intact, though slightly shrunken, and the whole lot is the most perfect pink and the softest of softs. Leave to cool; do not play with it. I have known some rhubarb to take an extra hour to cool down properly.

● Finally, get the chocolate sauce going. Set up a double boiler (a bowl set on top of a larger pan of water, on a small flame). Pour in half the double cream and stir occasionally until it has warmed up. Meanwhile, whisk the remaining cream with a tablespoon of sugar. Don't overwhip it and go and spoil everything now. Once the cream in the double boiler is warm, drop in the chocolate pieces and stir until smooth.

● For serving, I've done this as a mucky family supper (see page 163), but the first time I did it was as the finale of an uber-posh dinner, where we put the chocolate into martini glasses with the other components in little dishes beside it. Dip and scoop, suck and see.

Shelf Life: Rhubarb, 5–7 days; chocolate sauce, 2–3 days; shortbread, 5 days (or 2 months in the freezer). **Best Kept:** Rhubarb in the fridge. Chocolate sauce, in the fridge if it isn't all gone. Shortbread, in a cookie tin (or even freeze them).

rhubarb and raspberry TART

I always like to know where I am with my ingredients, and officially rhubarb is classed as a fruit, though technically it's a stem. Recently, blueberries have received much positive press, but the raspberry is also mighty. It is said to perk up your skin and hair, as well as the lesser seen (and therefore less cared about) sweat glands, bone marrow and mucous membranes, which are Very Important – without them working well, you're not going to have any skin and hair to obsess about anyway. To mix rhubarb with raspberries is a seasonal span, but the rhubarb was looking so unloved in the market I felt obliged to take it home and give it some. Anyway, flavourwise they are stunning together.

serves 6

FOR THE PASTRY

200g plain flour

70g caster sugar

100g unsalted butter (cold)

2 egg yolks

2–2$^1/_2$ tablespoons milk

FOR THE CUSTARD

300ml milk

1 vanilla pod, split in half and seeds scraped out

4 egg yolks

100g caster sugar

FOR THE FILLING

200g rhubarb, cut into 4cm batons

200g raspberries

● Make the pastry: in a food processor, spin the flour for a minute with the sugar. Split the butter into 6 knobs and drop them down the chute individually until the butter is completely incorporated, then immediately add the yolks one by one and a little milk to bring it all together to a pastry consistency. Scrape the pastry out, wrap it in clingfilm and put in the freezer for 10 minutes for a quick rest.

● Line your 20cm diameter tart case with the pastry. You can roll it out or you can just squash it into place. Keep any leftovers to fill any cracks that occur as it cooks. Whack the lined tart case in the freezer again for 15 minutes to harden up.

● Preheat the oven to 200°C/400°F/gas 6.

● Take the pastry case out of the freezer and bake in the oven for around 12 minutes.

● Gently heat the milk with the vanilla pod and seeds.

● Take the tart case out of the oven and fill in any cracks that have appeared in the pastry (they'll never know). No need to re-cook.

● Drop the oven temperature to 160°C/320°F/gas 3.

● Make the custard by beating the egg yolks thoroughly with the sugar. Pour in the milk, picking out the vanilla pod along the way, whisking all the time.

● Put the rhubarb in the bottom of the pastry case, then dot on the raspberries. Put the tart on the shelf in the oven and only now fill it up with the custard by pouring it from a jug – this just stops spillage on the way to the oven.

● Bake for 20–25 minutes until the custard is set. If it is still not set after this time, turn the oven down to 140°C/275°F/gas 1 and cook for a further 15 minutes.

● Let it cool a little before serving – with crème fraîche if you want.

Shelf Life: Not longer than a day. **Best Kept:** In a cool, but not cold, place – pastry doesn't like the fridge.

4 chilli SAUCES– one spicy, one sweet, one salty, one smoky

I love the message that chillies give out: that red means nothing but danger.

harissa

There are two women who know a lot more than me about Moroccan cooking: Paula Wolfert (author of the seminal *Moroccan Cuisine*) and Claudia Roden, in addition, of course, to the 16 million women in Morocco, plus another eleven-odd million female expats and émigrés worldwide... now I feel rather inadequate. Moving on, my point was a small one – both these great ladies start making their harissa by soaking the chillies in cold water for an hour or so, which makes me feel like a bit of a wuss because in this recipe there's no soaking; the sting is taken out of their tail by roasting them, which is a much more extreme way of mellowing the heat. I think the end result is that I go through my harissa faster, using more dollops per dish than they humanly can. This way you get an increased amount of herb and spiceage per forkful. I guess that's my theory, and even in the face of such informed opinion, I'm sticking to it. For now anyway.

makes 150ml

10 red chillies, halved and de-seeded

6 garlic cloves, peeled

1 teaspoon dried coriander seeds, toasted

1 teaspoon caraway seeds, toasted

2 tablespoons dried mint

35g coriander, picked and chopped

20g mint, picked and chopped

6 tablespoons extra virgin olive oil

S & P

● Preheat the oven to 200ºC/400ºF/gas 6.

● Put the chillies with the whole peeled cloves of garlic into a square of foil with some salt. Wrap it loosely, but make sure it's completely sealed into a bundle and pop it in the oven. Cook for 20 minutes.

● Whizz the coriander seeds, caraway seeds and dried mint in a coffee grinder, blender or pestle and mortar. Then put them in a bowl with the herbs.

● Take the foil parcel out of the oven. Open carefully and leave to cool for a minute. When they are cool enough to handle, remove the flesh from the skin of the chillies. This is easiest done with the back of a knife, dragging it slowly from the pointy end to the other to just scrape the flesh off the skin.

● Mash the garlic into the small bowl of ground seeds and herbs with a fork. Add the chilli and smoosh around until all are well mixed. Spoon into a jar and cover with the extra virgin and give it a shake just to make sure everybody is coated in oil.

Shelf Life: Good for 2 weeks. **Best Kept:** In a jar in the fridge.

sweet chilli sauce

Why buy it in bottles when homemade is so easy, has much more flavour and delivers a heat worth talking about? This chilli sauce lasts for months in the fridge, as long as it's in an airtight jar, so it's worth making in bulk.

Here's an odd one: in an _enoteca_ (wine shop) opposite the Pitti Palace in Florence, Susi and I were served pieces of Pecorino with chilli jam to dip them in as a nibble. Weird and not at all what I'd expect from the culinary introverted Italians, but none the less it was great. If you fancy doing that one, I'd leave out the lime and the leaves.

makes about 350ml

18 red chillies

9 large garlic cloves,
   peeled and finely chopped

180g caster sugar

juice of 2 limes (plus 6 lime
   leaves, if possible)

salt

● Take the tips off the chillies and chop them into small pieces or whizz them in the food processor with the garlic.

● Put the chopped chillies and garlic into a saucepan, along with the sugar, lime leaves and 500ml water.

● Bring to a boil, skim and put on a low simmer for ages (about 40–50 minutes), or until an almost jammy consistency is reached.

● Cool to room temperature and adjust the balance with the lime juice. Season with salt.

Shelf Life: 2 months. **Best Kept:** In a sterilized jar in the fridge.

crema di pepperoncini

This recipe came from Fred's boyfriend's mum, a Neapolitan lady of Parisian extract. A bit like her, this paste is fiery, stylish, and does exactly what it says – or so I hear from Fred because sadly I never met her.

The joy of it is two-fold: firstly, if you make a shed-load, you won't have to chop another chilli for months – a heaped teaspoon of this equals one regular red chilli. And secondly, as it macerates and reacts with the salt, the paste changes and takes on an interesting, deeper flavour.

makes 300ml, or thereabouts

400g red chillies, stems cut off and roughly chopped
80g rock or sea salt
6 tablespoons extra virgin olive oil

● Put the chopped chillies, seeds and all, into the food processor and pulse until all is chopped fine – not to a mush, though. Scrape the chilli purée into a 400–500ml jar.

● Mix the salt in, gently and evenly, and leave covered overnight.

● The next day it should have changed to a very slightly darker, deeper red. Stir in 4 tablespoons of extra virgin.

● Scrupulously clean the sides of the jar. This is a habit to keep up. Any bits that stay on the side of the jar could go mouldy.

● Cover the crema with the rest of the extra virgin and put a lid on it.

Shelf Life:
As long as you keep the insides of the jar clean and the crema is coated with oil, it will keep for 2 months.

Best Kept:
I am told that this can stay out in the ferocious heat of a southern Italian summer. It's certainly fine in my Hammersmith kitchen, but keep it in the fridge if you like.

chipotle ketchup

This turned out better than I ever thought it could, and has become flavour of the month in our house. My only sadness is that some of you may not be able to find chipotles. I am also aware that you may not even know what a chipotle is and, although I have tried very hard to keep the ingredients in this book accessible to all, this recipe still made the cut because it is so good. The worst part is that I can't even suggest a viable alternative.

Two things left to say. Firstly, chipotles are smoked jalapeños. And secondly, if you haven't given up already, there are two different ways you might find them: either dried, in a packet; or in a tin, called Chipotle in Adobo, which means they have been cooked in tomato, onion and salt*. Apparently you can also get them in vinegar in tins, in which case you'd have to de-brine them before making this recipe, or you might be able to get away with just reducing the amount of vinegar in the ingredients. Sweet, sharp and smoky. Very special indeed. Hotter than Hades.

makes about 400ml

5 tablespoons rapeseed or
   plain olive oil
8 shallots, peeled and sliced
8 garlic cloves, peeled and
   sliced
4 dried chipotle chillies (or
   1 x 200g tin of Chipotles
   in Adobo)
8 piquillo peppers, available
   in tins/jars from delis (or
   use 3 red peppers, roasted,
   peeled and chopped)
120ml red wine vinegar
90g brown sugar
a pinch of English mustard
   (optional)
S & P

* available from The Cool
Chile Company
www.coolchile.co.uk

● Heat the oil in a saucepan and then drop in the sliced shallots and garlic. Cook until they have softened, 10-ish minutes.

● If you have dried chipotles, re-hydrate them in water by simmering them for 10 minutes. Take the stalks off, remove the seeds, chop them roughly and throw away the water.

● Add the chipotles (if they are 'in adobo' then add the sauce as well) to the pan of shallots and garlic with the piquillo/roasted peppers.

● Pour over 120ml water and vinegar and stir in the brown sugar. Turn the heat down and simmer for at least an hour on a very low heat (if you have gas then use the smallest of your burners) until it is a very thick, ketchupy consistency. Now's the time to stir in the mustard, if you want even more fire.

● Blend if you choose. I kind of liked it un-blended and a bit chunky. Season with salt.

● Put the hot ketchup into a sterilised, airtight jar and seal immediately.

Shelf Life: 2 months. **Best Kept:** In the fridge.

smoky aubergine DIP

Aubergines are low in calories and high in minerals, with soothing influences on the liver and pancreas. They should never be eaten underripe (because they're a bit toxic like that) or raw (because that would be gross).

I'm a big fan of dips, and this one is unbelievably interesting and massively easy. The Turks like treating their aubergines like this, and our guru in the States, Alice Waters, does something similar where she just whacks them straight in the fire. It's like a better Baba (ganoush).

serves 6 (as a starter)

2 large aubergines

30g butter

2 garlic cloves, peeled and finely chopped

30g plain flour

$\frac{1}{2}$ teaspoon dried chilli flakes

3 tablespoons milk

2 tablespoons extra virgin olive oil, plus extra for drizzling

a squeeze of lemon

2 tablespoons tahini paste

a handful of flatleaf parsley, roughly chopped

1 ripe tomato, cored, de-seeded and flesh diced small

S & P

● Rest the aubergines on the metal frame above a medium gas flame (or under the grill, but you won't get quite the same smokiness) and blacken the skins, turning onto a different side as the skin goes crackly. They're done when the skin is scorched all over to such an extent that the flesh inside is nearly cooked; this will take 10-ish mins, depending on their size. Set aside and allow to cool.

● Melt the butter in a pan, add the garlic and fry gently for a couple of minutes. Stir in the flour and cook this roux for another couple of minutes over a very low heat, sprinkling in the chilli flakes along the way.

● Get all the scorched skin off the aubergines and chop the flesh roughly.

● Stir the milk into the roux until all is incorporated and smooth, then add the aubergine chunks and combine everything together. Keeping the heat down, cook for another 5–7 minutes, stirring occasionally.

● Pull off the heat and cool for a minute before stirring in the extra virgin and tahini. Taste and season with salt, pepper and lemon juice.

● Transfer to your serving dish whilst still a little warm – traditionally it would be spread thinly over the bottom of a little plate. Sprinkle with the chopped parsley and tomato, and finish with a healthy drizzle of olive oil. Serve with some kind of flat bread, or the Onion Seed Twists on page 115.

Shelf Life: About 4 days, keep it airtight as it has a tendency to absorb fridgy flavours. **Best Kept:** Covered with a plate at room temp for up to 12 hours, then fridge it.

strawberry VESUVIUS

To drink the right thing at the right time is just as important as the eating side of things. Here are three tastes of summer, all swirling around together with the express mission of making you feel lovely and drunk. Just a little something to liven up your party – sunshine in a glass.

serves 6

300g strawberries, hulled
70g caster sugar
300ml Pimms N°1
1 bottle chilled Prosecco/
  Champagne/Cava/
  sparkling wine
Triple Sec (optional)

● Put the strawberries, sugar and 300ml water in a saucepan and gently cook down to a compote for about 10–15 minutes.

● Once the strawberries have cooled, pour into a blender, add the Pimms and blitz.

● Pour the thin purée into the bottom of your champagne flutes – about 60ml in each.

● Gently top up with the fizz of whatever kind, going nice and slow to avoid a messy pink eruption, or fast if you want to see how this cocktail got it's name. I recommend Prosecco, but of course Champagne is the winner, but a little redundant with all that other gear in it; Cava is fine too; and then there's always good old sparkling wine to fall back on.

● Serve with a swizzle stick.

Shelf Life: Purée in the fridge 5 days; freezer 1 month. **Best Kept:** Purée in the fridge, or freeze in ice-cube trays...

tabasco gazpacho SHOTS with a TEQUILA float

My thought process on this one went like this: when in Mexico and shooting tequila (those were the days), you automatically get a shot of a blended, spicy tomato drink on the side, not a million miles from a Virgin Mary mix. It's delicious and the flavours really work with tequila. I've mixed that up here and halved on the washing up by letting it all go on in the same little glass.

The word Tabasco can be taken to mean several things: the region in Mexico, on the southern side of the gulf, the name of a chilli pepper (originating from the eponymous region of Mexico and now widely grown in Louisiana), or the famous spicy condiment.

There is hardly a more delicious way to celebrate the ripe tomato than this super-cool classic that really gets the party going. Easy, fun and just a bit dangerous.

makes 12 shots

3 tomatoes, blanched, peeled and de-seeded

1/4 of a cucumber, peeled and de-seeded

10g coriander, chopped

juice of 1 lime

1 red pepper, peeled with a veg peeler

1 garlic clove, peeled and chopped

10–15 drops Tabasco (this depends on how much you can take)

Tequila (or Vodka if you'd rather)

salt

● Blitz all the ingredients, except the booze, to a purée in a blender.

● Chill the concoction thoroughly.

● Adjust the consistency with enough water (around 150ml) to make it shootable, but not like water – we want some substance.

● Share the gazpacho between shot glasses and float a little bit of tequila on top – many years of trying this has made me slowly realize that too much is *not* a good thing.

Shelf Life: A day. **Best Kept:** This needs to be in the fridge.

autumn

If our whole lives were concertinaed into a year, autumn would be the time when we can relax and start enjoying it, having done all the hard work; by now it's either happened or it hasn't and there is precious little we can do either way. I don't know if this is why it has always been my favourite season, but for as long as I can remember I have a deeper emotional response to it than any of the others. Autumn, in my mind, is the time to use more butter and less olive oil, swap soft herbs for hard (rosemary and thyme, not basil and mint), and change from flip-flops to slippers.

Veg-wise this season's big news is, of course, squashes and pumpkins which come under the huge umbrella of the cucurbit family. Other cousins include gherkins, gourds, courgettes and melons. Butternut (still the most popular variety) is packed with beta-carotene, the precursor to vitamin A – vital for vision, for those long, dark winter nights, and essential in keeping your skin supple and elastic for the upcoming harsh weather.

Beta-carotene is a ferocious antioxidant. The knowledge we have of this nutrient is still comparatively small, but even the most traditional doctors are aware of its extraordinary disease-fighting qualities. Studies at the University of Arizona have shown that 30–60mg of beta-carotene taken daily boosts the immune-fighting cells like lymphocytes or T-helper cells in proportion, i.e. the greater the dose, the higher the immunity. But two months after the subjects stopped taking the dose, their immune-fighting cells were back to the pre-experiment levels. The quantities they were given are equal to about 200g carrots or quarter of a pumpkin per day – quite a lot, really, but you don't have to eat that much to feel the effects. The rule of thumb for finding veg with the highest quantities of antioxidants is to follow your eyes: the deeper the colour, the higher the antioxidant levels. In the case of beta-carotene, it is those with the most orange flesh (pumpkin, sweet potatoes, some carrots) or the deepest green leaves (spinach, kale) that can really make a difference.

And, being autumn, let's have a big round of applause for the orchard, now showing the fruits of its labours. The colours may not be as bright and deep as those in the field, but they are an equally appealing, demure shade of off-red mixed with a real green heading into russet brown, deep yellow and the kind of orange that great sunsets are made of. Russet apples are a particular favourite of mine, both in flavour and appearance: they look as though they were draped in lace a long time ago, so long ago that the weave has now become a part of their skin.

There are some other folks who I felt naturally belonged in autumn, though these days they are year-rounders. I could find no happier home for my nut recipes. I am aware that the vast majority of you will not be foraging for cobnuts, or harvesting wet walnuts from the copse down the way, but my natural tendency is always to look at things positively (which can lead to a bad case of not seeing things for how they really are). So let me carry on believing that you will gather your own chestnuts (whilst you carry on buying them pre-cooked in vac-packs). I don't mind if you don't.

The final group of potential misfits is so unassuming in looks – small, usually brown and hard as nails – but really knows how to deliver a body-blow (in a positive way) with their flavour and nutritional value. Seeds are slowly catching on as one of the best nibbles you can have, and a scattering on anything from porridge to salads makes a real improvement. But they can be so much more than a scattering: crushed into marinades, packed on top of roasting pumpkin to form a crust and incorporated into my Power Bar recipe. I've had a lot of fun with these little time-bombs. For that's what they are: plants in waiting with all the vitamins, minerals and protein necessary to start their life journey.

The key colours for this season are all around us: surely the changing of the leaves is one of nature's most dramatic and best-loved shows. The yellows, reds, browns and oranges that each tree bears and sheds are reflected in the markets with acorn, spaghetti and delcarter squash, ironbark and regular pumpkins and a plethora of wild mushrooms. Most cooks are happy to extol the virtues of wild mushrooms, with wild mushroom pasta or risotto being the *de facto* veggie choice on so many menus, but in my opinion the magical versatility of pumpkins is still missed by many. So much more than just an ornament for Halloween, pumpkins have always been used by the Persians in their traditional *khoresh* (stews), whilst the Turks make a stunning pud by candying them with walnuts. And then there are the Americans, who use their national vegetable in everything from breads to soups to pies to bakes, including the terrifying Thanksgiving tradition of baked pumpkin and marshmallow. Even leaving that classic aside, there are still innumerable ways to employ this most helpful of veg, and that's why it features heavily in my autumn collection.

AUTUMN superstars

Acorn squash – contain good sugars and mighty magnesium to guard against heart disease and mental dysfunction – good brain food, and the carotenoids encourage great skin too.

Almonds – are rich in calcium and phosphorus which has a balancing effect on the nervous system. They also contain oleic acid, which lowers cholesterol whilst strengthening the cardiovascular system, reducing the risk of coronary heart disease.

Apples – contain malic acid, which is one of the catalysts for the conversion of sugars and fats into energy so you use them and don't accumulate them. Aside from their antioxidant properties, the all-important pectin binds readily with cholesterol to facilitate elimination.

Butternut squash – together with the rest of the Cucurbit family, has phenomenal amounts of beta-carotene. This is very good for the skin, strengthening and helping to fight free radicals, keeping our outermost defence against the world strong, supple and regenerated.

Carrots – the old wives' tale is true; it's official, they do help your eyesight. It's all the vitamin A and trace elements in them. For maximum effect, they are best eaten raw or lightly cooked. Lets hear it for orac orange!

Chanterelles or girolles – have been hailed for aeons as a panacea for all manner of diseases. They are good for keeping the blood thin, which works against arteriosclerosis.

Chestnuts – are full of potassium, iron and vitamin E, and are believed to help repair artery damage. Not to be confused with horse chestnuts, which are just for conkers.

Chestnut mushrooms – also known as Paris mushrooms, are an effective anti-coagulant, thus keeping the blood flowing to feed our cells and also eliminate waste. Research continues into their effects on cancer patients.

Cobnuts – contain zinc (good for the libido) and they work with the pancreas to help regulate insulin, thus an equalising element for sugar distribution and absorption. Member of the hazelnut family.

Dates – are a powerhouse of complex sugars and protein. Very good for the heart and exceptional for the lungs and all bronchial complaints. These are the sun-powered oracs at their golden-brown best.

Pears – contain magnesium, phosphorus, sulphur and zinc. They aid uric acid elimination, making them very good for the joints. They have a calming effect on the digestion and help prevent bacteria levels from growing out of control in the intestines.

Porcini – are also known as ceps in France and *Boletus edulis* in the international horticultural language of Latin. Their combination with olive oil and pungent herbs such as thyme and rosemary makes for a famous Italian cure-all, particularly good for maintaining supple joints. There's something about mushrooms that's magical, so although Western nutritional data is scarce, ancient and alternative medicines both use them extensively. No wonder the fairies have festivals around them.

Prunes – contain a perfect package of preserved sugars and nutrients. Their orac value is still the same as when they were juicy plums. They also contain sorbitol, a natural aspirin, and yes, with their high fibre, they keep you regular. Prunes d'Agen are almost rude they're so delicious.

Pumpkins – are autumn's mascot. They are low in calories and high in oracs – the autumn veg to pick up on thos vital micronutrients as the reds and purples of summer pass into autumn's shadows.

Sweet potatoes – are packed with all the good sugars and complex carbohydrates. Their gorgeous hue, beta-carotene orange, shows that they are the best of the orac pack from beneath the earth. They have a low glycemic index and are good for coeliacs.

Wet walnuts – are high in omega 3s and ellagic acid, an antioxidant and cancer-fighter. Each walnut contains, weight for weight, about as much protein as an egg.

4 onion and cognac soup

This is essentially a beefed-up version of that old classic, French Onion Soup. The alliums are one of the most powerful families on the globe in terms of taste, nutrition and World Domination. No single species is used as such a cornerstone of cookery across so many different countries. This is my homage to them, as they are too often consigned to being a vital, but nevertheless back-seat flavour. White and red onions we know well and they're a staple of this season's cookery; we need them for the rich braises and stews that keep us warm. Spring onions, which we have all year round from Wales, make for a touch of green and freshness to contrast with the slow-cooked ones. And shallots add a sweetness that none of the others carry in their bag.

serves 6

1.7 kg assorted onions (red, white and shallots)

70 g caster sugar

30 g butter

2 garlic cloves, peeled and finely chopped

100 ml cooking brandy

1 litre beef stock (fresh, if possible)

10 g fresh thyme, tied together in a bunch

3 bay leaves

30 g Gruyère cheese, grated

6 thin slices of baguette

a splash of sherry vinegar

1 tablespoon chopped curly parsley

3 spring onions

S & P

● Peel and thinly slice all the onions, keeping the spring onions separate.

● Get a large-bottomed saucepan on a high heat. Have your sugar, butter and sliced onions all ready. Put the sugar into the pan and stir with a wooden spoon – it should caramelise quite quickly. Tip in all the sliced onions, except the spring, with the butter.

● Stir well for a few minutes until all are well coated. Sweat gently for 15 minutes until you see the onions begin to caramelise and the bottom of the pan is starting to brown.

● At this point, add the garlic and stir vigorously for a minute before pouring in the brandy, followed a couple of minutes later by the stock. Toss the thyme branches into the pan with the bay.

● Bring to the boil and then simmer very slowly for 30 minutes, after which time you should skim off all the scum that has risen to the surface. This is particularly important with a soup like this, as you want the stock to be clear. Continue to simmer very slowly for a further 45–60 minutes, or until the soup is a bit reduced and the onions are very, very soft.

● Just before time, put the Gruyère onto the slices of baguette and set them under the grill until the cheese is melted and the bread is toasted round the edges.

● Have a last play with the soup, seasoning it with S & P, and adding a splash of sherry vinegar to add depth of flavour. I also like to finish it with a drop or two of brandy right at the end. Divide between serving bowls and float a cheesy croûton in each one. Sprinkle on a bit of parsley and the sliced spring onions and off you go.

Shelf Life: 5 days (and gets better throughout that time). **Best Kept:** In the fridge or a cool larder.

butternut, bacon and sage soup

In the Americas, where it was (globally speaking) born, butternut squash is much appreciated for its flavour and beneficial qualities: vitamin E and trace elements of magnesium, as well as containing the carotene pigments you can see in the bright colour of the flesh. This soup is from the Italian peasant school, along the lines of a *ribollita* and it is a very gentle way to ease yourself out of summer soups and into something heartier, without feeling like all the sun has gone for the year.

serves 6

1 tablespoon olive oil

100g smoked bacon, cut into small dice

1 small red onion, cut into small dice

1 big carrot, peeled and cut into 1cm dice

1 celery stick, cut into small dice

1 red chilli, de-seeded and finely diced (or ½ teaspoon Crema di Pepperoncini, page 169)

1 small butternut squash, peeled, de-seeded and cut into 1cm cubes

1 tablespoon chopped sage

2 garlic cloves, peeled and finely chopped

1.2 litres chicken stock

2 bay leaves

30g dried porcini mushrooms, chopped (optional)

60g Parmesan cheese, grated (keep the rind for adding to the soup)

2 tablespoons chopped parsley

S & P

● In a heavy-based saucepan, gently heat the olive oil.

● Fry the bacon until it browns a bit, then throw in the onion, carrot and celery and reduce the heat.

● Put a lid on for about 5 minutes, stirring occasionally so that the veg softens but does not colour.

● Take off the lid, turn the heat up and then add the chilli, squash, sage and garlic. Stir thoroughly for a minute, making sure everything gets nicely coated with oil, then before it all starts to brown, pour in the chicken stock.

● Add the bay and then the porcini (if using) and some seasoning. If your piece of Parmesan has a good bit of rind on it, cut it off in one piece and submerge it in the soup for added flavour. Just remember not to serve it, as it's a bit much to chew on.

● Put the lid back on again, bring to the boil and skim, then turn down the heat and simmer gently for about 30 minutes, or until all the veg is tender.

● Turn off the heat and stir in the chopped parsley. Allow the soup to stand for 10 minutes before serving. Use this time to adjust the seasoning.

● Pour into bowls, sprinkle on the Parmesan and give it a good crack of black pepper.

Shelf Life: 3–4 days **Best Kept:** In the fridge.

duck, shiitake and watercress broth

This is such a great broth, with all the psychological goodness of a classic chicken soup, enhanced by the richness of the duck, and then the joy of the meaty mushrooms and peppery leaves.

And, my god, what nutritional value. Shiitake mushrooms are known as 'The Food of Emperors' because back in the days of Imperial China they were eaten only by the Emperor and his family. They are a superfood for the immune system, and have long been used in Eastern medicine to fight infectious diseases, particularly viral ones. They contain essential amino acids and lower cholesterol. Meanwhile, on the other side of the broth, watercress is the highest source of vitamins and minerals across any of the food groups. Respect.

serves 6

2 big duck legs
200g watercress (stalks and leaves), washed and roughly chopped
130g shiitake mushrooms, de-stalked and then thinly sliced
1 tablespoon dark soy sauce
30g beansprouts
juice of 1 lime
salt

● Preheat the oven to 160°C/320°F/gas 3.

● Put the duck legs into a tray big enough to hold the 2 legs (and deep enough to hold the 2 litres of water that you add later). Sprinkle them with a bit of salt and pop into the oven for 25 minutes until the fat begins to melt off.

● Pour off the fat and set aside for roasties if you like. Fill the roasting tray with the water and put the duck back in the oven for 1 hour.

● When the pinger goes off, lift the duck out of the liquid (which is now technically a stock) and leave until cool enough to handle.

● Throw away the skin and shred the duck meat, making sure you pick out all of the bones – be aware of the thin spikey one that runs alongside the big fat one. Strain the stock from the roasting tray into a saucepan, bring to the boil, skim it and drop in the pieces of duck.

● When the stock has come back to the boil, skim it and then add the watercress, mushrooms and soy sauce. Bring to the boil again, stirring all the time, and turn off immediately. (Once you have added the watercress, you should serve quickly, so if you want to wait, hold back the leaves until you are ready.)

● Divide the beansprouts between your serving bowls, pour over the broth and serve with a squeeze of lime.

Shelf Life: Not long once the leaves are in it, but for about 3 days without.
Best Kept: In the fridge.

two carrot salads
one JAPANESE

Last year I had one of the best holidays of my life in Japan. When we landed in Tokyo at four in the morning, all groggy with jet-lag and too many cocktails at 30,000 feet, this was the first thing we ate and instantly we came back to life. It was then that I knew I was in for three weeks of serious culinary treats, and this delightful little salad turned out to be about the most normal thing I was to taste until we got back to London.

The secret is in the dressing, one of those cases of a few simple flavours that come together and do something very special. You'll see this dressing in a couple of other places in the book, but I'm not apologising, just letting you know it's a good one to have in your repertoire as it can bring the most sluggish of salads up to Bullet train speeds.

serves 6

FOR THE SALAD
500g carrots, peeled and
   coarsely grated
30g root ginger, peeled
   and finely grated
1 red chilli, chopped
15g mint, chopped
50g sugar snaps, French
   beans or mangetout,
   thinly sliced diagonally
90g peanuts or cashews,
   raw if possible, roughly
   chopped

FOR THE DRESSING
1 tablespoon fish sauce
juice of 1 lime
1 tablespoon sesame oil
1 teaspoon sugar
1 tablespoon light soy
   sauce

● Preheat the oven to 200°C/400°F/gas 6.

● Mix the carrots with the ginger, red chilli, mint and the green veg of your choice.

● Put the nuts on a small baking tray and cook until golden brown in the oven – about 7–10 minutes.

● Whisk together the ingredients for the dressing.

● Take the nuts out of the oven and leave until cool enough to handle, then very roughly chop, leaving some nearly whole, and add to the salad.

● Pour over the dressing, toss well and let it sit for 5 minutes. Eat with chopsticks.

Shelf Life: It depends how you feel about soggy carrots... **Best Kept:** ...because carrots, soy and lime make a soggy mess after an hour or so. If you want to make it in advance, you could toast the nuts and make the dressing before, and then grate the carrot 1 hour before you're ready to eat. Any which way, before or after the preparation, keep the veg in the fridge – the dressing and nuts are fine out.

and one MOROCCAN

Years of school dinners made me shy away from grated carrot salads, but a short trip to Marrakech beat some sense into me. Although eating raw veggies is not that appealing in the cooler months, this salad and the one before give your body what it needs, whilst also keeping your taste buds on their toes.

Argan nuts are indiginous to Morocco and, when the nut is cracked, roasted and pressed, the oil that runs free from it is a whole new kind of amazing in the nut oil spectrum. I had a fantastic time smashing them with stones at a progressive women's co-operative near Essaouira, where they not only extract the oil, but take advantage of its beneficial skin properties to make soaps, shampoos and skin creams*. Their fats are polyunsaturated and therefore good for the heart, and joyfully the oil is now stocked in most supermarkets. Try it on crumpets with a thin stroke of honey for a wonderful breakfast.

I try to love mung beans as much as the other sprouting pulses, but that afternoon thirty years ago when I got one stuck up my nose in Science class still haunts me. It took the headmaster and two ambulance men what seemed like hours of puffing, pushing and prodding to get it out. The joke is mung beans are excellent for maintaining optimum energy levels during stressful situations – if only I'd been munching on some during the whole ordeal, it might not have been such a psychologically scarring experience.

serves 6

2 heaped tablespoons
flaked almonds
1/2 teaspoon cumin seeds
4 tablespoons pumpkin seeds
500 g carrots, peeled and
coarsely grated
2 tablespoons sultanas
100 g sprouting beans
10 g coriander, chopped
1 teaspoon sugar (optional,
but that's what they do
in Morocco)
juice of 1/2 orange
4 tablespoons argan oil (or
extra virgin olive)
S & P

● Dry fry the almonds and seeds in a frying pan. When they are toasted, tip onto a plate to cool.

● Mix together the carrots, seeds, nuts, sultanas, sprouting beans, coriander and sugar in a bowl. Stir in the orange juice and oil and season well.

● Let it rest for 30 minutes in an ideal world, not that we live in one.

Shelf Life: 2 days max. **Best Kept:** In the fridge.

* Coopérative Amal, Village de l'Arganier, Tamanar, Province d'Essaouira, Maroc. www.targanine.com

camilla's BIG garden salad with oyster mushrooms

Oyster mushrooms are a particularly good kind of 'shroom. They contain two of the Vitamin B group: B2, which is necessary for the metabolism of fats, sugars and proteins in the body, and B12 (riboflavin), which is good for your nerves and red blood cells. This variety of mushroom is also full of the trace element selenium, which is a very geeky name but nonetheless is to be revered as one of the most important antioxidants.

When my wonderful but truly eccentric godmother Camilla made this for us, I was very impressed with her use of hemp seeds, but then she is a child of the seventies.

I would be really impressed if you made your own rolls – well worth the effort.

serves 6

3 red peppers

60g seeds (hemp, sunflower, linseed, pumpkin, sesame, etc.)

600g mixed, crispy leaves (Trevisse, Curly Chicory, Little Gem, Frisée, watercress, etc.)

1 red chilli, finely chopped

80ml extra virgin olive oil

1 garlic clove, peeled and finely chopped

400g oyster mushrooms, cleaned and torn into large-ish pieces

2½ tablespoons red wine vinegar

3 tablespoons chopped parsley

juice of ½ lemon

S & P

● Preheat the grill.

● Cut the peppers in half and de-seed them. Lay them on a baking tray and grill on all sides until the skin is blackened.

● Put them in a bowl, tightly covered with clingfilm, and leave to cool. Then peel off the skins and rip the peppers into finger-sized lengths.

● Dry-fry your seeds in a large frying pan for a few minutes until they are toasted. When they are done, tip them out onto a plate to cool and wipe out the pan.

● Wash the leaves and drain well.

● In your large seed-toasting frying pan, sauté the chilli over a medium-low heat in a splash of olive oil for a minute, then throw in the garlic and cook for a further minute until all the little pieces begin to go golden. This imparts the power of the chilli and garlic into the oil. Increase the heat just a bit, add the mushrooms and sauté until golden brown and soft.

● Throw in the pepper pieces and add the vinegar – the acidity will fly straight up your nostrils – and let it reduce away. Toss in the parsley and finish with the lemon, the rest of the olive oil and some seasoning.

● Scatter over the leaves and finish with the seeds. Soft-hot and crisp-cold.

Shelf Life: Nope. **Best Kept:** Not at all.

vacherin with seasonal dippers

For those of you who have never had Vacherin, I feel slightly envious. It goes in the same bag as your first taste of caviar, of truffles, and of the one you love. It's a seasonal cheese, available from September to March, and that's because it is made from the milk the cows produce on their way down from their summer pastures high in the Alps. It comes in a little wooden box that you couldn't get it out of if you tried, and why should you when it is such a natural cooking vessel? Vacherin is delicious raw, but heat it gently in the oven and it becomes a gift of pure, molten love from the Alpine cows.

serves 6 as a fondue (like sharing starter), thus a perfect party dish

1kg new potatoes
2 tablespoons extra virgin
   olive oil
1 head celery
1 Vacherin, the smaller size
   (there are only 2), which
   is about 400g
4 pears or apples (750g),
   washed
200g black grapes
100g walnuts, finely chopped
S & P

● Preheat the oven to 180°C/350°F/gas mark 4.

● Wash your potatoes, but do not peel. Cut them in half lengthways. Toss the pots with the olive oil and some seasoning in a roasting tray and pop them into the oven. After about 15 minutes, give them a turn, shake and a wiggle.

● Celery is very low in calories (which is lucky because the Vacherin certainly isn't) and high in vitamins. Peeling it is your call: there's something quite lovely about peeled celery, but then you do lose all that roughage. There's no right answer to this one – take a bite, see how stringy it is and make your decision. Either peeled or not, cut it into finger-length batons, give it a quick wash, and make into a pile on your serving dish.

● Shake, rattle and roll the spuds again. You want a golden-brown, cooked potato, which should be about another 20 minutes.

● The Vacherin: all you need to do is put it on a baking tray, in its wooden box with the lid off, and then into the oven it goes for 15 minutes.

● Quarter the pears or apples and slice out the core and stem. Then chop them up into chunky, bite-sized pieces. They can now go onto the serving dish with the celery.

● Wash the grapes, take them off the stem and put them with the celery and apple.

● The chopped walnuts go into their own separate little dish.

● Take the Vacherin out. It should be hot, soft and gooey throughout, and if it's not, pop it back in for another 5-ish minutes. Put the Vacherin on the serving tray with its friends and bring to the table.

● To eat, tear through the top skin and dip in the pots, pears, grapes or celery and finish with a quick dab into the chopped walnuts. I particularly like a potato in molten Vacherin, walnut dip, and then a fresh pear chaser. If the cheese starts to solidify a bit and therefore is not adhering to the dippers, just whack it back in the oven – it'll be worth waiting a few minutes more to get that sublime, sexy texture back.

Shelf Life: N/A **Best Kept:** Don't keep it.

BISTRO mushroom salad

This salad is all about the mushrooms, and the eggs. My recommended mushrooms of choice for this dish would be girolles, one of the earliest of the wild mushrooms to appear each year. They are also known as chanterelles, or egg mushrooms, which has good implications within this dish.

serves 6 as a starter

6 slices streaky bacon
  (optional)
3 thick slices brown bread
3 GOOD (organic free-
  range) chicken or
  duck eggs
a splash of vinegar –
  preferably white wine
1 head frisée
1 bunch watercress
250g girolle mushrooms
1 tablespoon butter
2 garlic cloves, peeled and
  finely chopped
S & P

FOR THE DRESSING:
1 tablespoon capers
1 tablespoon chopped
  tarragon
1 teaspoon smooth Dijon
  mustard
1¹/₂ tablespoons red wine
  vinegar
4 tablespoons extra virgin
  olive oil
S & P

● Preheat the grill. Lay the bacon on a rack sitting on a baking tray and grill for 7 minutes until crisp. Don't wash up the bacon fat tray.

● Preheat the oven to 180°C/350°F/gas mark 4.

● Tear the bread into 2–3cm chunks. When the bacon is ready, take it out and set aside. Put the bread chunks into the bacon tray and roll them around in the fat. If you're not using bacon, drizzle them with light olive oil and a touch of salt. Bake the chunks in the oven for 20 minutes, moving them around halfway through the cooking time to ensure they are an even golden brown.

● Meanwhile, make the dressing. Finely chop the capers and put them in a bowl with the tarragon and mustard. Add the vinegar and whisk in the extra virgin. Season.

● Put a pan on the stove with enough water to boil the eggs. Add a splash of vinegar (stops the albumen exploding) and, once boiling, gently lower the eggs in. Cook for 5 minutes (chicken eggs) or 7 minutes (ducks'). Tip into the sink, making sure the shells crack (much easier for peeling) and run under cold water until cool. Peel.

● Throw away any unappealing leaves from the outside of the frisée, then tear apart right down to the heart. Trim the very ends off the watercress, but keep as much of the stalks as possible – these carry most of the flavour and nutritional value, which is high. Give both lots of leaves a good wash and then drain or spin-dry. Give the mushrooms a quick rinse, but only if they need it – they are like sponges and absorb water very readily. Trim off any soily ends and halve any huge ones.

● Melt the butter in a large-ish frying pan with a lid and add the garlic. Swirl it around in the bubbling butter for a minute until both the garlic and the butter just begin to turn golden brown, then add the mushrooms. Season, toss and put the lid on for a couple of minutes. Toss again and then fry on a high heat (without the lid) for another 3 minutes, or until the mushers are soft.

● Coat the leaves lightly with the dressing and arrange on plates with the croûtons scattered around. Roughly chop the bacon and throw in with the mushrooms, then spoon over the leaves. Add the eggs, cut in half, on top, with a crack of pepper and a touch of sea salt on the yolk.

Shelf Life: If you have any leftover mushrooms a day or two – forget the rest.
Best Kept: In the fridge, but not really designed for keeping.

fusilli with smoked haddock and AUTUMN nut pesto

As the weather gets worse and the seas get choppier, so the fish swim deeper for a quieter life. Therefore, there is less fish caught, and so in order to get our recommended and desired intake throughout the winter it makes sense to use preserved fish from the happier fishing months. We have already discussed the joys and benefits of smoked salmon and mackerel (see page 29), but haddock is also a fish that suits smoking, just like Steve McQueen. It's actually better for it. I've also done this pasta in summer with a classic basil pesto (see page 124) for a lighter feel, which works beautifully.

serves 6

600g good (un-dyed) smoked haddock, pin-boned

600–900ml milk, depending on the size of your baking tray

200g white onions, sliced

2 bay leaves

10 peppercorns, whole

500g dried fusilli

6 tablespoons Autumn Nut Pesto (see page 228)

1 lemon, cut into 6 wedges

2 tablespoons extra virgin olive oil

S & P

● Preheat the oven to 180°C/350°F/gas 4.

● Lay the haddock skin-side down in a small roasting tray and pour over the milk to come two thirds of the way up the fish. Submerge the onion, bay and peppercorns in and around the fish. Cook for 10–15 minutes in the oven, then carefully put the haddock on a plate (the test of whether it's cooked yet is that it should just begin to break up as you lift it out). Leave until cool enough to handle.

● Save a splash of the haddocky milk for step 6. (The rest can be turned into a great, creamy soup: just bring to the simmer, add a few peeled and cubed potatoes, half a leek, finely sliced, and a herb or two and/or a touch of saffron; when the pots are cooked, blend and you could finish it with a touch of cream and quite a lot of S & P.)

● Meanwhile, bring a large pan of water to the boil for the pasta. When it is boiling, add a healthy sprinkle of salt and the pasta. Stir, and cook as per the packet.

● Flake the haddock, discarding any small bones, as well as the skin.

● When the pasta is cooked, drain thoroughly for a few minutes (any excess water will ruin the sauce). Now tip half the pasta back into the pan, add half the pesto, half the haddock and a good splash (about 100ml) of the poaching milk. Combine well. Repeat with the rest of the pasta/pesto/fish, adding just enough of the milk and the extra virgin to bring it all together to a creamy consistency.

● Now taste and season with salt (if needed) and a good crack of pepper. Serve immediately with wedges of lemon to excite the pesto.

Shelf Life: 1 day, but like all pastas, best eaten fresh. **Best Kept:** Fridge or larder, depending on the weather.

sweet potato WEDGES
with paprika SALT

Both for colour and goodness, go for orange sweet potatoes over white ones. They contain carotene in their bright flesh as well as vitamin A, which is absent in the white variety. These autumnal gifts from nature are her way of building up our immune system and helping the body deal with viral infections through the tough months to come.

Don't expect them to be super-crisp – you have to deep-fry them for that – think more soft with crunchy bits, which ultimately is more textually interesting. Forget chips: these are the way forward.

serves 6

2kg sweet potatoes, washed and gently scrubbed if necessary (but not peeled)
3 tablespoons olive oil
1 teaspoon smoked paprika
3 teaspoons sea salt

● Preheat the oven to 220ºC/425ºF/gas 7.

● Cut the sweet potatoes in half widthways and then cut in half again and then into wedges. The size of the spuds varies enormously, but you're aiming for finger-length wedges about 3cm high on the skin side. Put them into a big mixing bowl.

● Pour over the olive oil, then mix the smoked paprika and sea salt and coat the wedges entirely.

● Lay the wedges with ample space on two 20cm x 35cm baking trays and put them into the oven for an initial 20 minutes. After this time, turn the potatoes wedges over and cook for a further 10 minutes. Eat hot, perhaps with sour cream.

Shelf Life: 3 days. **Best Kept:** Covered at room temperature. They are okay cold but much better reheated.

soft CHEESE baked with QUINCE in vine leaves

Often, over the years spent in the kitchen, I've noticed that it's the recipes I've struggled with that have brought me the most pleasure in the end. These little parcels caused me quite a lot of stress, but it was all in my head because actually they are so simple. Natural bundles of warm love.

serves 6

some cocktail sticks

100ml calvados

100g golden granulated
  sugar, plus extra for
  sprinkling

2 quinces, washed

12 fresh vine leaves (or
  12 preserved ones in jars,
  or you can use fresh, big
  leaves such as sycamore
  from the garden)

a little melted butter, for
  brushing

3 x 70–90g individual soft
  cheeses, such as Bath
  Soft Cheese, Cornish
  Gevrik or Capricorn

● Heat the calvados in a pan and dissolve the sugar in it.

● Grate the quince on the large holes, skin on, and discard the core. It will discolour immediately, but don't let that trouble you.

● Tip the grated quince into the pan and coat it in the liquid. Put a lid on and keep on a very low heat for 40 minutes, stirring occasionally. It's done when the quince has broken down and taken on the texture of a thick apple sauce.

● Preheat the oven to 160°C/320°F/gas 3.

● If you have fresh vine leaves, or are using something from the garden, just blanch them in boiling, salted water for a couple of minutes to make them supple. The ones in jars or vac-pacs tend to be in brine, so just soak them in cold water for an hour, changing the water halfway through.

● Lay two leaves on top of each other, but with about half of the bottom leaf showing. Brush with a little melted butter and sprinkle lightly with sugar. Repeat with the other 10 leaves.

● Cut the individual cheeses in half across the middle so you have 6 circles of cheese and sit in the middle of each leaf. Share the quince compote between them, putting a blob on top of the cheese.

● Bring the edges of the leaf up and around the cheese and secure with a couple of cocktail sticks – the aim here is to try not to leave any gaps at the sides, or your cheese could escape.

● Put the leafy bundles on a lightly oiled tray. Bake for 10–15 minutes and serve just like that, all wrapped up in the leaves. Remember to take the cocktail sticks out first (and tell your guests not to eat the leaves).

Shelf Life: It'll never be the same again, but will last for about 3 days.
Best Kept: In the fridge.

Nice with a piece of toasted walnut bread

chicken and MUSHROOM pie

I'm still torn between a mash top and a pastry top on this, so I'll leave it to you. If you do go down the mash route, then go light on the dairy in it as the pie is pretty rich. This can be a great two parter: make the base and the pastry well ahead of time and refrigerate; just allow an extra 20 minutes in the oven if cooking the pie from cold. Or make the whole thing and freeze it for a time when you really need some pie in your life, and we all have those moments.

serves 6

FOR THE PASTRY

300g plain flour

150g butter

3 egg yolks

milk, to bind

1 egg yolk and 1 tablespoon
double cream, for the
egg wash

S & P

OR FOR THE MASH

1.5 kg potatoes, peeled

40g butter

S & P

FOR THE FILLING

1.5 kg free-range chicken

2 carrots

2 celery sticks

1 onion

100g butter

4 garlic cloves, peeled and
finely chopped

350g oyster mushrooms,
cut into bite-sized pieces

3 heaped tablespoons
plain flour

1 tablespoon Dijon mustard

20g tarragon, finely chopped

S & P

● In a food processor, spin the flour and add the butter down the chute in 6 knobs. Then add the egg yolks one by one. Pour in enough milk to bring the pastry together and season. Wrap in clingfilm and refrigerate until needed.

● Put the chicken in a suitably sized pot and cover with water. Add the carrot, celery sticks and onion, all peeled but whole. Bring to a relaxed boil, skim (v. important) and then immediately turn down to a low simmer/steam. Cook for about an hour – or until tender (i.e. so when you pick up a leg, it falls off the carcass).

● Strain 1.5 litres of the chicken stock into a saucepan and set over a low heat – this is for the pie filling. The remaining stock can be left to cool, to keep in your fridge or freezer. Put the chicken and veg on a tray to cool. Get your mash on now, if you are heading that way.

● In a heavy-based saucepan (30cm) with medium-high sides, melt the butter and turn up the heat to make it frothy. Add the garlic and then the mushrooms with some seasoning and fry together for a good few minutes. Reduce the heat and stir in the flour, which will stick to the mushrooms. Cook for a few minutes, then add the hot stock one ladleful at a time. After each ladle of stock, stir with a wooden spoon until the sauce is smooth before adding some more. When all the stock is incorporated and you have a smooth chickeny sauce, stir in the mustard and some seasoning.

● Pick off all the meat from the bird, discarding the skin and bones, and add to the sauce. Chop the cooked vegetables into chunky pieces and put these in with the chopped tarragon. Season again and pour into your pie dish (25cm x 35cm).

● Preheat the oven to 180°C / 350°F / gas 4.

● Roll out the pastry to make a lid and secure to the edge of the pie dish with some egg wash and a good pinch with your fingertips. Make some leaves or pretty shapes with the pastry offcuts and stick down with egg wash. Brush the top generously with the last of the egg wash and remember to make a hole to let the steam escape. Bake in the oven for 30–40 minutes. Eat with a few crispy leaves.

Shelf Life: Cooked, 3 days; uncooked, 2 days (or 2 months in the freezer).
Best Kept: Cooked, in an outdoor pantry; uncooked, in the fridge.

OXTAIL and red lentil risotto

I am bonkers about oxtail. The flavour of the rich meat, braised and nurtured for hours; the sexy texture of all that flubbering flesh. And I really like the trick of cooking the lentils as if they were fat little grains of rice.

serves 6

FOR THE OXTAIL

4kg oxtail

750ml red wine

50g fresh thyme sprigs

4 bay leaves

2–3 carrots, cut into bite-sized chunks

12 round shallots, peeled and cut into quarters

1.5 litres good beef stock

4 tablespoons sherry vinegar

S & P

FOR THE RISOTTO

1 litre chicken stock

2 tablespoons olive oil

3 garlic cloves, peeled and roughly chopped

280g celery, cut into small dice

450g red onion, cut into small dice

300g red lentils

350g whole leaf spinach, roughly chopped

1 tablespoon chopped thyme

45g Parmesan cheese, grated

50g butter

S & P

● The day before, marinate the oxtail in the red wine, thyme and bay. Turn twice in the 24 hours to make sure the meat absorbs all the flavours.

● The next day, preheat the oven to 180°C/350°F/gas 4.

● Drain the oxtail, reserving the marinade. Season the meat and put it, cut-side down but not touching, on a roasting tray (or two, if they don't all fit in one). Brown in the oven for about 40 minutes, then turn to ensure even colouring. Pour off any fat and discard or keep in a jar for roasties. Return to the oven for a further 40 minutes.

● Take out of the oven and reduce the heat to 150°C/300°F/gas 2. Pour off most of the remaining fat. Add the carrots, shallots and marinade. Sizzle, sizzle. Then add the stock with 1.5 litres water and give it a good stir. Cover with foil and put back into the oven for a further 3–4 hours. Turn it after the second hour and add the sherry vinegar. The meat is ready when it is falling off the bone but still needs a tug to come away completely. Take it out of the oven, taste and season. Give it a 20-minute rest with the foil on – it'll need time to relax after all that hard work. Now for the risotto….

● Put the chicken stock on until steaming, but not simmering.

● In a large, heavy-bottomed saucepan, heat the olive oil and fry the garlic, celery and onion until they are just soft – about 10 minutes. Add the lentils and stir until all is coated in the oil and they are beginning to fry gently. Begin to feed the risotto: give it a ladleful of hot stock and listen for the satisfying sizzle. Stir briefly and let the hot liquid be absorbed before adding any more – the poor lentils have been craving some liquid, and only when it's all gone do you give them another ladleful. If you fancy your oxtail juices a little bit thicker, drain off half of their cooking liquor now and reduce it by two thirds. I like the wetness though.

● Feed the risotto one ladleful at a time and repeat. There should be about 5 batches, depending on the size of your ladle, and the cooking time should be around 20–25 minutes from the first feed. You want the lentils to lose their roundness and begin to break up. Red lentils have a magic trick whereby they do nothing, do nothing and then turn to mush. With attentive feeding, stirring and starving, you will know the right moment. With the last feed, add the chopped spinach and the thyme. Stir in the Parmesan and butter and check the seasoning – this one will take quite a lot of salt and pepper. Serve in shallow bowls: a spoonful of creamy lentils with your well-rested oxtail, veg and juices.

Shelf Life: Oxtail: In the larder for 2 days, fridge for 4 days or freezer for 2 months. Red lentil risotto, 2 days in the fridge. **Best Kept:** Oxtail, in the cold larder or for longer in the fridge or freezer. Red lentil risotto, best eaten then – but will keep in the fridge.

bonfire BEEF (in a teatowel)

I was told this recipe by a very overexcited Spanish man, in Spanish, which is a language I don't really speak. The core facts of it were sufficiently crazy to get me really excited, and I have to say the results have never let me down. What happens is that the rock salt forms a solid shell around the beef, which has a twofold, magical effect. Firstly, the flavours of the herbs and garlic go soaring into the beef, and I mean soaring, because there's nowhere else for them to go. It's a lock-in, and that applies to the moisture inside the meat too, which is the second part of the magic. Normally when you cook anything, the water inside it heats up and evaporates off, which leads to big-time dryness, but in this case that is never going to happen.

This recipe wins on so many fronts: what it does to the meat is sublime and it's easy, dramatic and fun. The only drawback is that you must do it with prime fillet, so it's one for special occasions and a bit of an audience. Being a fire and not an oven, the heat is slightly out of your control, but as long as it's throwing out quite a lot of heat, my cooking times are about right. If your fire has died down, stoke it up and add an extra 10 minutes cooking per side.

serves 6 – 8

an old tea towel (it will
never be the same again)
1 metre good thick string

around 500g table salt
around 1kg rock salt
80g rosemary, on the
   branch
80g thyme, on the branch
4 garlic bulbs
1.5kg beef fillet, the fat
   end please
freshly ground black pepper

● Light your fire; both coal and wood work for me. Coal tends to be a bit more heat-consistent, but I slightly prefer the connotations of wood – your call.

● Boil a large saucepan of water with so much table salt in it that no more will dissolve. Submerge the tea towel and a metre of string in the water and boil for 10 minutes or so. Put a plate on it to keep the towel down. Drain.

● When it's cool enough to handle, lay out the tea towel – folded in half – and pour on the rock salt to make a layer 2cm thick. Rip the herbs up, roughly chop the garlic (no need to peel) and lay them over the salt. Be generous, as these are the key to the beef's flavour.

● Heavily pepper your fillet. Put the beef just above the centre of the towel and, as adeptly as possible, wrap the meat up. If you move confidently, without hesitation, you'll get a better result. It's massively important that the fillet is totally surrounded by the salt. Secure your bundle tightly with string (it may help to do this with a friend). Sit your parcel in the really hot embers of the fire and cook for around 10 – 15 minutes on each side – there are too many variables to give an exact time, but obviously the hotter the embers, the quicker it cooks.

● Give it a good rest (10 minutes) still all wrapped up, then open up your pride and joy. Brush off the excess salt and eat however you want, with a salad or simple veg, as sarnies, or whatever. The flavour of the meat has to be tasted to be believed.

Shelf Life: 3 days. **Best Kept:** At room temperature for as long as you dare.

veal CHOP with porcini, SAGE and balsamic potatoes

Italian porcini or French ceps are way superior in the world of fungi. So slippery, sexy and flavourful, they have about as much in common with button mushrooms as courgettes do with pumpkins. They cope with the dehydration-rehydration process well, maintaining nearly all their flavour and only losing a bit of their slipperiness. Like a lot of autumn produce, their bank of minerals supports a strong immune system – very handy as the weather gets nastier.

serves 6

1kg new potatoes, washed and cut in half lengthways
4 tablespoons olive oil
4 red onions
1 bulb of garlic
90g butter
20g fresh sage, roughly chopped
150ml cheap balsamic vinegar
6 x 225–250g veal chops (or boneless cutlets)
4 fresh porcini/ceps, thickly sliced (or 25g dried)
200ml Madeira
juice of 1/2 lemon
S & P

● Preheat the oven to 190°C/375°F/ gas 5.

● Put half the olive oil into a wide ovenproof frying pan and set over a medium heat. Lay the potatoes cut-side down in the oil, season and sauté for about 10 minutes.

● Thickly slice the red onions and cut the garlic bulb in half. Add to the potatoes. Stir in 60g of the butter and let everything brown together for 5 minutes. Throw in the sage, pour in the balsamic and give it a good stir. Put in the oven for 25 minutes, mixing halfway through to move those around the edge to the middle and vice versa.

● If you are using dried porcini, put them in a bowl and cover them with boiling water. Leave to stand for 10 minutes.

● Put another giant frying pan on the heat and add the remaining olive oil. Season your chops. When the oil is smoking hot, lay 3 of the chops in the pan and let them brown on one side before turning them over to finish on the other side – about 5 minutes per side. When they are done, take them out of the pan and put them on a plate covered with foil to keep the heat and moisture in. Put the pan back on the heat, repeat for the other 3 chops and then stick it back on the hob again.

● Now for the 'shrooms. If you have fresh porcini, lightly fry them first in the veal fat and then pour in the Madeira and allow it to reduce by half. If you have dried mushrooms, add the Madeira first and reduce a little before adding the rehydrated mushrooms and half the juice they were steeped in. Let everything simmer together for another 3–5 minutes.

● Take the potatoes out of the oven and give them a good shake about.

● Keep reducing your sauce gently until a delicious consistency has been reached, then turn off the heat and finish by vigorously stirring in the last of the butter, a squeeze of lemon juice and some seasoning. Put the potatoes on your serving plates, sit the veal chops on top and generously spoon over the mushroom sauce.

Shelf Life: 2–3 days. **Best Kept:** In the fridge.

baby PUMPKINS love lamb

This requires time but minimum input for an impressive and fulfilling endgame. It works well with acorn squash too, but whichever member of the cucurbit family you use, the bit that makes this recipe special is giving the pumpkin/ squash all the flavours of the braised lamb to work with as it bakes.

Such tender sweetness is too rare in this fast-moving world of ours.

serves 6

50g pine nuts

3 tablespoons olive oil

1kg diced lamb

2 white onions, cut into large dice

3 garlic cloves, peeled and roughly chopped

2 bay leaves

1 tablespoon ground cumin

1/2 tablespoon dried chilli flakes

1 tablespoon dried mint

150g dried apricots, roughly chopped

250ml tomato juice

1 litre chicken stock

6 x 400–700g individual-sized pumpkins or acorn squash

40g pumpkin seeds

3 tablespoons pumpkin seed oil

S & P

● In a large, heavy-based pan, fry the pine nuts in the olive oil for a few minutes until golden, then take them out with a slotted spoon. Tip in the lamb with some S & P and continue frying for 15 minutes, letting it pick up some colour along the way. Stir in the onions, garlic, toasted pine nuts, bay, spices, mint and apricots and cook for a further 10–15 minutes, until the onions have softened.

● Pour in the tomato juice and stock, bring to the boil, skim and turn down to a very relaxed simmer for 1–1¹/₂ hours, leaving uncovered and stirring occasionally. It's ready when the chunks of lamb are very soft when you squeeze them; it should still be pretty wet, and if it's not, stir in a glass of water.

● Preheat the oven to 180°C/350°F/gas 4.

● Cut the tops off the pumpkins/squash (to make lids). Scoop out and throw away the seeds and stringy bits. You may also need to trim their bottoms a bit so that they sit flat.

● Taste the lamb and adjust the seasoning, then pack into the pumpkins. Replace the lids, put in a lightly-greased ovenproof dish and bake in the oven for 45–60 minutes. The exact time depends on the size and type of pumpkin/squash used. They are ready when you squeeze the outside and the flesh feels soft inside. From now until serving, nothing is going to go wrong so give yourself plenty of time to cook them properly. The pumpkins can be kept in the oven at 150°C/300°F/gas 2 to no ill effect.

● Pull them out of the oven and take the tops off. Share the pumpkin seeds between them and drizzle a little of the pumpkin seed oil over the tops of the stew, with a sprinkling of sea salt. Bake for a further 15 minutes, topless, but put the lids back on before serving.

● Totally delicious, but pretty heavy going, so serve or follow with a green salad.

Shelf Life: 2–3 days. **Best Kept:** In the larder or fridge.

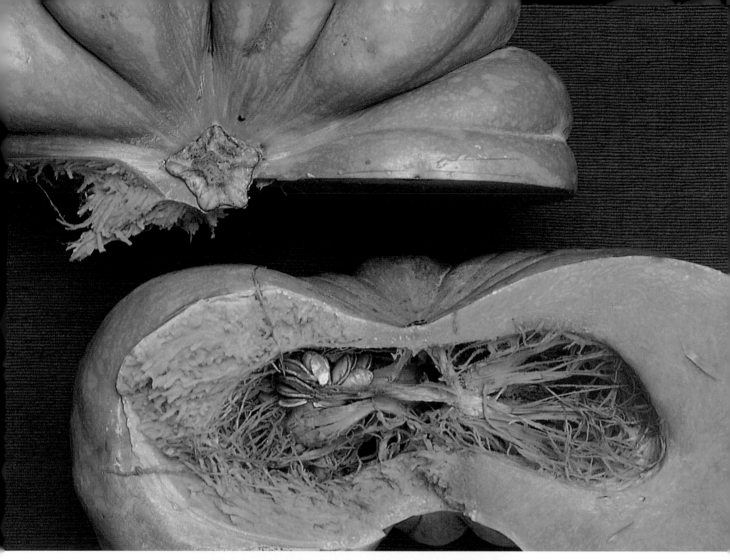

pheasant risotto

Game birds really give you a sense of the changing seasons – strung up in butchers' windows their orange, gold and brown feathers reflect the colours of the leaves on the ground so perfectly. Having said that, I have always had a slightly love-hate relationship with pheasants, loving the idea of them, but so often feeling miffed at the result: dry breasts, my pet hate when it comes to poultry.

However, the fact that one of my favourite poems is about this bird (*The Pheasant* by Alexander Pope), as is one of my favourite books (Dahl's *Danny The Champion of the World*), I persevered until I sorted out a recipe that did justice to the emotional place they hold in my heart. So this is a dish for all those who, come the right time of year, fancy doing a bird or two, but are fearful that the fruits of their labours will be disappointing. However, recognise that this is a two-way stream: you need to attend to the birds in order for them to pleasure you. In other words, it's a bit of a labour of love.

serves 6

a brace of pheasants, 800g–1kg each, breasts and legs removed (and you need the carcasses for the stock)

FOR THE STOCK

2 pheasant carcasses

1 red onion, peeled and roughly chopped

1 celery stick

250ml red wine

FOR THE PHEASANT

2 white onions, sliced

300g carrots, peeled and cut lengthways then sliced

2 celery sticks, thinly sliced

3 bay leaves

20g thyme, tied in a bunch

4 garlic cloves, peeled and thinly sliced

50ml extra virgin olive oil

● Preheat the oven to 180°C/350°F/gas 4.

● Roast the veg and carcasses for the stock in a 30cm x 40cm roasting tray in the oven for 40 minutes.

● Take the tray out, pour in the red wine, stir well, then top up with 2 litres water. Put back in the oven for a further $1^1/_2$ hours. You may need to add a bit more water halfway through; the idea is to keep the bones covered to make a stock with maximum flavour. (You could make the stock up the day before.)

● Strain this stock into a saucepan, and throw away the bones and veg. Give the roasting tray a quick clean.

● Put the onions, carrots, celery, bay leaves, thyme, garlic and olive oil back in your roasting tray. Stir well and put into the oven for 30 minutes until all is well browned.

● Pour in the red wine and nestle the legs between the veg. Give a little dash of S & P, and then top up with 1 litre water and 500ml of your lovely pheasant stock. Braise in the oven for 1 hour.

● Take the tray out of the oven and set the legs on a plate to cool down – you will be picking the meat off them later.

● Strain off the cooking liquor and put the braising veg aside for later.

● Pour the cooking liquor into a medium-sized saucepan and add 1.5 litres of the pheasant stock, topping up with water if necessary. Bring up to steaming point. This will be used for poaching the breasts and feeding the risotto.

300ml red wine
S & P

FOR THE RISOTTO
2 tablespoons extra virgin
   olive oil
500g risotto rice
30g butter
30g Parmesan cheese,
   grated
S & P

● Tip the braising veg into a large, heavy-bottomed saucepan, big enough to hold the finished risotto. Turn the heat onto medium and add the olive oil. Stir until you get a good sizzle going, then pour in the risotto rice and mix until all is well coated.

● The braising liquor/stock combo is steaming – no bubbles here please, as it will upset the cooking times. Check the seasoning and slip the pheasant breasts into it, just like that. Poach the breasts ever so gently for 10 minutes, then turn them over and let them keep poaching as you use the liquid around them to feed the risotto.

● Meanwhile, turn the heat on the risotto down to low. Now it is time to begin the loving feed and starve that is the hallmark of a good risotto, using the liquid that the pheasant breasts are poaching in. For the first feed, pour in 2 ladlefuls of your stock (my ladle holds 120ml) – the rice is very hungry for it now. Stir and allow the rice to absorb the stock before adding the next ladleful; you will add single ladlefuls from now on whenever the last has been absorbed. Keep stirring the risotto regularly to prevent it catching on the bottom. Cooking times vary, but it should be round about 30 minutes.

● Between feed and starve moments, turn your attention to the pheasant legs. Throw away the skin and shred the meat off the bones. Then chop it up roughly and stir it into the rice.

● When you add the last ladleful of stock, lift the breasts out onto a chopping board and leave them to rest for 5 minutes while you finish off the risotto.

● Once the meat has had time to relax, remove the wing bone if still attached and slice the breasts in long, thin slices – aim for 6–8 per breast. Cover the slices with foil, tucking it around them tightly to keep them warm.

● Nearly there now: the risotto is cooked when the rice is al dente, no liquid is left in the bottom of either pan, and there is a creaminess to the whole thing. Turn the heat off and stir in the butter, Parmesan and some seasoning – heavy on the pepper. Now leave to rest for a few minutes, lid on.

● Serve your risotto with the slices of poached breast on top and a big green salad to follow.

Shelf Life: The stock and the cooked pheasant will keep for 3–4 days in the fridge. A stock-based risotto can be yum cold, or even reheated. Just heat it up in a bit of simmering water on the hob or blow it up in the mike with no more liquid. Will probably take a bit more salt. **Best Kept:** The stock can be cooked the day before, if need be, and refrigerated. Finised risotto also in the fridge.

snapper, sweet potato BUBBLE and chilli drizzle

This is one for the Caribbean Crew. Because sweet spuds are native to the same shores as the snapper, it makes sense to use them here, but if sensible doesn't appeal to you, do it just for the flavour and great colours.

The bubble and squeak is simply the best I've ever had, and I've been a devoted bubbler for years.

serves 6

800g sweet potatoes,
  preferably the ones that
  are orange inside
80ml extra virgin olive oil
6 red chillies, whole
6 garlic cloves, peeled and
  finely chopped
4 spring onions, thinly sliced
¼ Savoy cabbage, cut
  into 1cm dice
50g coriander, roughly
  chopped
2 tablespoons plain flour,
  plus extra for dusting
2 limes (1 for juicing, 1 cut
  into wedges)
4 tablespoons light olive oil
6 red snapper fillets
S & P

● Preheat the oven to 180°C / 350°F / gas 4.

● Put the sweet potatoes, unpeeled, in a small baking tray. Drizzle over a tablespoon of olive oil, season with S & P and coat well. Bake in the oven for around 50 minutes. When they're properly cooked, you'll see a caramel-coloured goo oozing out of them. Check they're cooked by sliding a knife in.

● Once the spuds are in, wrap the chillies (whole) and half of the garlic in foil with a touch of salt, making a nice tight, flat, little package.

● Pop the foiled chillies and garlic into the oven and cook for 20 minutes.

● Remove the chilli parcel from the oven and leave it to cool slightly. Keep the oven on.

● Peel the chillies – easiest done by cutting them in half lengthways, laying them skin-side down on a board and scraping the flesh off with the back of a knife. Depending on how daring you feel, remove some/all of the seeds. Using a fork, mash the garlic with the chilli flesh in a small bowl. Stir in the other half of the coriander, squeeze over the juice of one lime and incorporate all the extra virgin. Season.

● When the spuds are cooked, take them out of the oven (but leave the oven on) and put on one side until cool enough to handle, but not stone cold. Peel and coarsely mash the flesh with a masher or fork (not in the food processor, which will break up the fibres too much and leave you with baby food). Stir in the spring onion, Savoy cabbage (raw), half of the coriander, the remaining garlic and the flour. Season and then cool the mix for a minimum of 30 minutes in the fridge.

● When the time is up, take it out, form it into 6 patties and dust with flour.

● Heat 3 tablespoons of light olive oil in a large, heavy-bottomed, ovenproof frying pan to just about smoking. Gently lay your patties in the hot oil. Sizzle sizzle.

● Heat up a griddle pan for the fish. If you haven't got one, you'll be using the grill (but sadly you'll miss out on those groovy black lines).

● Turn the patties over and pop them in the oven for 10 minutes whilst you cook the fish.

● Lightly oil the skin with the last of the olive oil, then season the fish on both sides. Place the fillets skin-side down in the griddle pan. The fish will tell you when it's ready to be turned because the skin will start to come away from the griddle – about 4 minutes. Premature turning will lead to ripped skin, which spoils the aesthetics.

● Turn the fish and cook for a further 2 minutes, flesh-side down.

● Presentation is simple: bubble on the plate, fillet on top, drizzle of the roast chilli and a healthy wedge of lime.

Shelf Life: 2–3 days. **Best Kept:** In the fridge.

butterflied TROUT
with hazelnut crust

Clearly someone has to take the bones out, and the better the place you buy your fish from, the more likely it is they'll do it for you. If you have to do it yourself, believe me I have tried to explain it clearly but really you need a visual on this one. My friend Vicky, who's not a completely natural cook, recipe-tested this at a time when this book was just a lot of word-processed print-outs. So at sea was she with the Advanced Boning 101 course needed to do this that she ended up finding a short video on the net by a man in Norway showing you how to bone out a herring. Might still be up there if you are having difficulties.

As with almonds, cashews, macadamia, pecans, pistachios and walnuts, hazelnuts are an antioxidant that lowers cholesterol. They are energy boosters, high in fibre, and are a suggested preventative for those susceptible to kidney stones.

This recipe would go well with some blanched broccoli, still crunchy, and plain boiled new potatoes as it's quite oil-rich. Or for the hotel-stuck-in-the-seventies feel, buttered sliced carrots, a wedge of lemon and a sprig of frisée.

serves 6

200g hazelnuts, roughly chopped

6 x 300–400g trout, gutted and scaled

3 tablespoons butter

30g fresh dill, finely chopped

2 lemons (1 for juicing and 1 cut into wedges)

S & P

● Preheat the oven to 180°C / 350°F / gas 4.

● If your hazelnuts are shelled, just roast them in the oven until they go golden and you can smell that delicious smell. If your hazelnuts are not shelled, roast them for 10 minutes, then tip whilst still blazing hot into a tea towel, bring the edges up around them and rub them furiously against each other. Leave to cool (but don't forget they're in the tea towel and grab it – a common and boring accident). When you open it, you'll find about 80 per cent of the skin has rubbed right off. Depending on the colour they are once the skin has come away, you may want to toast them for a few more minutes.

● Cool and pulse the roasted, shelled hazelnuts to a very coarse powder in a food processor and then spread them evenly over a baking tray. Season.

● Now for the fish: cut the head off just below the fin, immediately next to it. Trim off all the other fins using a pair of scissors. With a very sharp filleting knife, put the point in right at the end of the gut cavity, blade facing down towards the tail on one side of the backbone, then turn your blade around so that it's now facing the head.

● Staying on the same side of the backbone and right next to it, work your way up to the head end, cutting through all the little bones that come off the backbone. Do the same for the other side. Use scissors to cut off the now isolated backbone, and at this point your fish will lay flat. Having ditched the backbone there are two other sets of bones to get out: the carriageway bones, which you can see all of, and the pin bones, which you can see only the tips of sticking out in a line down each fillet. Carriageway bones first: lay the fish north-south with the tail near you. Starting with the left fillet, with the blade of your knife facing towards the head, use just the tip of it to go under where you cut the carriageway bone from the flesh. Start at the tail end and work all the way up to the top so you have a 0.5cm flap, then turn the blade around and, working just underneath the bones, slice the whole row of bones out, working towards the outside of the fish. Throw away the strip of bones. Now do exactly the same with the right fillet.

● Nearly there: run your fingers gently up and down the fillets to locate the line of pin bones and pull them out with tweezers or your fingernails. Lastly, use scissors to neatly trim the sides of the fish. Well done – I think you're amazing and I promise the other 5 will be quicker.

● Preheat the oven to 220°C/425°F/gas 7.

● Season the flesh of the trout and lay the fish flesh-side down in the toasted hazelnuts. Give them a good press with the flat of your hand to make sure the nuts stick to the flesh.

● Get two baking trays big enough to hold 3 trout in each one. Splash a good bit of water on them – this will keep the fish from sticking. Lay your trout on the trays, hazelnut-side up.

● Divide the butter into 12 little knobs and put 2 pieces on each of the fish. Put the trays in the hot oven and cook for about 8 minutes. Have warm plates ready.

● When they are cooked, carefully lift the fish off the trays with your special flipper.

● Drizzle the leftover butter from the tray all over the fish and finish with a liberal sprinkling of dill and a squeeze of lemon. Serve with a lemon wedge on the side.

Shelf Life: A couple of days. **Best Kept:** I don't anticipate leftovers, but if so it's a job for the fridge.

baked SWEET potato
with sour cream 'slaw

Sweet potatoes are a blockbuster source of beta-carotene, with 130g of cooked flesh containing a massive 14mg of the stuff. But this recipe is also a chance to beef up your intake of raw veg. Cabbage is every nutritionist's wet dream – a great antioxidant, which speeds up oestrogen metabolism. And beetroot, as well as being my favourite surprise 'slaw ingredient, gives cabbage a run for its money in terms of antioxidant qualities, whilst also being loaded with potassium.

Our wonderful family friend and celebrity psychiatrist Jeanie C-R rightly pointed out that for carnivores this would be scrumptious with a few thick slices of quality baked ham.

serves 6

7 x 350g sweet potatoes, the ones with the orange flesh
6 knobs of butter (optional), to serve

FOR THE 'SLAW
100g frozen peas
1 raw beetroot, peeled and grated
¼ white cabbage, thinly shredded
2 spring onions, thinly sliced
2 season's best apples

FOR THE DRESSING
200g sour cream or mascarpone cheese
juice of 2 limes
a pinch cayenne
1 flat teaspoon smoked paprika
S & P

● Preheat the oven to 180ºC/350ºF/gas 4.

● Sit a pan of salted water for the peas on the stove on high heat.

● Put 6 of the sweet potatoes, evenly spaced, on a baking sheet and put in the oven for 50 minutes. They are done if they feel soft when you squeeze them; often some black, sticky caramel goo comes out too.

● Whilst they are cooking, make the 'slaw. Cook the peas in boiling water for a couple of minutes, then drain and cool.

● Peel and coarsely grate the remaining sweet potato.

● In a bowl, mix the peas, grated sweet potato and beetroot together with the cabbage and spring onions. Wash and slice the apples and chuck them in too.

● Make the dressing by whisking together the sour cream/mascarpone, lime juice, cayenne, smoked paprika and some salt.

● Toss the grated fruit and veg in the dressing and mix well together. Season again, adding a splash of water if the 'slaw looks a bit sticky – this will immediately make the consistency more creamy.

● When the spuds are cooked, cut them open and season with a little salt and plenty of pepper. Slip in a knob of butter if you fancy it. Serve with the 'slaw on the side or dolloped on top – one of those instances when the hot and cold thang works so well.

Shelf Life: 2 days. **Best Kept:** 'Slaw in the fridge; spuds at room temp.

baked open RAVIOLI

Ravioli are an effort to make, involving not only growing your own pasta but also using a ravioli press. This cheaty version uses sheets of lasagne, filled on one half and the other half flipped over. The joy of this recipe is that the work can be done in advance, leaving you to put the ravs in the oven when you want.

serves 6

1 large butternut squash, peeled and cut in half lengthways, discard the seeds and stringy bits and cut into 2cm slices
8 garlic cloves, peeled
100ml extra virgin olive oil
700g whole leaf spinach
grating of nutmeg (optional)
12 sheets lasagne
250ml double cream
75g Parmesan cheese, grated (keep the rind for adding to the cream)
25g sage, finely chopped
250g ricotta cheese
S & P

● Preheat the oven to 180°C/350°F/gas 4.

● Put the squash and 6 of the garlic cloves in a roasting tin, drizzle with a little olive oil and season. Roast in the oven for 35 minutes or until the flesh is soft, giving it a stir halfway through.

● Meanwhile, heat a large saucepan with the rest of the olive oil and, when the oil is hot, throw in the spinach. Quickly turn it over and keep stirring for a few minutes until it is all wilted. Turn the heat down to medium and let the liquid boil away – there will be a lot of it – it will take about 10 minutes for the water to evaporate. Season and add a scratch of nutmeg if you choose, then roughly chop on a chopping board.

● Cook the lasagne as directed on the packet. When al dente, carefully remove each sheet one by one and put them all in a bowl of cold, lightly oiled water.

● Pour the cream into a small saucepan and set over a low heat. If you have the rind left over from the Parmesan, add this now just for flavour infusion. Chop the remaining 2 garlic cloves and add to the cream with half the chopped sage.

● Check your spinach: if it is still seeping out loads of water, squeeze out the excess in handfuls. Once you are happy with it, stir the spinach into the cream and season.

● Check that the roasted squash/garlic is cooked. If it is, take it out of the oven and mash lightly with a fork or a masher. Put the ricotta, the remaining sage and half of the grated Parmesan in a bowl, stir in the mashed squash/garlic and season to taste. Turn up the oven to 200°C/400°F/gas 6.

● Begin to layer up the ingredients. Take a 30cm x 40cm baking tray and cover it with about 3mm water. Take one sheet of lasagne, lay it on the tray and put a blob of squash/ricotta mix in one half. Fold the other end over the filling, flatten with the back of a spoon and place a dollop of the spinach-cream on top. Now take another sheet and lay half of it on top of the spinach-cream and let the other half flop over the side. Do like you did before: blob of squash mix, flip the other half of the pasta sheet over and then finish with a good spoonful of the spinach-cream on top. Push your completed stacked rav into a corner of the tray. Repeat for the other five stacks. Sprinkle over the remaining Parmesan and put in the oven for about 25–30 minutes, or until your ravs turn a golden brown.

Shelf Life: Make it and eat it. **Best Kept:** Not.

ALICE b TOKLAS' hashish fudge

This is a classic recipe from 1954, which I came across in one of my Mum's cookbooks. It's a bit of a giggle and you're never quite sure how tongue-in-cheek she's being – in the intro Alice recommends it as 'an interesting refreshment for a Ladies' Bridge Club' – can she be serious? Nowadays, the medicinal qualities of marijuana are understood better and it is used as effective, natural pain relief by people with arthritis, MS and IBS, as well as the less drastic symptoms of period pains. Very figgy, spicy and sticky.

makes about 20 pieces

1 teaspoon black peppercorns

1 teaspoon coriander seeds

a scratch of nutmeg

$^1/_4$ teaspoon ground cinnamon (I don't like cinnamon, so I substituted the seeds from a vanilla pod, which worked out really well)

a handful of stoned dates (ha ha)

a handful of dried figs

a handful of flaked almonds

a bunch of Cannabis sativa leaves (or you can just crumble in some hash or weed)

140g light brown sugar

125g butter

Shelf Life: Weeks and weeks. **Best Kept:** In an airtight box in the larder or fridge.

● Toast the peppercorns and the coriander seeds in a small frying pan on a high heat until they start to smell wonderful. Put them with some nutmeg scrapings and the cinnamon (if you wish) into a pestle and mortar/coffee grinder and pulverise.

● Chop the fruit and nuts and mix them in a bowl. Sprinkle on the spices and add the cannabis in whatever form you have – if it's leaves, they will have to be pounded first (i.e. in the pestle and mortar with the seeds and cinnamon), but hash or weed can be crumbled in with the other spices.

● Dissolve the sugar and the butter in a heavy-based saucepan over a low heat. When the sugar has melted, the mixture will be separated: melted butter floating on top of a slightly bubbling brown sugary goo. Slowly bring to the boil – don't let it catch on the bottom of the pan – stirring briskly with a wooden spoon until the mixture starts to boil and come together. Keep stirring until it is a thicker, foamier texture. Mix in the fruity bits, take off the heat and beat thoroughly. The fruit will break down and make it even smoother. (If you are left with a little melted butter in the pan, drain it off, and use some kitchen paper to de-grease the fudge mix.) Line a tray with a piece of buttered greaseproof paper and push the fudge into it, or Alice suggests rolling it into individual, walnut-sized pieces. Cool to room temperature in the larder overnight, in the fridge if you're in a hurry, or in the freezer if you're desperate.

COX granita

If you can make ice you can make granita, because that's all it is, just flavoured water ice – but instead of doing it in cubes on a tray, you texture it by disturbing and layering the freezing crystals. But before that you have to get some fun into it because frozen water, however interestingly textured it may be, won't please the critics.

For such a simple thing, I advocate keeping the flavours clean. Here we go for a classic taste of British autumn, but in spring you can do this with mint (and vodka?) and in summer with strawberries. It's all about catching the granita before it solidifies beyond the pleasure point.

A granita makes a light way to round off a meal, but if you're really out to impress serve as a great inter-course or pre-dessert refresher, all for stupidly little effort. Make the base whenever you want, but for best results pop it in the freezer about an hour and a half before you need to eat it.

What a healthy pudding – all the nutritious value of eating raw apples and a couple of thimblefuls of water to boot.

serves 6

70g caster sugar
1.3kg Cox's Pippins (or
   600ml best organic
   apple juice)
juice of ½ lemon

● Put the sugar and 120ml water into a small saucepan, stir slightly so the sugar is all wet, and bring to a rapid boil for 1 minute. Take off the heat and allow to cool down completely.

● Put an 18cm square tray with sides at least 5cm high (or something similar) in the freezer.

● Juice the apples in a juicer and mix with the lemon juice. Alternatively, if you don't have a juicer, chop the apples into chunks and whizz in a blender with the lemon juice, then strain – make sure you really push the juice through with the back of a spoon. You should end up with about 600ml juice.

● Mix the juice with the cooled sugar syrup and pour into your cold tray. Set in the freezer for about 1½ hours, stirring every 30 minutes to pull the freezing bits away from the sides of the tray.

When you serve the granita you want it to be crystallised and solid, but not rock hard. If you forget about it and it sets as hard as an iceberg, let it warm up for about 20 minutes on the counter. Then break it up with a fork, chisel or machete and put it back in the freezer to re-set.

Shelf Life: Best on the night, but will keep for a few weeks in a Tupperware container. **Best Kept:** In the freezer.

french PEAR tart

Pears are a great fruit to see us through the winter, with plenty of natural sugar that is released slowly into our bodies, and no less than five minerals: copper, iodine, phosphorus, sulphur and zinc – that's a truckload of elements hitting your system. This tart involves a little precise slicing so you will find the laying out easier if you have a slightly obsessive nature.

serves 6

FOR THE PASTRY
180g plain flour
60g icing sugar
90g unsalted butter
2 egg yolks
splash of milk

FOR THE MIDDLE
8 big pears (doesn't matter
   if they're a bit bruised,
   which pears do easily)
70ml Poire William (along
   with Vieille Prune, this is
   Fred's and my fave kitchen
   tipple) or brandy
60g demerara sugar
2 nice big pretty pears
   for the top, the red-
   skinned are kind of fun
4 heaped tablespoons
   apricot jam, to glaze

● In a food processor, spin the flour and icing sugar for a minute to aerate them and then drop the butter down the chute in 6 separate knobs. Once the butter has been incorporated, add the egg yolks individually, with a pulse between each one, and then turn the pastry out onto your surface and work in the milk. Wrap in clingfilm and put in the freezer for 10–15 minutes.

● Peel and core the 8 pears and cut into large-ish chunks. Put the pear, the Poire William or brandy, demerara sugar and about 1cm water into a heavy-based saucepan with a lid and set over a medium heat. When the pear pieces begin to break down, take off the lid and boil away any excess liquid so you are left with a chunky compote.

● Preheat the oven to 200°C/400°F/gas 6.

● Line your 20cm x 3cm deep tart ring. Keep any surplus pastry wrapped in clingfilm in the freezer; it'll be good for up to a month. Put the lined tart ring in the freezer for 10–15 minutes. Once the pastry case has hardened up, take it out of the freezer and put it straight into the oven for around 10–12 minutes. When it's golden brown, take it out and tip in the cooled pear compote. Level off the top with the back of a spoon.

● Turn the oven down to 180°C/350°F/gas 4.

● Now for the famous fanned top of this French tart. Quarter and core 2 pears lengthways. Using a small sharp knife, slice one of the quarters lengthways as thinly as possible – it's much easier if you slice a quarter at a time. The end game is 3 concentric circles of over-lapping slices. So start by laying out the fat end touching the pastry and the thin end pointing towards the middle. Then when you've been all the way round, start the second circle inside that one with the pears facing the other way. The third and final central circle is the hardest to lay down evenly – just do your best. There's no trick, it just takes a bit of patience.

● Meanwhile, melt the apricot jam with 1 tablespoon of water over a low heat. Whisk for a minute so it becomes smooth. When the top of the tart is covered with pear slices, brush liberally with the jam and put in the oven for 10–15 minutes, until the slices have softened. You could grill the tart for added coloration, but be careful not to burn your masterpiece. Serve with whipped cream, crème fraîche, good natural yogurt or vanilla ice cream – your call.

Shelf Life: Best within 48 hours. **Best Kept:** Out on the table to show off to your friends and family.

prune DATE and HONEY powerbars

So this is like a modern flapjack, but crumblier. It accentuates all that can be great about flappers (oats, dried fruit and seeds) and minimises the refined sugars. You can swap my suggested ingredients for whatever you have in the cupboard – apricots or figs instead of dates and prunes, walnuts for almonds, and use whatever seeds you have knocking around. My new favourites are alfalfa seeds – itsy bitsy crunchy things. The key to the flavour of the flap is the ratio of oats: butter: honey. A good rainy afternoon activity for all.

makes about 14 pieces, depending on what size you like them

160g butter
6 tablespoons clear honey
300g oats
80g flaked almonds
70g sultanas
70g dried apricots, chopped
80g dried prunes, chopped
100g stoned dates, chopped
1 teaspoon fennel seeds
1 tablespoon pumpkin seeds
1 tablespoon hemp seeds
1 tablespoon linseeds

● Preheat the oven to 160°C/320°F/gas 3.

● Melt the butter with the honey.

● Toss all the dry ingredients together in a big bowl, then pour in the melted butter and honey. Line a 20cm x 30cm tin with buttered greaseproof paper and pack the mix into it, pressing it down with the back of a spoon.

● Cook for 45 minutes, or until slightly brown. Take out of the oven and allow to stand for 5 minutes before cutting into oblongs. Cool to room temperature before taking out of the tin.

NB The Powerbars may sometimes be a bit crumbly because of the varying absorbency of the dry ingredients. I don't mind this, but if you do you could make a note to add a bit more butter next time you make them. I wanted to try and make them replacing the butter completely with omega 6 oil, but never quite got there – maybe psychologically it was a bit too healthy for me; however, I can't see why it wouldn't work.

Shelf Life: 5 days. **Best Kept:** In an airtight container.

ginger, ALMOND and choc chip cookies

The ginger-chocolatey thing is a solid partnership: crystallised ginger can be quite hot and fiery and therefore helps cut through the sweetness of the chocolate. The fire in ginger is an indication of its famed antiseptic qualities, the ability to ward off colds and chills, as well as fighting off toxins. I'm not saying you will get all of that out of a biscuit, but it's good to bear in mind.

These are versatile little babes because you can make the mix and cook them there and then or you can roll them out and pop them in the fridge for baking later. You can even freeze the dough and experience the joy another day, for joy it is when you eat them fresh out the oven and the chocolatey bits goo all over your lips. They are ideal fuel for autumnal leaf catching and garden clearing, or break them over vanilla ice cream for an instant pudding.

makes 24-ish, or 12 really exciting big ones

120g unsalted butter (at room temperature)

150g soft brown sugar

1 egg, beaten

1–2 drops of vanilla essence

160g plain flour

1 level teaspoon baking powder

280g flaked almonds, hand-chopped or coarsely ground (do this in the food processor, but don't walk away and pulverise them)

120g chocolate drops

50g crystallised ginger, roughly chopped

salt

● Preheat the oven to 160°C / 320°F / gas 3.

● Using a mixer, cream the butter and sugar until light and fluffy. Work in the egg and vanilla essence.

● In a separate bowl, sift the flour, baking powder and a pinch of salt and then stir in the almonds.

● Carefully stir the flour and almonds into the egg/butter mix, sprinkling in the choc drops and ginger as you go.

● If possible, rest for 1 hour in the fridge.

● Use a tablespoon to scoop out 24-ish apricot-sized chunks of dough (or divide into 12 for the joke-sized ones) and place them on a greased baking tray with plenty of space between the balls. You might need 2 trays if they don't all fit on one.

● Bake the regular ones for about 12 minutes, the super-sizers for a further 6–8 minutes – they should be just browning round the edges.

● Take the tray out and let the cookies sit for a couple of minutes – but don't let them cool down completely – before using a palette knife to move them onto a cooling rack.

● Snarf as many of them as you can whilst they're still warm.

Shelf Life: Raw mix in the fridge for 1 week; in the freezer for 1 month. Cooked cookies – don't think this is going to be a problem. **Best Kept:** Raw mix in the fridge; cookies in an airtight tin.

maple SYRUP and brazil nut biscuits

Brazil nuts are a true Superfood. They have much going for them (protein, unsaturated fat, minerals and B-complex vitamins) but there is also a special relationship between two of their components, vitamin E and the mineral selenium. Each one enhances the performance of the other as an antioxidant fighting free radicals, and thus helping to decrease the signs of ageing and boosting immunity to disease.

Brazil, where the nuts come from, is home of the Amazonian rainforest, and for centuries these elongated rugger balls of natural defence have helped keep the indigenous population in good fettle.

makes 24-ish biscuits

250g plain flour

1 level teaspoon baking powder

100g Brazil nuts, split in half lengthways

120g butter

180g maple syrup

100g brown sugar

salt

● Preheat the oven to 160°C / 320°F / gas 3.

● Sift the flour, baking powder and a tiny pinch of salt in a bowl.

● Melt the butter in the maple syrup and sugar – don't get it too hot.

● Pour the wet ingredients into the dry ones, leaving the nuts out of the equation.

● Roll the dough into small balls and put them on a greased baking tray.

● Squish the chunky Brazil nut halves into the balls of dough, thus flattening them out a bit, and bake for 15-ish minutes.

● As with all biscuits, allow them to cool on the baking tray for a few minutes before moving them with a palette knife to a wire rack.

Shelf Life: 5 days. **Best Kept:** In an airtight container (you might need to hide them).

orange BLOSSOM, cashew and semolina CAKE

I have to say this is my favourite: a truly stunning cake with the most incredible, crumbly texture. All the ingredients bring something to the party – semolina for colour and consistency, cashews for moistness and all their good oils, and orange flower water to keep the whole thing fragrant and light. Really stunning on its own, or makes a fab pud with a bit of fruit and a blob of crème fraîche. Yellow cake like you've never had it before.

serves 6+

FOR THE CAKE
200g butter (at room temperature)
250g golden demerara sugar
250g ground cashew nuts, raw and unsalted
3 eggs
zest and juice of 2 oranges
110g fine semolina
1 level teaspoon baking powder
a good splash of orange blossom water (about 2 tablespoons)
salt

FOR THE ROSEMARY SYRUP
15g rosemary, in little sprigs
2 tablespoons caster sugar

● Preheat the oven to 160ºC / 320ºF / gas 3.

● Cream the butter and the sugar together with a mixer until light and pale. Mix in the ground cashews. Add the eggs, one by one, waiting until each is fully incorporated before adding the next. Stir in the orange zest and juice, followed by the semolina, baking powder and a pinch of salt.

● Grease a 25cm cake tin with a little butter, then dust lightly with flour. Shake the flour all round the inside so that there is a fine dusting, and then tip out the excess.

● Spoon the cake mix into the tin and then put into the oven on a tray to bake for around 1^{1}/$_{2}$ hours. (The reason for the tray is that when I did it some of the mixture oozed out of the bottom of the tin – it could just be that my tin was broken, though it didn't look it, but it's better to be safe than on your knees scrubbing the oven.)

● When the time is up, do the skewer test to check it's cooked through. If a little bit of the cake mixture sticks to the skewer, pop the cake back in for another 10–15 minutes. When it is done, cool in the tin while you get on with the rosemary syrup.

● Put the rosemary sprigs in a small pan with the sugar and 5 tablespoons of water. Cook over a very low flame for 5–10 minutes until the rosemary has softened and the sugar has turned into a thick, clear syrup.

● Now sprinkle the orange blossom water over the cake. Then loosen it around the edges of the tin with a knife and transfer it to a wire rack. Wait 5 minutes and then brush the rosemary syrup over the cake and dot the candied rosemary sprigs across the top.

Shelf Life: Up to a week and, believe me, it just keeps on getting better.
Best Kept: Uncovered, at room temperature.

AUTUMN à la mode

Dried apricots are a great way to bump up your fruit intake through the more sluggish months: loaded with trace elements (zinc, iron, manganese and copper), rich in fibre and jumpin' with vitamins A, B and C. Just be careful not to go for the really bright orange ones that may have been treated with sulphur – the organic, darker ones have much better natural sweetness.

Frangelico is an outrageously delicious Italian liqueur made out of hazelnuts that you will never regret having in your booze cupboard. If you can't get hold of it use Amaretto (made from almonds).

In the States when you order 'pie à la mode', it means your pie comes with ice cream – a translation I'm sure the French would find bewildering and amusing in equal portions. I've even overheard people in diners say, 'pie, hold the mode', meaning no ice cream. This is a really long way round explaining the name of this recipe. Suffice to say that the flavours are bang on for this time of year. Obviously serve with ice cream.

serves 6 and some for later

70g hazelnuts, shelled
150g dried apricots
¼ teaspoon ground cinnamon (or half a stick)
1 tablespoon caster sugar (or 1½ tablespoons honey)
3 tablespoons Frangelico

● Preheat the oven to 170°C/325°F/gas 3.

● Toast the hazelnuts for 10–15 minutes, until golden brown.

● Put the apricots, cinnamon, sugar (or honey) and 300ml water into a small saucepan and bring to the boil, then knock it down to a very slow simmer. Cook like this for 15 minutes.

● Ditch the cinnamon stick, pour the whole lot into a blender and blitz until smooth.

● Add the Frangelico and leave to cool.

● Smash the hazelnuts roughly with the side of a knife. The sauce is delicious either hot or cold on ice cream and topped off with a sprinkling of chopped hazelnuts. And perhaps on a cool day you might consider heating it for a perfect little autumn-warming shot.

Shelf Life: Good for 6 days. **Best Kept:** In the fridge.

all purpose PEANUT sauce

This is an extremely handy little number to have knocking around your fridge. Use it as a salad dressing (see Hispi Slaw page 26), a dip for crudités, with grilled chicken skewers (commonly known as satay) or as a spread for rice cakes or sarnies.

The kind of oils in peanuts are, of course, the good kind, but as ever too much of a good thing will lead to American Lard-ass.

Shrimp paste is famously one of the worst smelling ingredients to be found in the kitchen. I once had the pleasure of watching the deck-hands on a flotilla up the Irrawaddy make this from scratch, starting with catching lots of little fish, then laying them out on racks with salt sprinkled on them. Over the course of a week under the hot Burmese sun the little fish went seriously off and their flesh started breaking down; my cabin was directly above where the fish were laid out, and I have never had such fruity dreams. Once the fish have reached just the right point of degeneration, spices were gathered and ground along with the honking fishies. When the right consistency was reached the whole thing was sealed under wax (to keep the smell in and the air out) which you will find is true too of the one you will buy in your local Asian store.

makes about 400ml

150g organic peanuts, raw and unsalted

2 red chillies, cut into small dice

3 garlic cloves, finely chopped

1 tablespoon peanut or vegetable oil

1/2 teaspoon Thai shrimp paste, dissolved in 1 tablespoon hot water (optional but does add depth of flavour)

1 tablespoon Thai fish sauce

juice of 1 1/2 limes

100g crunchy peanut butter (really is worth getting organic)

splash of sesame oil

● In a small frying pan, dry-fry the peanuts on a medium heat until they get some colour. Tip them out on a plate to cool. Now fry the chillies and garlic gently in the peanut/vegetable oil. Either in a food processor or by hand, chop the peanuts and then put them into a big bowl with the chilli, garlic and any oil that has not been soaked up.

● Add the shrimp paste dissolved in water, fish sauce, lime juice, and peanut butter. Slowly start whisking in warm water (about 150ml) until you reach a good coating consistency. Finally, stir in a bit of sesame oil and then refrigerate for at least 30 minutes so the flavours have a chance to settle down. If the peanut sauce has seized up a bit, stir in a splash of warm water, which will get it back to the right consistency.

Shelf Life: Will keep for up to a fortnight in a sealed jar.
Best Kept: In the fridge.

apple and PEAR chutney

Now is the time to make hay with our best native autumn fruits, and there is no better way to do it than with this simple chutney. During the winter in our house, we have a tradition of Carpet Picnics, which involve sitting on the sheepskin rug in front of a roaring fire with some good cheeses, Bath Olivers, a decent bottle of red and some of my fine chutney. All those endless books about BBQ cooking and picnic food are really only relevant for such a short time in our climate, and a Carpet Picnic together with recipes such as Bonfire Beef in a Tea Towel are year-round ways of bringing the Great Outdoors into the Also Great Indoors.

makes about 500ml

4 good-quality apples
  (preferably not Grannies),
  something tasty like
  Cox, Worcester or Pippin
3 pears – Williams and
  Comice both work fine
4 tablespoons walnut oil
  (or another nut oil, or
  plain olive oil)
1 large white onion, cut into
  small dice
30g thyme, on the branch,
  tied with string
3 bay leaves (fresh are
  much better)
2 celery sticks, cut into
  small dice
5 cloves
1 teaspoon ground ginger
2 teaspoons ground
  allspice
1 cinnamon stick, broken in
  half, or 1/2 teaspoon ground
100g demerara sugar
120ml red wine or cider
  vinegar
S & P

● Peel your apples and pears and then cut the flesh into 1cm dice, throwing away the core and seeds.

● Put the (walnut) oil in a pan and sweat off the onions, thyme, bay and celery for 10 minutes.

● Keep on a medium heat whilst you add the spices. Once the spices are well incorporated, cook for a further 5 minutes to allow their flavours to expand.

● Tip in the pear and apple pieces and stir well. Increase the heat a bit, and then add the sugar and vinegar.

● Allow the chutney to simmer away slowly until there is only a tiny residue of liquid left – the slower the better. I cooked mine for 1^1/$_2$ hours on the lowest flame of the smallest burner.

● Season with S & P and spoon into a sterilised jar.

● Try to serve at room temperature, with your favourite cheeses or ham. The flavour improves over time, so make it in advance.

Shelf Life: About a month in the fridge – but as with all homemade preserves that contain no additives or life-extending chemicals to kill off the natural formation of mould, we home folk need to keep the sides of the jar tidy when we use it.
Best Kept: In an airtight jar in the fridge or a cold larder.

autumn NUT pesto

Nuts are like seeds: little life-forces that already contain everything they need, given the right conditions (i.e. food and water), to become magnificent trees of their own one day. This means an exceptionally high amount of protein, and a starter-pack of vitamins and minerals. They have good unsaturated fats, which means that they're able to react and therefore be used by the body (as opposed to just sitting there being fat, like saturated fats do).

The joy of this pesto is that it will last over a month in the fridge and is very versatile. It can be stirred into pasta, turned into chicken stuffing (add breadcrumbs), used to dress veggies (meaning vegetables, not vegetarians) or added to cooked pulses. Such a good return on your investment of time.

makes about 1 litre

500g walnuts in the shell
(or 100g shelled walnuts)
150g chestnuts in the shell
(or 100g of the vac-packed ones)
150g cobnuts (or 100g hazelnuts)
430ml good extra virgin olive oil
120g streaky bacon, thinly sliced (optional)
5 garlic cloves, peeled
80g rosemary, roughly chopped
35g thyme, roughly chopped
50g flatleaf parsley, roughly chopped
1 teaspoon dried chilli flakes (optional)
S & P

● If your nuts are not shelled....

WALNUTS AND COBNUTS: these need to be shelled in the time-honoured way, and even if you have been lucky enough to get wet walnuts, in which case this will be extra delicious, you'll probably still need a pair of crackers.

CHESTNUTS: make a little slit in them from top to bottom and drop them into a pan of boiling water. Simmer for 5–10 minutes, then strain and peel once they are cool enough to handle.

Once you are sitting in front of a large pile of shelled nuts, the rest is plain sailing.

● Put one third of the olive oil in a pan on a very gentle, low heat with the nuts, bacon and garlic cloves. The heat needs to be gentle to give an all-round, infused flavour so do it slowly.

● Cook for around 20 minutes, stirring regularly. The aim is for everything to slowly and gently turn golden in the oil.

● Once the nuts have begun to colour, add the chopped herbs and another third of the oil, along with the chilli flakes (if using).

● Let the flavours keep infusing for about another 10 minutes, then take off the heat and leave to cool for 15 minutes.

● Pulse the whole lot in the food processor to a very coarse paste. Stir in the rest of the olive oil and some seasoning before transferring the pesto to an airtight jar. If necessary, cover the solids with a little extra oil to form a thin, airtight barrier which you should maintain each time you use it .

Shelf Life: 1 month and counting. **Best Kept:** In the fridge.

za'atar ALMONDS

Contrary to popular belief, the West Coast of the USA (and not Spain) is the biggest almond producer, with a whopping 80 per cent of the world's almond trade. In the nineties, Britain's stongest man attested his strength to the handful of almonds he ate every day, and he could pull a bus with his hair.

Za'atar is a fabulously simple blend of spices that is usually found with bread in Lebanese cookery. It's a mix of thyme (dried), sumac, salt and sesame seeds, and it's a real example of the end result being far greater than the sum of the parts. You can either make your own blend, or buy it ready-made from Middle Eastern groceries. Roasting almonds in it makes for a top nibble.

makes nibbles for 6 people

500g whole almonds, either blanched or skin on depending on personal preference – a mix can look nice

1 egg white, lightly whisked until just frothy and white

FOR THE ZA'ATAR

1 tablespoon dried thyme
1 tablespoon sumac
1 tablespoon sea salt
1 tablespoon sesame seeds

● Preheat the oven to 200°C/400°F/gas 6.

● First make the za'atar. In a pestle and mortar or a coffee grinder, grind the thyme, sumac, sea salt and sesame seeds to a fine powder.

● Whisk the za'atar into the egg white, stir in the almonds and mix until well coated.

● Oil a 30cm x 40cm sheet of greaseproof paper and put it on an a baking tray.

● Spread the almonds out, evenly spaced and not piled up, on the oiled greaseproof and put in the oven.

● Roast for 15–20 minutes, or until a deep golden brown. Don't worry if the za'atar turns quite dark – the flavours work best at that nutty point that happens shortly before burning (but don't burn it). You may need to break the nuts up a bit, or they might just split up naturally.

● It's nice to serve them warm, but room temperature works too.

Shelf Life: Weeks. **Best Kept:** In a dish for munching.

christmas

Now it's come to the bit where I have to justify having five seasons, and that I'm aware I'm on slightly shaky ground. The idea really came from something I heard on the radio a while back, that for some reason stayed with me. It was the old rocker Susy Quattro talking about a Christmas single she had put out in the seventies, and how she felt differently about the record with 30 years of hindsight.

Her points were simple, yet I'd never really taken them on board before. On the downside was the fact that the record was only ever going to get played for a maximum of three weeks a year (though that doesn't apply to high street chains who think Christmas starts before Bonfire Night). But on the upside, come the festive time, all the Christmas tunes get dusted off and played again. Every year. Without fail. Even the dire ones. So they become etched into our festive play list, greeted with a groan and a smile and over many, many years receive more air play than they would had they not been Christmassy.

In this age, in which cookery books are flooding the market, they tend to come and go pretty quickly – endless books with pretty-boy-fishing-in-chef's-whites on the cover now sitting less prettily on the remainder shelves. There are very few new classics, and I guess I thought that if you reach for this book only on three days of the year to get that excellent stuffing recipe, that's better than it not getting used at all. I'd rather be a perennial than an annual, and Susy said that even though it wasn't her biggest hit, her Christmas tune is now probably her best known. Damned if I can remember the name of it, but I sure know all the words.

But then there are other reasons for giving Christmas its own chapter: by definition winter is the slowest season; warmth and light are required to keep the world moving, so, in the cold, dark days of midwinter, nothing changes. Or rather it does, but painfully slowly. So, by removing December from our seasonal equation we have one less month of nothing happening to think about. And anyway, December is nothing like the rest of winter. January, February and March are the cold and depressing ones, where everybody stays in and goes a dull grey colour.

However, from the last day in November the tone of the people could not be more contrasting. It's a party time, a free-licence to get drunk, and is referred to in our business as the Silly Season. Restaurant kitchens start swimming in roast potatoes, big birds and gravy, not to mention hungover chefs (remember we don't get to start our partying until all you lot have gone home, which hurts if you're on an early the next day). Even at home it's all about the food, booze and pressies as the great day draws closer. Now, tell me, is this picture of excess and merriment anything like the frugality and dark calm of what is to follow?

It's a shorter chapter than the others, but all the recipes have a special significance to a bygone family Christmas. Some are antidotes to the great British roasting explosion and others are there to maybe teach you something new. You'll notice that I have put the seasonal colour principle aside, and I dip into imports (mainly those great citruses that appear around now) really for the first time. I haven't done a list of seasonal ingredients, as it is you and your family who are this season's superstars.

two terrific stuffings

Stuffings absorb the juices of the meat they are being cooked in – that's what makes them so special. However, ideally it should be a symbiotic relationship: a really great stuffing should add to its host. Bacon, butter, duck or olive oil, whatever your fat, it is in this case essential. If you are a devoted stuffing lover then my tip is get a goose: not only will you be good for grease, but goose fat is also the only kind of animal fat that's not associated with heart disease; it displays the same pattern of saturated, monounsaturated and polyunsaturated fats as olive oil. The only drawback is that the ratio of stuffable cavity to useful meat is about 2:1, but luckily these stuffings are mighty filling. Last Christmas I did both stuffings and filled a goose with half each. By the end of lunch, the goose had done its work and it was definitely our turn to feel as though we'd just come back from the taxidermist.

ALMOND, lemon and coriander stuffing

This one adds a bit of Moroccan spice to a meal that otherwise could turn into a bit of an English roastathon. It may not all fit in if your bird is little, so push any leftovers into a baking dish and cook separately.

serves 6

600g white bread, torn up

250g red onion, finely chopped

juice and zest of 2 lemons

75g flaked almonds, toasted

60g pistachios, toasted

1 red chilli, finely chopped

1½ teaspoons ground cumin, toasted

30g coriander, chopped

6–8 tablespoons extra virgin olive oil

S & P

● Combine all the ingredients in a large bowl, seasoning well. It'll taste even better if left for a few hours to allow the flavours to mingle.

Shelf Life: Both stuffings are good for a couple of days raw and a couple more cooked. **Best Kept:** At this time of year I always keep my cooked meat out of the fridge, so I guess that applies to the stuffings as well. There's just no need to take up all that fridge space with a cumbersome carcass, and besides, you're much more likely to pick at it if it's in full view.

SAGE, chestnut and smoky bacon stuffing

This one is pretty trad, but there's a reason why the classics are classics.

serves 6, handsomely

4 tablespoons olive oil

180g smoky bacon, cubed

2 white onions, finely
  chopped

600g white bread, torn up
  (use either no crust or
  soft crusts)

1¹/₂ tablespoons chopped
  sage

1 tablespoon chopped thyme

250g fresh (shelled) or
  pre-prepared chestnuts,
  roughly chopped

75g walnuts, toasted and
  chopped

3 tablespoons melted butter
  (optional, but preferable)

S & P

● Warm a medium-sized frying pan over a low heat. Add the olive oil and bacon and fry very gently. The object here is to render the fat and let the bacon go golden brown.

● Then add the chopped onions and cook until soft and just picking up a bit of colour, about 10 minutes.

● Meanwhile, in a large bowl, combine the bread, herbs and nuts.

● When the onions and bacon are golden, add to the bread mixture and combine until all is glistening. I have never found a better way of making sure it is all mixed thoroughly than by squishing it together with my hands. If you want to add the melted butter, do it now – it will help to make it crisper as well as richer.

● Season very well and stuff.

smoked salmon and
tapenade palmiers

So this is designed to be a canapé/nibble to keep the starving crowds off your back while you co-ordinate everything else. Although I am at present kid-less, I have cooked all but two of the last eighteen big family Christmas lunches, and that's over half my life, so I am well qualified on tips to get you through the day. A bottle of kitchen Champagne (referring not to its quality but more the physical location of the bottle) would come high on my list, alternated with sips of Vieille Prune.

Palmiers are those mad, French, curled-in horseshoe-shaped pastries that, as long as you have a slab of puff and aren't planning on making your own, are a doddle to make and look impressively, well, French. Boosting them with a salty, strong tapenade really works. I'd treble the tapenade recipe and keep some in the fridge, as it'll last till Valentine's.

makes 25–30 palmiers

FOR THE TAPENADE

3 garlic cloves, peeled

juice of ½ lemon

1 tablespoon chopped
   flatleaf parsley

2 sprigs of thyme, leaves
   picked

20g anchovies in oil

150g good black olives,
   stoned

2 tablespoons extra virgin
   olive oil

FOR THE PALMIERS

500g puff pastry

150g smoked salmon, sliced

● Put the garlic, lemon juice, parsley, thyme leaves and anchovies in the food processor. Pulse for a few seconds until you have a smooth paste.

● Then add the stoned olives and pulse again a few times, until all is combined and the olives are still in little bits, not a paste. Scrape the tapenade out into a small bowl and mix in the olive oil.

● On a well-floured surface, roll out the pastry into a rectangle roughly 40cm x 30cm, and about 5mm thick. Turn the rectangle so that the longest side is facing you.

● Visually split the pastry horizontally into two halves. Lay a single layer of smoked salmon slices across the top half (furthest away from you) and spread the tapenade in a thin layer on the other half (closest to you). Make sure you get right out to the edges.

● Now, working from the long tapenade edge nearest to you, begin to gently but firmly roll the whole side up to the centre, or to where the salmon starts.

● Repeat from the opposite side (furthest from you), gently rolling the side with the smoked salmon on towards the centre. You should end up with something that looks like a double scroll. Dab a bit of water in between the rolls and give them a gentle squish so that they adhere along the seam.

● Put on a flat tray, seam-side down, wrap the whole thing in clingfilm and rest in the fridge for 15–20 minutes.

● Preheat the oven to 180°C / 350°F / gas 4.

● You are going to need 2 greased 35cm x 25cm baking trays. Take your salmon and tapenade roll out of the fridge and lay on a board. Using a sharp knife, cut off the messy ends and set them on the edge of the baking tray – chef's tasting snack.

● Cut the palmiers off the roll in 1cm thick slices and lay them down flat on the baking tray, leaving a good space between each one. You can get a glimpse of your handiwork and an idea of how pretty they will be when they're cooked – a swirl of pink salmon and a swirl of black tapenade held together with curlicues of pastry. Continue cutting and laying flat on the baking trays until all are cut.

● Put into the oven for 10–15 minutes until golden brown. Depending on your oven, they may need a quick flip over and a minute or so on the other side. Uncooked pastry is so easy to spot: you'll know as soon as you look at the bottom whether it's cooked or not. Serve warm. If they do go cold, just whack them back in a gentle oven.

Shelf Life: Raw, rolled and/or cut 1–2 days; cooked, less than 24 hours.
Best Kept: Keep the raw log whole (or cut) in the fridge until needed. Once cooked, keep at room temp.

christmas in LENINGRAD

Peroshki are little pies of Russian origin, but they are also rampant all over New York City. My version makes one big one that you cut into slices – much less work and less of the heavy pastry to fill you up. The recipe is loosely based on one by Claudia Roden, my Jedi Master, a lifelong family friend and the only person in the whole world who makes me get butterflies when I'm cooking for her. I don't know how much she had to do with me becoming a chef, but she's certainly done her bit since.

serves 6

FOR THE DOUGH
2 small eggs, beaten
190g mashed potato
375g self-raising flour
an egg yolk, to glaze
a sprinkling of sesame seeds
S & P

FOR THE FILLING
300g cream cheese
6 tablespoons sour cream
120g cottage cheese
a bunch of chives, finely
    chopped
1 spring onion, finely
    chopped
1 egg
S & P

TO SERVE
300g smoked salmon, sliced
    (optional)
a tub of sour cream
1 lemon, cut into wedges

● Stir the beaten eggs into the mash with some seasoning. Sift the flour into a separate bowl and slowly stir in the eggy mash. Knead lightly together until you have a nice elastic dough. This feels good.

● Make the filling by mixing all the ingredients together, then refrigerate for 30–45 minutes to let them set a bit.

● Preheat the oven to 180ºC / 350ºF / gas 4.

● Roll out the potato dough on to a lightly floured (preferably marble) surface to the size of a piece of A4 paper. Spread the filling over the top, leaving a 5 cm border all the way round.

● Roll up lengthways (like a roulade), which is easier said than done. My theory is that food always knows when you're nervous, so be firm and decisive and don't panic if the filling splodges out a bit. Then put onto a well-oiled baking tray with the seam down. Pinch the ends so that they're sealed, then brush the whole thing with the remaining egg yolk and sprinkle with sesame seeds.

● Bake for 20–30 minutes until golden brown.

● Take your baby out of the oven and leave to rest for 5 minutes before carefully cutting it into roughly 2.5 cm slices with a serrated knife.

● Serve with smoked salmon draped over/around it, not forgetting the sour cream and proverbial lemon wedge.

Shelf Life: 2 days. **Best Kept:** Keep it out for up to 4–6 hours, after which time you ought to put it in the fridge.

NOT roast potatoes

Sometimes the line between classic and boring becomes a thin one, and this is one of those times. I'd sell my granny for a good roastie (goose/duck fat please) but sometimes, just sometimes, I get a little bored of them: after a rough calculation (spuds x parties x people x years in the business) Fred and I reckon that between us we have roasted about 16$^{1}/_{2}$ tonnes of spuds.

So this is a different way of approaching your Christmas carb, not at all low-fat, but Christmas isn't really about that. While the bacon and sage thing is a bit old hat, when it is fronted by some spuds and backed up with some Gruyère, you really are set up for a great dauphinoise. More of a contender than a pretender.

serves 6

1 tablespoon olive oil
150 g smoked bacon, cut into 1 cm dice
4 garlic cloves, peeled
3 tablespoons chopped sage
2.5 kg regular big potatoes
a small knob of butter
230 g Gruyère cheese, grated
6 tablespoons crème fraîche
1 litre chicken stock
S & P

● Heat the olive oil in a frying pan over a low heat and brown the bacon. Finely chop 3 of the garlic cloves. When the bacon is golden brown, add the garlic and sage and cook for a couple of minutes more, then turn off the heat.

● Peel and wash the spuds, then slice them as thinly as possible. I do this on a mandolin, but by hand is okay – it'll just take a little longer to make and cook.

● Preheat the oven to 200°C / 400°F / gas 6.

● Rub the inside of your ovenproof dish (27 cm x 20 cm and 7 cm deep) with the remaining garlic clove and then with a knob of butter. Cover the bottom of your dish with a few slices of spud, then sprinkle on some cheese, some bacon mix and some seasoning (more pepper than salt). Layer up the remaining spuds, cheese and bacon, saving a good handful of Gruyère for the top so it will go crispy. Once the dish is loaded up (it's okay if it's a bit domed, as it will level out in the oven), mix the crème fraîche and chicken stock together in a bowl and then gently and slowly pour over the spuds.

● Butter the underside of a piece of foil and then cover the whole thing loosely. It's a bad idea for the foil to be tight on the cheese because it can stick and then you'll lose your fabulous topping. Put the dish on a baking tray and set in the oven for 1–1$^{1}/_{2}$ hours, until a knife goes through it with little or no resistance; cooking time depends on the thickness of your spud slices, of course. When the potatoes are cooked, take off the foil and set under the grill for a few minutes to get the top crispy. Stand for 5 minutes before tucking in.

Shelf Life: 4–5 days. **Best Kept:** In the fridge or larder – depends on how hot your house is and whether or not you have a larder.

LIME chicken kebabs with saffron jewelled RICE

This is a lesson on how to get the most out of your Boxing Day. As we all know you are what you eat, and if on Boxing Day all you put out in the obligatory family buffet is yesterday's brown leftovers, then you and your kin will find yourselves behaving like yesterday's brown leftovers.

On the other hand, dazzle your nearest and dearest with this array of Middle Eastern wonder and your day will be uplifting and full of laughter and excitement.

Make the marinade on Christmas Eve, roll the chicken in it on Christmas morn and throw the easy rice together on Boxing Day – it'll take about as much effort as re-heating all those bloody leftovers, and the effect of serving something fresh and colourful will have pleasant repercussions throughout the day.

serves 6

FOR THE SKEWERS
6 chicken breasts (skin off)
2 pinches of saffron
3 tablespoons extra virgin
  olive oil
3 garlic cloves, peeled and
  sliced
zest and juice of 2 limes
6 x 15 cm long kebab
  skewers, wooden or
  metal, or long bay twigs

FOR THE RICE
450g basmati rice
  (I prefer brown but this
  is a white rice dish)
160g butter
2 tablespoons plain yogurt
a pinch of saffron
1 tablespoon dill seeds
S & P

● Cut each chicken breast in half lengthways and then cut each strip into roughly 3–4 chunks, depending on the size of the breasts.

● In a small saucepan, bring 2 tablespoons of water to the boil. Add your two pinches of saffron and take off the stove. Leave to cool.

● In a large bowl make the marinade with the olive oil, garlic, infused saffron, lime zest and juice. Drop in the pieces of chicken, coat well and leave to soak up the flavours in the fridge for 24 hours.

● The next day, skewer up your kebabs (it's a good idea to pre-soak the wooden ones to avoid splintering and burning). You want 6–8 chunks on each skewer (one breast per person).

● Rinse the rice under cold running water for a couple of minutes. Get a pan of salted water on a rolling boil and cook the rice in it for 5–7 minutes. Drain.

● Melt the butter on a low heat in a non-stick frying pan (26 cm diameter and 6 cm deep) with a tight-fitting lid, then stir in the yogurt and saffron. Do not try to make this go all creamy – you just need to heat all of them together, before they start to catch on the bottom.

● Gently spoon in the semi-cooked rice, making sure it's level but also compacting it right down into the edge of the pan with the back of a spoon.

3 large tomatoes, halved
  across the middle
3 large dill pickles, cut
  in half
1 lime, cut into 6 wedges
a few sprigs of fresh dill
1 pomegranate, seeds
  removed (see page 250)
6 egg yolks (optional)

● Dampen a tea towel, wrap it around the lid and cover the rice (this aids the steaming process and helps keep the rice light). Cook like this for 15 minutes, keeping the heat dead low.

● Lightly toast the dill seeds in a dry pan, giving them the odd shake – about 2–3 minutes.

● Preheat the grill for the chicken.

● After the rice has been on for 15 minutes, very gently stir in the toasted dill seeds but be careful not to disrupt the delicious crust which is forming on the sides and bottom of the pan. Replace the eccentric-looking lid and cook for another 20 minutes, still on the same heat.

● Meanwhile, season the kebabs with S & P and set them under the grill along with the halved tomatoes, cut-side up. Grill for 12-ish minutes, turning the kebabs halfway through.

● Check the crust on the rice is golden brown and crispy. If it's not looking as gorgeous as you might have wanted, just increase the heat a smidgen and keep her on for another 10 minutes or so. Pull off the heat and set aside to cool a little without the lid.

● To serve, use a palette knife or your special flipper to carefully tease the crust away from the pan around the sides and bottom. Then very calmly turn out the rice onto a flat plate and cut into wedges. Serve a tranche of golden-crusted rice with a kebab, a grilled tomato, half a dill pickle, a wedge of lime, a few sprigs of dill and a generous sprinkling of pomegranate seeds.

There is an option to serve a raw egg yolk to stir into the rice, like the Persians do. I love this touch because it makes the rice even more rich and delicious, but it does make some people squeamish.

Shelf Life: Rice in the fridge for a day; chicken for 2. **Best Kept:** All of this is best eaten hot.

VENISON and prune casserole, chestnut mash and cranberry jelly

This recipe combines three late winter superstars. Becoming a prune is the greatest thing that could ever happen to a plum, and their addition to a slow-cook like this is massive; flavour, texture and richness. It's worth spending money on good ones as the cheap kind are often brushed with paraffin, boiled in brine or soaked with lye to make them look plump and appealing.

Chestnuts contain polyunsaturated fats, which are the best kind in the world, and help to keep your cholesterol down.

The North American cranberry season reaches its zenith in late November, and as this is an East Coast crop (mostly from Massachusetts). Fresh ones are usually available in the UK a couple of weeks later.

Most available venison is English and is very lean – good for the heart but a little low on flavour (fat is flavour, after all) so I've put in some optional bacon for the animal fat lovers amongst us.

As with all stews, best made a day ahead.

This is the longest recipe in the book, but it's not difficult and is very, very satisfying. It is much easier if you can make the jelly the day before.

I'm not sure if this is allowed, but I'd like to dedicate this recipe to Jane and William Dorrell for being the best of friends to my family for so many years, and never more so than now.

serves 6

FOR THE MARINADE
300ml red wine
1 white onion, diced
1 teaspoon thyme, picked

FOR THE VENISON
1.5kg haunch of venison (or braising steaks to the same weight) diced into 5cm chunks
150g butter
2 large onions, medium diced

● First marinade the venison overnight in the wine, onion and thyme.

● The next day, preheat the oven to 150°C/300°F/gas 2.

● In a heavy based pan (something like a Le Creuset is perfect) heat a third of the butter and gently fry the onions, bacon and rosemary in it for about 10 minutes until they just begin to brown.

● As that is going on, tip the meat into a colander, saving the marinade, and season well. Lay down a few sheets of old newspaper and, holding the colander above it, throw over the flour and shake the colander so that all the meat is coated but the excess is falling away. Throw your newspaper and flour in the bin, thus saving money on a plumber later. When they are done spoon the oniony-bacon mix out and set aside, leaving the yummy bacon fat and flavour in the pan. Keep the pan on the heat.

200g smoked streaky bacon, sliced or diced 2cm thick

2 sprigs of rosemary, picked, and roughly chopped

60g plain flour

2 large carrots, sliced into 2cm thick rounds

250g good quality prunes, roughly chopped

5 garlic cloves, peeled and sliced

300ml red wine

1 litre beef stock

3 bay leaves

40g flatleaf parsley, picked and roughly chopped

S & P

FOR THE MASH

1.8kg mashing potatoes, something like King Edwards or similar, peeled and quartered

250g chestnuts, shelled and cooked weight, roughly chopped

200ml milk

S & P

FOR THE CRANBERRY JELLY

15g gelatine, either leaf or powder

350g cranberries

130g sugar

● Add the meat to the pan and fry gently on a medium heat, stirring regularly so that the flour doesn't burn on the bottom, but it's bound to stick a bit.

● Throw in the carrots, prunes and garlic and fry them until you can smell the garlic.

● Tip the onions and bacon back in and then pour in the red wine and the leftover marinade. Let the whole lot come to the boil, then pour the stock over to cover the meat so that it comes to about 3cm above it. It needs to be submerged. Season with S & P, add the bay leaves then cook in the oven for 2¹/₂ hours. You can look at it, either out of fear or curiosity once an hour, but no more. The meat is done when it is very tender, but not falling apart; it should still hold its shape.

● Put the cranberries, sugar and about 700ml water in a pan and simmer for 20 minutes.

● Line a sieve either with some muslin or a clean J-cloth and sit it over a bowl.

● Prepare your gelatine (soaking in cold water for leaves or dissolving for the powder).

● Pour the cranberries and all the syrup into the sieve and leave to drain – don't push or you will cloud your jelly. Whisk the gelatine into the still warm cranberry liquor. Transfer either to your serving vessel or a sterilised jam jar, cover, and refrigerate for at least 2 hours, or until set. (You can re-use the remaining cranberry solids that are left for cranberry sauce at a later date; they still have flavour.)

● About an hour before serving put on the mash: big saucepan, cold water and salt. And the spuds. If using fresh chestnuts, put them peeled into the water with the potatoes, so they cook. Bring to the boil and simmer until the spuds are cooked i.e. they fall off a knife when spiked. If you are using the precooked chestnuts, add them once the spuds are cooked, which is logical.

● Drain and mash. Melt the butter with the milk and then stir into the mash. Season well.

● Let the stew sit for at least 10 minutes – it needs a bit of quiet time to sort itself out. Then skim off any excess fat that may be sitting on the surface and taste for seasoning. I'd serve this in shallow bowls with a handful of watercress and a scattering of the parsley.

Shelf Life: Casserole 5 days; jelly 2 weeks; mash 1 day **Best Kept:** Jelly in the fridge; casserole and mash in the fridge or in a cool place.

BLOOD orange
and rose water JELLY

Puddings fall into two categories: those that aim to kill you – jam roly-poly – and those that let your waistline live on. This one definitely falls into the latter category, leaving you feeling pleasantly invigorated and revived. For some reason the acidity of the citrus juice affects the setting of the jelly, so you need a booster of leaf gelatine as well. Don't even bother trying it without unless you enjoy jelly soup. It would be foolish to regard jellies as passé – this wobbly bastion of Britishness is definitely shimmying up for a comeback.

This won all the prizes three Christmases ago and had admirers aged from two years old to seventy five. My chocolate roulade, lemon tart and Christmas Pud were all passed by in favour of this light and refreshing jelly. So simple too.

serves 6

1 packet tangerine jelly
juice of 10 clementines
4 leaves of gelatine
2 tablespoons rose water
3 blood oranges
6 Medjool dates, cut into
   thin slivers (optional)

● Tear up the jelly and put it in a bowl.

● Soak the gelatine leaves in cold water.

● Check the volume of clementine juice you have and take that away from the volume of water required to make up the jelly (refer to the packet). Boil the remaining water and pour onto the jelly cubes and whisk furiously.

● Now whisk in the soaked gelatine leaves and check everybody has dissolved.

● Cool the jelly mixture to room temperature, then add the fresh juice and rose water.

● Tip the jelly into 1 large or 6 small jelly moulds or straight into glass goblets, and put in the fridge.

● Meanwhile, carefully skin the blood oranges with a knife, not fingers, so you remove all the white pith as you go. Then break them down into segments. (I describe how to do this with a grapefruit on page 128 and the principles are exactly the same.)

● Once the jelly has started to solidify, after about 2 hours, gently drop the orange pieces in, and hopefully they won't sink to the bottom but will stay suspended. Refrigerate overnight.

● If applicable, turn the jelly/jellies out, and serve with a few slivers of date if you want to go down the road to Damascus.

Shelf Life: 1–2 days. **Best Kept:** In the fridge, on a pedestal.

gently souchong'd WINTER
fruits with praline cream

For some reason that I've never really understood, I was always taught to float a tea bag when stewing fruits. Without really questioning it, I have adapted the idea – believing that the flesh of the fruit works well in a wintery way with the smoky taste synonymous with Lapsang. Smells like bacon, which has got to be good.

And then there's the praline cream – how can something so smooth also be so crunchy. In Japan, texture is as important as flavour, and in this recipe the cream certainly adds more to the dish than just taste.

Winter is a hard time to get your fresh fruit quota, so we reach into the storecupboard in search of nutritious goodies and warming spices...

serves 6

FOR THE POACHING LIQUOR

3 cm piece of root ginger,
  split in half

90 g brown sugar

2 Lapsang Souchong tea bags

1 vanilla pod, split in half
  and seeds scraped

2 bay leaves

1 piece of star anise

1 cinnamon stick

1 clove

4 cardamom pods

1 mace blade

FOR THE PRALINE CREAM

150 g caster sugar

125 g flaked almonds

300 ml double cream

FOR THE FRUIT

3 apples

3 pears

180 g dried prunes (pre-
  stoned weight), stoned

75 g dried cherries

6 dried figs

12 dried apricots

TO SERVE

75 ml whisky (I like 'Paddy'
  Irish Whisky)

● Put all the ingredients for the poaching liquor into a saucepan with 700ml water, bring to a relaxed simmer, then turn down and let steam quietly for 20 minutes.

● Put the sugar for the praline cream in a small, heavy-based saucepan, measure in 4 tablespoons of water and stir briefly so that all the sugar is wet. Set over a low heat until it begins to turn into a deep, amber caramel, giving it a gentle swirl (not stir) from time to time. This may take a while, so if you are either in a hurry or impatient, like me, turn the heat up a bit but don't go far. Stir in the flaked almonds so they are well coated, take it off the heat and pour onto a sheet of lightly oiled greaseproof paper to cool.

● Once cooled, peel off the paper and smash the praline up with a rolling pin to a coarse crunchy texture. Loads of fun.

● Strain the fruity liquor in a large, shallow saucepan and re-heat.

● Cut the apples and pears into quarters, removing the core and stem. It's up to you whether you want to peel them or not: Fibre vs French.

● Put the dried fruit that needs rehydrating, such as the prunes, cherries, figs and apricots, in the poaching liquid first and stew them gently for 10-ish minutes. Then add the apples and pears and simmer, covered, for a further 10-ish minutes, or until they are tender.

● Whip the cream until just thickened, then stir in the praline pieces, which will instantly thicken it up a lot more.

● Once the fresh fruit is cooked, but before it loses its shape, turn the heat off. Use a slotted spoon to lift out the fruit onto a serving dish. Then, as Bob Marley says, 'simmer down' the syrup until it reaches a good saucy consistency.

● Serve hot with the whisky stirred in at the last second. Pass the praline cream round in a bowl.

Shelf Life: Nearly a week, as the fruit is pretty much preserved in the syrup; cream 1 day. **Best Kept:** Cooked fruit out and covered; cream in the fridge.

SALADE sheherizade

This ticks many boxes: short prep time, simple ingredients, a bit different and also good for you. I keep a 'get out of jail free' tin of halva in the fridge at all times, and combining that with the best seasonal imports makes for a pleasing pud. If you can't get hold of orange blossom water, I'd run with orange juice with the honey dissolved in it.

Pomegranates are the hottest antioxidant on the market at the moment. Truly, they are dazzlingly jewel-like in appearance and god-sent for their health benefits. And the best part is that I've just learned the easiest way to de-seed a pomegranate. For years this had been a thorn in the side of an otherwise perfect fruit, but thanks to my sister Binky's friend Lourdes, now there is only joy. Quarter the pomegranate, hit the outside skin with the back of a heavy spoon, and the seeds just 'pop' out. So much simpler and tidier than trying to dig them out with your fingers like precious jewels from the earth.

serves 6

10 clementines with the
   leaves, for pretty
150g halva – the one with
   pistachios works really
   well
1 pomegranate, seeded
1 tablespoon orange blossom
   water (or orange juice)
2 tablespoons runny honey

● Choose a plate that will contrast with the colours of the completed dish. You have the orangest of clems with ruby jewels of pomegranate and pistachio-speckled halva.

● Using a very sharp knife, cut the ends off the clems so you just hit the flesh and they can sit flat on their top or bottom. With a serrated or a really sharp paring knife, hold the clem with one hand and carefully cut away the skin and pith in a gentle arcing motion, top to bottom in sections. The idea is to just cut away the skin and membrane without losing a lot of flesh. Continue until you have a naked fruit.

● Now that you have your perfectly pithless clems, roll them on their sides and slice each one into 4–5 rounds. Put them on the serving plate in whatever fashion grabs you.

● Cut the halva into 2cm x 1cm rhomboids, or diamonds, or just crumble it over the top of the clems.

● All that is left to do is to sprinkle over the pomegranate seeds and drizzle with orange blossom water. Just before you serve, give a final drizzle with some of your favourite honey, but nothing too perfumed. I know my sister Floss would like a bowl of yogurt with this but I think it is unecessary.

Shelf Life: It starts to lose its magic after 2–3 hours. **Best Kept:** In the fridge.

organic chocolate soufflé

I promise this won't be difficult – a little tense on the nerves, but not technically challenging. I know you won't believe me, but please have a go anyway; you'll be so proud of yourself.

To be fair, the ease of your task and your confidence will be greatly increased if you have proper soufflé dishes, which are like oversized ramekins. I'm not suggesting you go out and buy half a dozen at the princely sum of a fiver each, but think of your ponciest cooking chum and ask if you can borrow theirs – the ones I borrow off James are a very impressive 10cm across and 6.5cm deep.

serves 6

9 eggs, separated
255g caster sugar, plus
   extra for dusting
675ml milk
75ml double cream
65g unsalted butter, plus
   extra for greasing
50g cornflour
60g best organic cocoa
   powder

● Preheat the oven to 200°C / 400°F / gas 6.

● In a mixer, whisk the egg yolks and 180g of the sugar until white-ish and fluffy.

● Heat the milk and cream until nearly boiling. Slowly pour over the egg and sugar mix, whisking all the time until totally incorporated.

● Melt the butter in a pan (big enough to hold the whole mixture) and stir in the cornflour to make a roux-ish affair.

● Whisk the egg custard mix into the roux, and bring to the boil, stirring continuously to avoid lumps.

● Beat the cocoa into the custard unti it's smooth – zero lumpage, then turn off the heat and let it cool down slightly. Meanwhile, whisk the egg whites with the remaining 75g sugar to a stiff peak meringue, but be careful not to overbeat, ie. beyond the stage when the whites become silky.

● Brush the insides of 6 soufflé dishes or ramekins with melted butter. There is an old wives' tale that if you grease the mould from bottom to top in upward strokes it helps the soufflé to rise: I'm really not convinced it makes any difference, but when it comes to soufflés everyone has their own superstitions. I would tell you mine, but then I'd be jinxed. Dust lightly with caster sugar and refrigerate for 5 minutes.

● Mix a third of the egg whites into the chocolate and beat well (to even up the consistencies a bit). Then fold in the remaining two thirds super-gently – up and over, swapping the bottom with the top in gentle arcing movements.

● Load up the ramekins to the brim. Then run your thumbnail around the inside of each ramekin to create a little ridge.

● Cook for 20 minutes (depending on how soggy you like the middle) without opening the oven and serve the puffed-up soufflés IMMEDIATELY.

Shelf Life: 3 minutes. **Best Kept:** Shurley shome mishtake…?

bibliography

Andrews, C., *Catalan Cuisine: Europe's Last Great Culinary Secret;* Grub Street Publishing, 1997

Batmanglij, N., *The New Food of Life: Ancient Persian and Modern Iranian Cooking and Ceremonies;* Mage Publishers, U.S., 1997

Bown, D., *Herbal: The essential Guide to Herbs for Living* (Chelsea Physic Garden); Pavilion Books, 1991

Cousin, PJ. and Hartvig, K., *The Complete Guide to Nutritional Health;* Duncan Baird Publishers, 2004

David, E., *English Bread and Yeast Cookery;* Penguin Books Ltd., 1979

Devi, Y., *The Best of Lord Krishna's Cuisine;* Bala Books, 1991

DK Pocket Encyclopedia Cooks Ingredients; Dorling Kindersley

Edwards, J., *The Roman Cookery of Apicius;* Rider Books, 1985

Fearnley-Wittingstall, H., *The River Cottage Year;* Hodder & Stouton, 2003

Khaing, M. M,. *Cook and Entertain the Burmese Way;* 1975

McEvedy, F., *The Step-Parent's Parachute;* Time Warner Paperback, 2005

McEvedy, C. and S., *The Classical World;* Hart-Davies

My Ma's cookery book, *orange photo album with collected recipes*

Roden, C., *A New Book of Middle Eastern Food;* Penguin Books Ltd., 1986

Roden, C., *The Book of Jewish Food;* Penguin Books Ltd; 1999

Round, J., *The Independent Cook: Strategies for Seasonal Cooking;* Pan, 2001

Safron, J., *The Raw Truth: The Art of Preparing Living Foods;* Celestial Arts, 2003

Stobart, T., *The Cook;s Encyclopaedia: Ingredients and Processes;* Grub Street Publishing, 2004

Toklas, A. B., *The Alice B. Toklas Cookbook;* Michael Joseph, 1954

Toussaint Samat, M., *History of Food;* Blackwell Publishers, 1994

Tsuji, S. and Hata, K., *Practical Japanese Cooking: Easy and Elegant;* Kodansha Europe, 1986

Van Straten, M., *Superfoods;* Doring Kindersley, 1990

Van Straten, M., *The Oracle Diet;* Kyle Cathie, 2002

Waters, A., *Chez Panisse Vegetables;* HarperCollins, 1996

index

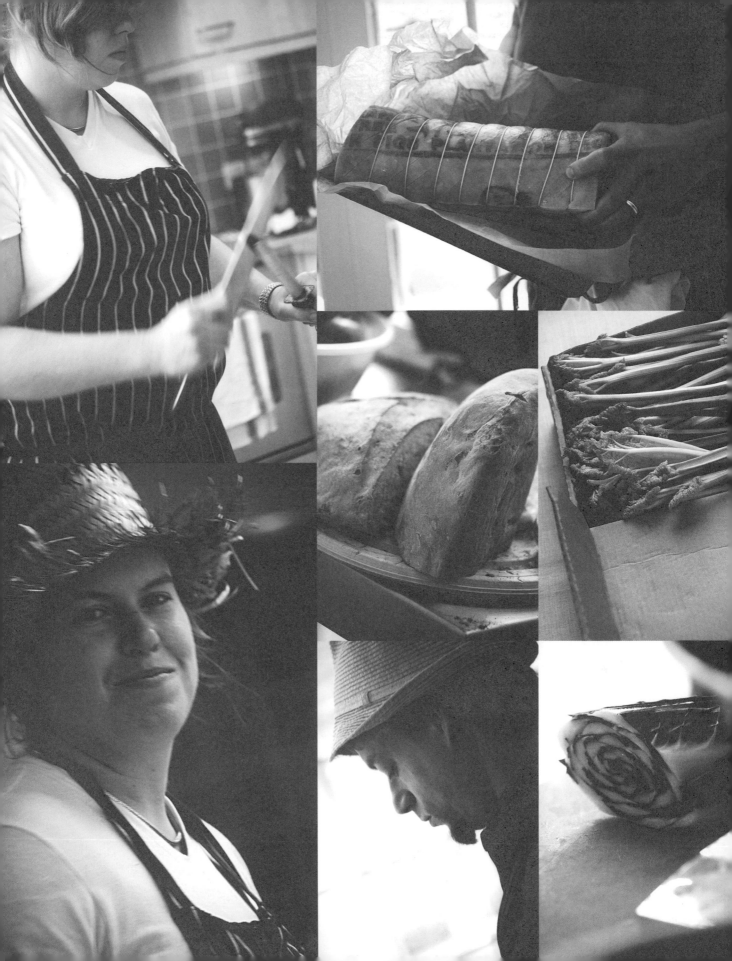